GW00696645

LOYALTY
IS MY
HONOUR

LOYALTY
IS MY
HONOUR

GORDON WILLIAMSON

LONDON   NEW YORK   SYDNEY   TORONTO

I would like to take the opportunity of thanking each and every one of the contributors for their time, patience and cooperation during the production of this publication. Their unstinting efforts over the course of many months turned an idea into reality, and I am indebted to them all.

Gordon Williamson

This edition published 1995 by BCA
by arrangement with Brown Packaging Limited

CN 5312

Editorial and design by Brown Packaging Limited
255-257 Liverpool Road, London N1 1LX

Printed and bound in Spain

PHOTOGRAPHIC CREDITS

b= bottom, l= left, r= right, t= top.

Bundesarchiv: FC, 2/3, 6/7, 10, 26/7, 29, 30, 39, 42/3, 47, 50/1, 52, 53, 54, 55, 56, 61, 64, 66, 70, 72, 75, 76t, 76b, 92, 101, 107b, 117.
Robert Hunt Picture Library: BC, 78/9, 80, 81, 83, 87, 93, 96, 107t, 108, 115t, 121, 126, 129, 131, 153,171, 173, 176.
Private Collections: 8, 9, 13, 16, 19, 20, 22, 23, 24, 25, 28, 31, 32, 33, 34, 35, 36, 37, 38, 40, 41t, 41bl, 45, 46, 48, 49, 57, 58, 60, 62, 67, 68, 69, 71, 73, 74, 86, 88, 95, 99,100, 104t, 104b, 110, 111, 112, 113, 114, 115b, 116, 118, 119, 120, 122, 124, 125, 127, 130, 134, 135, 138, 141, 143, 144, 145, 146, 151, 152, 155, 156, 157, 158, 159t, 159b, 160/1, 162, 165, 167, 168, 170, 174, 175, 177, 178, 179, 180t, 180bl, 181.
TRH Pictures: 14/5, 21, 84/5, 89, 91, 102/3, 128, 132/3, 136, 139, 147, 163, 164, 166.
United States National Archives: 148/9.

Previous pages: The Waffen-SS mounts an honour guard as Reinhard Heydrich (second from left), the new Protector of Bohemia and Moravia, takes over in Prague in October 1941. Note also Reichsführer-SS Himmler (centre).

CONTENTS

INTRODUCTION

Out of the turmoil in Germany following World War I came a new political ideology, National Socialism, and a hypnotic leader: Adolf Hitler. Like all dictators, Hitler formed a praetorian guard, the Schutz Staffel (Protection Squad), to protect him. The SS was characterised by iron discipline and ruthlessness, qualities shared by its military wing, the Waffen-SS.

This book goes to press over five decades since the end of World War II in Europe in May 1945. Much has changed in the last half-century, not least the world's attitude to Germany. In 1945 the country was a pariah in the world community, occupied and divided by foreign powers, and economically as well as militarily broken. Today Germany is respected, united, a powerful global economic force and one of the most committed supporters of the European Union.

As Germany has earned its new place in the world, attitudes to the men who fought in the German armed forces during World War II have mellowed. The soldiers of Rommel's Afrika Korps, or the young Luftwaffe pilots who took on the 'Few' of the RAF in the summer of 1940, are now generally recognised as having been no less brave, skilled and honourable than those who fought for the Allies. In Germany, too, credit has been given where it is due. Many of the more famous individual leaders of the old Wehrmacht have been rehabilitated to the extent that ships, garrisons and military units of the post-war Bundeswehr have been named after them. Rommel, Mölders, Marseille and Dietl are but a few examples.

But the passage of time has seen no such softening of attitudes towards one branch of the German armed forces, or, more precisely, one branch of the Nazi Party's war machine.

Waffen-SS soldiers of the Das Reich *Division photographed in Russia in the summer of 1941, during the early stages of Operation 'Barbarossa'. It was in Russia that the Waffen-SS displayed its characteristic mix of unmatched bravery and ruthlessness.*

ABOVE: Reichsführer-SS Heinrich Himmler congratulates some of his Waffen-SS soldiers. Despite his position as head of the SS, Himmler took no part in the direction of his Waffen-SS divisions in wartime. As a result, to the men who wore the death's head badge he was rather remote.

For the Waffen-SS, any form of rehabilitation has been very conspicuous by its absence.

The reason for this is not hard to find or understand. The Waffen-SS was the armed wing of Hitler's National Socialist Party. It was not part of the regular Army, although its divisions fought alongside those of the Wehrmacht. It was an offshoot of the same paramilitary empire that ran the concentration camps, policed the ghettoes, organised slave labour, rooted out, tortured and killed German dissidents, controlled education and, most notoriously, manned death squads and filled the extermination centres where Jews, Gypsies, homosexuals, and the old, the infirm and the demented were systematically done to death in their mil-

lions. Whatever the purely military virtues of the Waffen-SS, these fighting echelons are inevitably linked in the public mind with the gross monstrosities perpetrated by their parent organisation.

The surviving veterans of the Waffen-SS thus find themselves in an unenviable position. While they were indeed some of the toughest soldiers the world has seen, whose feats of arms were impressive by any standard, they are usually deemed guilty by association of the SS's crimes against humanity. These men themselves consider that they were soldiers first and foremost. And they did indeed fight with a tenacity and an elan that has rarely been seen in modern warfare. They feel that there is a fundamental difference between the part the Waffen-SS played in World War II and the actions of the rest of Himmler's gruesome apparatus. Among others, the death squads of the SD Einsatzgruppen, the inquisitors of the Gestapo, the sadists of the Death's Head concentration camp units, and the inhuman administrators of the Final Solution led to the SS as a whole being condemned at Nuremberg as a criminal organisation. Those who served as soldiers in the Waffen-SS believe that history has judged them, as individuals, unfairly.

In the course of researching various aspects of military history over the years, I became acquainted with a considerable number of former Waffen-SS soldiers. On first contact, they were almost invariably reluctant to talk about their experiences – fearing that in the end they would always be portrayed in a negative light, whatever they might say. This book came about as a result of my suggesting to these veterans that, if they truly felt they had been grossly maligned, it was time for them to tell their own side of the story.

BELOW: The ceremonial face of the Waffen-SS. Standing rigidly to attention, men of the Leibstandarte SS Adolf Hitler *take the salute in Munich in November 1935. The chevrons on the right arms indicate those who were members of the SS or the Nazi Party before January 1933.*

From their accounts, and sometimes from reading between the lines, readers can judge for themselves the degree to which these young men were purely soldiers. They have taken the opportunity to discuss what motivated them to join the Waffen-SS, the training that moulded them into elite troops, their combat experiences, and their treatment as prisoners after the defeat of Germany. They make no attempt to whitewash the Waffen-SS, or to excuse or justify those members of the Waffen-SS who, they freely admit, were undoubtedly guilty of appalling atrocities – not all of them committed in the heat of battle or in outraged response to some enormity perpetrated by the enemy. To them, too, the evils of Nazism are clear. For those who contributed to it, this book is essentially about what, for most, was the reason for joining the Waffen-SS in the first place: the business of being a first-class soldier. It is a compilation of purely military experiences, as remembered by men who spent their war as frontline combat troops.

ABOVE: Waffen-SS troops try to warm themselves during the onset of winter in late 1941. Waffen-SS divisions displayed a tenacity and steadfastness during the Russian counteroffensives in late 1941 and early 1942 that were higher than many of their Wehrmacht counterparts.

Mention should be made of the age of contributors. The reader will note that most of the accounts come from men who were NCOs and junior officers, i.e. those who were in their teens and 20s during World War II. There is a very good reason for this: the majority of the senior commanders of the Waffen-SS who survived the war are now dead.

Their stories are a legitimate part of modern history and deserve to be told. To see these recollections in context it is useful to know how the Waffen-SS came into being as an element of the SS as a whole, and to understand its relation to the regular German Army. First, it is necessary to see how the SS itself was born and grew.

Under Heinrich Himmler's leadership the SS grew into a vast empire whose activities ranged from running the death camps to business interests as diverse as fish farming, mineral water production and a porcelain factory. Its beginnings, however, were extremely modest.

Political violence was both commonplace and bloody in Germany in the aftermath of World War I. When Hitler began his campaign in the early 1920s to make his tiny National Socialist Party the major force in German politics, its was not unusual for Nazi meetings to degenerate into running battles with left-wing opponents. To protect their orators the Nazis created the Sturm Abteilung (Storm Troops), or SA. Many of its members came from the Freikorps: armed right-wing bands of ex-soldiers whose disillusion with both the Army (then called the Reichswehr) and post-war politicians made them loyal only to their own individual leaders. In turn, the SA's leader, Ernst Röhm, saw the SA as his own private army, and was on occasion highly critical of the Nazi leadership.

Birth of the SS

As a result of his botched attempt to oust the government of Bavaria in 1923, Hitler spent nine months in jail. In this time he became even more alarmed as the number of Röhm's followers grew from 2000 to over 30,000. He needed a paramilitary group that would be unswervingly faithful and obedient to him alone – not least to protect him from the possible machinations of the SA. But in the increasingly polarised atmosphere of German politics, Hitler could not do without the physical force of the SA. His answer was to create an elite personal bodyguard, in 1925.

The Schutz Staffel (Protection Squad), or SS, numbered only 10 men and an officer in each political district in Germany, and was officially under SA command. Each recruit was chosen for his fitness, sobriety and lack of criminal record; and, crucially, each swore allegiance not to the Nazi Party but to Hitler himself. For four years the SS languished as the victim of the SA's jealousy. Then, early in 1929, Heinrich Himmler took over its leadership.

Himmler was devoted to Hitler, fanatically concerned about racial 'purity', obsessed with Germany's pagan past, and a formidable organiser. Under his direction, recruits now had to prove their 'Aryan' lineage for three generations, the SS became operationally independent of the SA, and its uniform, insignia, ranks and rituals were established. When the SA rebelled against Hitler's leadership in 1930 and again in 1931, the SS remained entirely loyal. As a reward, the SS became the Nazi Party's prime security organ, and at once began to develop an apparatus for identifying and disposing of dissidents. Sympathisers saw it as a respectable alternative to the SA rabble. By 1932 the SS was some 30,000 strong. But the SA now had 400,000 members.

The Nazis' private troops outnumbered the Reichswehr by more than four to one. Many of the the generals sympathised with the Nazis, but distrusted the unruly SA – and all were absolutely opposed to any dilution of their role as the sole bearers of arms in defence of the nation. And the Reichswehr was a unique political and social force in Germany: in Alan Bullock's words, it 'took precedence over every other institution' in the land. It was quite capable of staging a coup if sufficiently threatened, and could have counted on wide-ranging popular support if it had done so. Even after he became Chancellor in January 1933, Hitler could not afford to lose the Army's support while he took the last few steps to absolute power.

In a speech in February 1934 Röhm finally overreached himself. Proclaiming the SA to be the true army of National Socialism, he proposed that the regular Army should be relegated to a training organisation. To both the Nazi party and the Reichswehr, this was nothing short of treason. In June 1934 Hitler settled the problem once and for all. First, the entire body of the SA – which by now had mushroomed to Three million men – was sent on leave. On 30 June, Röhm and the leaders of the SA were wiped out, along with others deemed inconvenient or obstructive to the regime. As many as 1000 people may have lost their lives. The killings were carried out by members of Hitler's super-elite personal bodyguard, the *Leibstandarte*, and the guards' unit at the concentration camp at Dachau, the SS Totenkopfverbände or Death's Head company.

The 'Night of the Long Knives' broke the SA. On 26 July, the SS was elevated to the 'standing of an independent organisation' within the Nazi Party. The way was open for Himmler's organisation to burgeon into a state within the state. As such, like any other state, it needed an army.

Six days after the announcement of the SS's new status, all officers and men in the Reichswehr were required to swear a new oath of loyalty – to 'render unconditional obedience to Adolf Hitler' and to be 'ready as a brave soldier to risk my life at any time for this oath'. Not the least effect of this compromise of the much-vaunted honour of the German officer corps was to render the generals incapable – in the name of honour! – of overthrowing the Nazi regime. It also pre-empted any objections they might have to the Party raising its own armed forces.

Arming the SS

Nonetheless, Hitler trod carefully. In March 1935, he broke with the Treaty of Versailles and announced the re-introduction of conscription and the expansion of the Army to some 36 divisions. Their mauled pride thus restored, the generals could hardly complain when, at the same time, Hitler announced the formation of the SS-Verfügungstruppe (Special Disposal Troop), or SS-VT, to be the core of a full-scale fighting division. To deflect the Army's fears, this unit and the Death's Head battalions were put on the police budget.

Hitler's own reasons for raising armed SS units were consistent with his general determination to regiment and militarise German society. 'In our Reich of the future,' he told Himmler in 1934, 'the SS and the police will possess the necessary authority in their relations with other citizens only if they have a soldierly character. Through their past experience of glorious military events and their present education by the NSDAP [Nazi party], the German people have acquired such a warrior mentality that... it will be necessary for our SS and police... to prove themselves at the front in the same way as the Army and to make blood sacrifices to the same degree as any any other branch of the armed services.'

The existence of the SS-Verfügungstruppe, and thus of the Waffen-SS, may have owed more to Hitler's fantasies of a Nazi mystique than it did to any actual, pressing, military requirement. But at the heart of that mystique was the fact that Hitler could depend on the unswerving loyalty and obedience of the SS troops.

Thus the annexation of Austria in March 1938 was ostensibly the business of the German 8th Army, but the *Leibstandarte*, *Deutschland* and *Germania* Regiments of the SS-Verfügungstruppe went with it, and the SS were on hand to carry out mass arrests, the looting of art treasures, executions, and the inevitable persecution of the Jews. In October 1938, the German force that took over Czechoslovakia included the same regiments and the *Der Führer* Regiment, which had been raised in Vienna.

Willing Volunteers

Neither of these operations met with any resistance. In September 1939, the SS-Verfügungstruppe had its baptism of fire in the invasion of Poland. It then consisted of the motorised, battalion-strength *Leibstandarte*, three infantry regiments (two motorised), an artillery regiment, and signals, reconnaissance and pioneer (combat engineer) battalions. All these units except the *Deutschland* motorised infantry regiment took part in the invasion, split up among different Army formations. The SS suffered high casualties in the campaign, which the Army generals put down to recklessness, inexperience and poor leadership. Himmler retorted that the Wehrmacht (as the German military, including the army, navy and air force, was known after May 1935) had left its most difficult and dangerous tasks to SS units. There was some truth in both comments, but the aggressive and daring tactics adopted by the SS troops, their commitment to one another and their willingness to fight to the bitter end had been proven. Impressed, Hitler agreed to the formation of three fully-equipped SS divisions. In March 1940, the SS-Verfügungstruppe was officially dubbed the Waffen-SS. Its next task was to join the invasion in the West – the subjugation of France, Belgium and the Netherlands.

The campaign in the West opened on 9 May 1940 and, after considerably more savage and heroic fighting than is sometimes realised, ended with the fall of France on 25 June. Once again opinions differed as to the performance of the Waffen-SS. The inexperienced divisions took heavy casualties, while the units that had been blooded in Poland had learned from their experience and suffered far less. But there had been severe lapses of discipline – a foretaste of what was to come on the Eastern Front. British prisoners of war were murdered by 4 Company, 2nd Infantry Regiment of the *Totenkopf* at Le Paradis, and by men of the 2nd Battalion, *Leibstandarte*, at Wormhoudt. The *Totenkopf* also shot numerous 'racially inferior' French colonial prisoners of war. It was inevitable that such atrocities would occur. The soldiers of the Waffen-SS were trained to be aggressive tactically, to eschew caution and to believe that killing at close quarters and being killed was integral to the soldier's creed. This being the case, it was difficult for them to show mercy towards the enemy, much less those which their indoctrination insisted were subhuman.

The Wehrmacht's doubts and disdain were dismissed by Hitler, Himmler, and the SS troops themselves. Hitler sanctioned the formation of a new division, while reassuring the Army that the strength of the Waffen-SS would never exceed 10 per cent of the peacetime Army – that is, six divisions.

This went the way of most of Hitler's promises. The Waffen-SS's performance in 1941 and 1942 in the Balkans and in the advance into the Soviet Union was appallingly costly in terms of its own casualties, but there was no doubting its bravery and, no less important, its stubborn tenacity in battle, no matter what the odds. The relentless training of the SS soldiers and their immersion in the tactics of modern mobile warfare had paid off handsomely. Even the Army could no longer withhold its admiration. In 1942, two more divisions were raised; by the war's end, the Waffen-SS boasted 38 divisions, of which about 25 operated at full strength.

The Wehrmacht's misgivings about the role of the Waffen-SS and its predecessors were not based entirely on an assessment of its combat efficiency. The Army was well aware that Germany had a limited pool of manpower, and it had no desire to see the best potential soldiers creamed off into the SS formations. The Wehrmacht agreed that service in the Waffen-SS in peacetime could stand in lieu of the two years' military service demanded of every able-bodied young man over 20 years old, but when war broke out the Army wanted first call on the nation's youth. The SS was open to volunteers aged 17 and over, but was entitled to only a small percentage of those called up for Army duty.

The Wehrmacht's conscripts, however, came only from the *Reichsdeutsche* – German nationals within the nation's

ABOVE: *The glamour of the Waffen-SS and its promise of adventure found favour among many non-German young men, and they enlisted in their thousands to fight in the East in the anti-Bolshevik crusade. These men are Dutch recruits of the Freiwilligen Legion Niederlande.*

borders. The Waffen-SS sidestepped the restriction on numbers by recruiting from among the so-called Volksdeutsche – ethnic Germans in the occupied territories, where the Wehrmacht's writ did not run. Foreign nationals were also accepted as volunteers, provided they were of suitably 'Nordic' stock and could show their 'Aryan' descent. These were inducted into their own units – for example the 5th SS Panzer Division *Wiking* was made up from Dutch, Flemish, Danish and Norwegian nationals.

By the war's end, there were nearly one million men wearing the uniform of the Waffen-SS. By then, any pretence of maintaining racial 'purity' among the foreign contingents had disappeared. So-called 'subhuman' Slavs, 'non-Aryan' (i.e. Latin) French and Walloons, and Balkan Moslems had all been recruited. Their motives were often far removed from any love of Germany, let alone National Socialism, but they were prepared to fight. Their quality ranged from the gallant and honourable men of the Baltic units to the psychopaths of Kaminsky's Russian brigade.

As we shall see in Chapter One, the German and northern European nationals who contributed to this book volunteered for the Waffen-SS for diverse reasons. Given the size and variety of the Waffen-SS in 1945, it is understandable that they resent being lumped together with men who were a disgrace to humanity. One hopes the fact that these veterans wore the uniform of the Waffen-SS will not prevent the reader from looking at their accounts with a fair and open mind. This is their story, in their words.

WHY THE DEATH'S HEAD?

O ne question asked of all of the contributors to this book was: 'What motivated you to volunteer for service in the Waffen-SS as opposed to the regular armed forces?'

Some readers may be surprised that very few considered that political pressure or their own political beliefs contributed in any way to their decision.

At the same time as looking at the reasons they gave for joining the Waffen-SS, it is worth glancing at the society in which most of these veterans grew up.

Before wartime casualties made wider age bands for military service necessary, the SS-Verfügungstruppe, and later the Waffen-SS, recruited only candidates between the ages of 17 and 22. In 1940, just after the start of the war and the victorious conclusion of the Polish campaign but before the losses on the Eastern front, the typical SS recruit would have been born in 1920.

This young man would have been too young to have appreciated much of the political significance of events in Germany as they actually occurred in the early 1920s, or to have been aware of the birth of the SS itself in 1925. But even as a child he could not have avoided the evidence of unemployment and poverty everywhere, and especially would have seen and felt the effects of the raging super-inflation that struck Germany –

The man who intoxicated a nation. A rear view of Adolf Hitler during one of the Nazi Party's mass rallies held before the war. Always surrounding the Führer were the elite black-uniformed SS men, who were loyal unto death to him, and only secondarily to the Fatherland.

his family no doubt suffered from this as keenly as most other Germans in the 1920s. As the 1930s opened and he approached teen age, he would have been equally aware of the appalling political violence in the country, as SA stormtroopers battled with communist activists in the streets. Germany then appeared to be lacking leadership and on the brink of anarchy and chaos.

The restoration of order

On Hitler's accession to power in January 1933, things would have seemed to improve almost immediately. Political order was restored, inflation brought under control, unemployment banished apparently at a stroke and the Ger-

man people given back some of the pride and self respect that they had lost at the conclusion of World War I. It would be strange then, if, in his formative years, the average young German was not impressed by the apparent achievements of the National Socialists. Certainly the press and many prominent individuals in most countries of the world, including Great Britain, praised the restoration of order in Germany.

Soon, the military once again took pride of place in German society and innumerable parades of police, military and paramilitary formations filled the streets. The sight of SS troops in their black parade dress could not have failed to appeal – as was intended – to the German love of uniform and the trappings of military ceremony.

⚡⚡ THE NEED TO BE SPECIAL

GERD ROMMEL
SS-ROTTENFÜHRER

SS-Panzer Aufklarüngs Abteilung 10
10th SS Panzer Division *Frundsberg*

EDUARD JANKE
SS-UNTERSCHARFÜHRER

11th SS Freiwilligen-Panzergrenadier Division *Nordland*

ERWIN BARTMANN
SS-UNTERSCHARFÜHRER

1st SS Panzer Division *Leibstandarte SS Adolf Hitler*

FRIEDRICH-KARL WACKER
SS-STURMMANN

16th SS Panzergrenadier Division *Reichsführer-SS*

RIGHT: Friedrich-Karl Wacker in the uniform of the Deutsche Jungvolk. This youth organisation catered for boys between the ages of 10 and 14.

'At the time, my greatest wish was to fight with the panzer [tank] troops. In 1942 conscripts were primarily being directed towards anti-aircraft artillery or the infantry. But by volunteering for the Waffen-SS, I was able to join a panzer unit. There were absolutely no political motivations whatsoever.'

GERD ROMMEL

'Why did I volunteer for the Waffen-SS and not the Wehrmacht ? Simple – I wanted to serve in an elite formation.'

EDUARD JANKE

'I came to the *Leibstandarte SS Adolf Hitler* on 1 May 1941. As a Berliner there was never any doubt in my mind that I would volunteer for this unit. I had often seen them on parades in the city, on guard at the Reichs Chancellery and so on. Good uniform, comradeship and above all they were all very tall men, at least 1.82m [6ft] tall.'

ERWIN BARTMANN

'I had already gained a very favourable impression of the SS from seeing the *Leibstandarte SS Adolf Hitler* during parades in Berlin before the war. In their impressive uniforms and with their impeccable drill they looked very smart indeed. In fact, all branches of the military looked first class in their walking out uniforms even long before the war. Clean, well behaved and very smart.'

FRIEDRICH-KARL WACKER

Such an attitude may seem superficial. But it is difficult to appreciate, from a distance of six decades and from an entirely different political and cultural tradition, how central the military was to German society. It really did take precedence over every other institution in the land. And the Nazis had played cleverly on the face-saving, almost universally held myth that in 1918 the German Army had been 'stabbed in the back' by Jews, liberal and left-wing politicians and profiteers at home, rather than the truth: that it had been defeated by the Allied armies at the front. Whatever reservations the generals might have had about the Nazis, and they had many, most ordinary Germans were delighted at Hitler's restoration of the military's status and the decision to rearm Germany.

However, there is no escaping the fact that the Waffen-SS was the armed wing of the Nazi Party, not of the German state. But by 1940, it was virtually impossible to tell the difference, especially for a young person whose formative years had been immersed in Nazi ideology. From 1933 everyone was subjected to Nazi propaganda. Much of it was specifically and purposely directed at the younger generation. One can only conclude that what to an outsider would have seemed like political pressure became, for those maturing under the regime, entirely normal.

The process started in school. In April 1934, Bernhard Rust, a fanatical devotee of all things Nazi, was appointed Reich minister of science, education and popular culture. He had already boasted that in the equivalent post in Prussia he had 'liquidated the school as an institution of intellectual acrobatics'. Germany's schools were taken from under the wing of local authorities and put in Rust's charge.

Teachers were obliged to join the Nazi Teacher's League, whose task was to execute 'the ideological and political coordination of all teachers in accordance with the National Socialist doctrine', and were retrained in the party's principles – with a heavy emphasis on Hitler's racial views. Jews were forbidden to teach, a fact that could hardly have gone unnoticed by their pupils. Likewise, they may have noticed when the history books were rewritten and, as William Shirer put it, the Jews cast as 'breeders of almost all the evil there was in the world'. The Germans, of course, were portrayed as the world's master race.

The indoctrination of youth

The Nazification of education and knowledge knew no bounds. Einstein's theory of relativity, the foundation of modern physics, was called a 'Jewish plot to pollute science and... destroy civilisation'. Modern physics was declared 'an instrument of... Jewry for the destruction of Nordic science'. Science, 'like every other human product', was 'racial and conditioned by blood'. Even mathematics had to be judged 'racially'.

There was no escaping these outpourings, and Hitler made no secret of what he was doing. In a speech in November 1933 he dismissed opponents of his New Order:

'What are you? You will pass on. But your descendants now stand in the new camp. In a short time they will know nothing else but this new community.' Hitler's desire to brainwash German youth was not to be satisfied by perverting education and by ceaseless propaganda in the media. The key tool was the Hitler Youth.

In June 1933, within six months of coming to power, the Nazis had taken over (at gunpoint) the Reich Committee of German Youth Associations, the overseer of some 10 million members of youth organisations. By 1936, when the average Waffen-SS recruit was still only 16 years old, all non-Nazi youth organisations were illegal. Hitler declared that 'German youth...shall be educated physically, intellectually and morally in the spirit of National Socialism...through the Hitler Youth.' This was only the beginning of a regimented existence that ended at the earliest after two years' military service, though longer for most.

For a boy, membership of the Hitler Youth had three stages. From six till 10 years old, a boy was a Pimpf, the Nazi version of a Wolfcub. At 10 he graduated to the Jungvolk (Young People) and took an oath: 'to devote all my energies and all my strength to the saviour of our country, Adolf Hitler. I am willing and ready to give up my life for him, so help me God.' Aged 14, he joined the Hitler Youth proper. Activities included sports, camping, Nazi ideology and military training. At 18, he would start compulsory labour service, and then be eligible for military service. While joining the Hitler Youth became compulsory for 17-year-olds only in 1939 (and for 10-year-olds in 1941), the organisation still boasted 7,728,529 members by the end of 1938 – more than 70 per cent of all German youth, both boys and girls.

To the boys themselves, there was probably nothing questionable about their time in the Hitler Youth. And the smart uniforms, military-style drill, discipline and training exercises – quite apart from the political and racial indoctrination – doubtless helped to instil absolute loyalty towards the Nazi regime.

William Shirer, who witnessed the early years of Hitler's rule and of World War II from inside Germany, has some illuminating things to say about this aspect of the Hitler Youth: 'Though their minds were deliberately poisoned, their regular schooling interrupted, their homes largely replaced so far as their rearing went, the boys and the girls... seemed immensely happy, filled with a zest for the life of a Hitler Youth.... No one who travelled up and down Germany in those days and talked with the young in their camps and watched them work and play and sing could fail to see that, however sinister the teaching, here was an incredibly dynamic youth movement.'

The seeds of fanaticism

The 'sinister teaching' had, it would seem, been thoroughly absorbed, so that a nihilist totalitarian regime, whose major interests were colonising eastern Europe and a rabid anti-Semitism, could seem unexceptionable. Certainly no German born in 1920 could claim to be unaware of the Nazis' relentless anti-Semitism, or of the fact that it was enormously popular. In 1933 Jews were excluded from the civil service, the entertainment industry, public office, farming, and journalism. The next year they were forbidden to work in finance. In 1935 they were deprived of citizenship altogether, and sexual relations between 'Aryans' and Jews were forbidden. From then on, signs saying JEWS NOT WELCOME (and worse) appeared on shops, restaurants and even pharmacies all over Germany.

On 9 November 1938, institutionalised terror reached a new level with the destruction of thousands of Jewish businesses, nearly 200 synagogues, and the murder of at least 36 Jewish people during 'Crystal Night' (the murderers, who were known, went deliberately unpunished by the Nazi courts). The orgy of hatred was presented as a spontaneous popular demonstration but, as an official report noted: 'The public, down to the last man, realises that political drives like [this] were organised and directed by the Party, whether this is admitted or not.' As compensating for the pogrom would have bankrupted the German insurance companies, the Nazis fined the Jewish community one billion marks for 'causing' the outrage, and confiscated their businesses. Jews were thus effectively excluded from the German economy. No church or military leader spoke out in public against any of this state-sponsored barbarity. On 30 January 1939, Hitler told the Reichstag that in any new

ABOVE: Friedrich-Karl Wacker in the uniform of the Reiter-Hitler Jugend, the mounted section of the Hitler Youth. The spurs on his boots can just be seen. Above the armband is the district badge stating Ost-Berlin, *and on his belt he wears the Hitler Youth knife.*

war the Jews of Europe would be exterminated. The road that led to the death camps was plain to see.

But so were other brutal aspects of the Nazi state. In May 1933, students under the eye of Dr Göbbels had made a bonfire of thousands of books as a prelude to the announcement of a massive censorship of literature. Hitler made no secret of his responsibility for the murder of Ernst Röhm, ex-Chancellor Schleicher and others in June 1934. Equally visible was the willingness of the German military to be identified with the Nazi regime, whatever the lingering doubts of the officer corps. The new Soldiers' Oath of allegiance to Hitler in August 1934 was one of the earliest signs

of this compromise with the new order. By grim coincidence, or something worse, the 1935 Nuremberg rally, at which Hitler deprived the Jews of their citizenship, was the first at which detachments of the Wehrmacht paraded with the massed ranks of Nazi Party faithful.

No one growing up in Germany in those years could pretend that they did not know what kind of government they enjoyed, or what kind of country theirs had become. Yet Germans seem to have set a far greater store by the new orderliness of life, the shows of political strength, and the glamour of a massive rearmament programme than they did by their own civil liberties, the treatment of the Jews, or the wilful destruction, from within, of one of the most admired and sophisticated cultures in the world.

Then there were the foreign successes before the outbreak of World War II, which seemed to vindicate Nazi policies: Germany annexed Austria and gained the Sudetenland and Memel without a shot being fired. When war came there were more successes: Poland fell within days; the campaign of 1940 drove the British from the European mainland and put France and the Low Countries in German hands in a matter of weeks. The Blitzkrieg carried all before it – German arms seemed invincible.

So, all in all, it is unsurprising that many young Germans would look to the military as a promising career. Apart from the prestige that the military traditionally enjoyed in German society, and the exaltation of soldierly virtues by organisations such as the Hitler Youth, a young man in about 1940 had no choice about being conscripted into the services. To many, perhaps hardly consciously, it must have seemed no more or less than a sensible career move to volunteer for the Waffen-SS. The organisation enjoyed the protection and favour of the Party; it quite rightly had the status of a military elite; and it also offered a long-term career when the war was over.

Below: Foreign volunteers also flocked to the banner of the Waffen-SS. Newly recruited Danish volunteers stand in front of a poster that exhorts volunteers to 'fight against Bolshevism under the Danish flag' in Freikorps Danmark.

As the war progressed, and the Waffen-SS proved itself on the battlefield, the newspapers and movie newsreels would show the troops of the Waffen-SS at the front. Soon the titles of its elite divisions and the names of their commanders would become household names. The esprit de corps, the sense of comradeship, and the military prowess of the Waffen-SS were widely known and, even after the tide of war turned against Germany, there were large numbers of volunteers willing to serve in its ranks.

Most of those who formed the earliest intakes into the SS-Verfügungstruppe and Waffen-SS were either killed in action during the course of the war, have died in the intervening years since 1945, or are now of extremely advanced years. The majority of those who have contributed to this work are of the younger age group who volunteered for service after the war started and were still in their teenage years or early 20s when Germany was defeated in 1945. Their comments on what motivated them to volunteer for the Waffen-SS are nonetheless illuminating.

One of the commonest reasons quoted for seeking to serve in the Waffen-SS was the desire to become part of a military elite.

SS YOUTH AND IDEALISM

KARL-HEINZ DECKER
SS-STURMMANN
(UNTERFÜHRERANWARTER)

SS-Panzergrenadier Regiment 25
12th SS Panzer Division *Hitlerjugend*

HEINZ KÖHNE
SS-UNTERSCHARFÜHRER

1st SS Panzer Division *Leibstandarte SS Adolf Hitler*

WERNER BUSSE
SS-UNTERSCHARFÜHRER

SS-Panzer Regiment 10
10th SS Panzer Division *Frundsberg*

HANS-GERHARD STARCK
SS-OBERSCHARFÜHRER

1st SS Panzer Division *Leibstandarte SS Adolf Hitler*

ABOVE: Youth organisations were an esential part of the Nazi Party's drive to militarise and indoctrinate German society. Boys such as these later joined the Waffen-SS.

'Like all young German boys, I was in the Hitler Youth. I came from a farming background and had a great love of horses. My ambition was to join the cavalry. Then, one day, we were told about a new Waffen-SS division to be formed from the Hitler Youth. I was told that if I volunteered for this I would immediately be put forward as a candidate for NCO training. That was how I joined 12th SS Panzer Division *Hitlerjugend*.'

KARL-HEINZ DECKER

'I believe that every young man who was accepted into the Waffen-SS was very proud of this achievement. In my muster group there were some 500 young men who were prepared to volunteer for this elite force, but only 28 were of a suitable calibre. Merely being accepted was already a great honour, because the selection procedure was so rigorous. And for us it fulfilled our military service obligation.'

HEINZ KÖHNE

'Although I was a member of the Hitler Youth like most young German men, at no time was any pressure put on me to join the Waffen-SS rather than the Army, Luftwaffe or Navy. I chose to volunteer for the Waffen-SS because it was known to have a greater atmosphere of comradeship, and also because it was an elite force, more dedicated to Germany's cause.'

WERNER BUSSE

'My motivation in joining the Waffen-SS lay partly in my age. All my friends in school were a year or two older than me.

At the age of 17, in March 1942, I passed my leaving exams. Because I wore glasses, the Luftwaffe wouldn't accept me and nor would the paratroops. In the Hitler Youth I had trained on infantry courses at Doberitz with the Infantry Training Regiment and in Potsdam with 9 Infantry Regiment, but these courses only lasted a few days or a week at the most. I was good at sport and physically very fit, so I decided I would be an infantryman. I didn't have any great feeling for the Army so I volunteered for the Waffen-SS, joining the Signals Replacement Battalion in Nuremberg.'

HANS-GERHARD STARCK

⚡⚡ THE LURE OF AN ELITE

RICHARD FUCHS
SS-UNTERSCHARFÜHRER

5th SS Panzer Division *Wiking*

MATHIEU KLEIN
SS-HAUPTSTURMFÜHRER

1st SS Panzer Division *Leibstandarte SS Adolf Hitler*

WERNER VÖLKNER
SS-ROTTENFÜHRER

3rd SS Panzer Division *Totenkopf*

FRIEDRICH-KARL WACKER
SS-STURMMANN

16th SS Panzergrenadier Division *Reichsführer-SS*

RIGHT: An SS-Verfügungstruppe recruiting poster.

Merkblatt
für den Eintritt als Freiwilliger in die ⚡⚡=Verfügungstruppe
(Ausgabe Juli 1938)

Wann
erfolgt die Einstellung in die ⚡⚡-VT?
Am 1. Oktober. Meldeschluß für die Einstellung im Oktober: 1. Februar.

Wer
kann eingestellt werden?
Bewerber vom vollendeten 17. Lebensjahr bis zum voll endeten 22. Lebensjahr; mit 22 Jahren jedoch nur noch in besonderen Ausnahmefällen.

Mindestgröße für Leibstandarte-⚡⚡ Adolf Hitler .... 178 cm
Mindestgröße für Standarte-⚡⚡ »Deutschland«, Standarte-⚡⚡ »Germania« und Standarte-⚡⚡ 3 .... 171 cm
Mindestgröße für Reitzüge, Pionier- und Nachrichtensturmbann .... 173 cm

Was
ist Voraussetzung für die Einstellung?
Jeder Bewerber muß:
a) die deutsche Staatsangehörigkeit besitzen.
b) wehrwürdig und tauglich für die ⚡⚡, d. h. sittlich, geistig, körperlich und rassisch einwandfrei und weltanschaulich Nationalsozialist sein,
c) den Nachweis seiner arischen Abstammung bis zum Jahre 1800 erbringen,
d) unverheiratet sein und noch kein Eheversprechen gegeben haben,
e) seine Arbeitsdienstpflicht erfüllt haben,
f) die schriftliche Einwilligungserklärung seines gesetzlichen Vertreters vorlegen, sofern er minderjährig ist,
g) als Lehrling in der Berufsausbildung seine Lehrzeit bis zum Einstellungstage mit Erfolg beendet haben oder die Einwilligung seines Lehrherrn zur Lehrzeitverkürzung beibringen,
h) die erforderliche Zahnbehandlung vor der Einstellung auf eigene Kosten durchführen,
i) normale Sehschärfe besitzen (kein Brillenträger),
k) nachweisen, daß er unbescholten und gerichtlich nicht vorbestraft ist *).
Wer diesen Bedingungen nicht entspricht, kann nicht eingestellt werden. Erneute Gesuche mit der Bitte um ausnahmsweise Einstellung sind zwecklos.
Darüber hinaus ist eine Einstellung von ehemaligen Wehrmachtsangehörigen oder Bewerbern, die bereits einen Annahmeschein der Wehrmacht erhalten haben, grundsätzlich ausgeschlossen.
Die Führerlaufbahn in der Schutzstaffel steht jedem ⚡⚡-Angehörigen offen, der nach mindestens 1jähriger Dienstzeit die Befähigung zum Führeramt beweist. Entsprechende Gesuche können dann a. d. D. eingereicht werden. Voraussetzung ist in jedem Falle die Verpflichtung auf 4 Jahre Dienstzeit; eine Bewerbung als Führeranwärter von vornherein wird nicht angenommen.
Die Einberufung zum Arbeitsdienst wird nach festgestellter ⚡⚡-Tauglichkeit von den Ergänzungsstellen veranlaßt.

Wie lange
dient der Freiwillige?
Die Dienstzeit bei der ⚡⚡-VT. beträgt 4 Jahre einschließlich 3 Monate Probezeit. Die ersten 2 Jahre rechnen als Erfüllung der allgemeinen Wehrpflicht.
Freiwillige, die bei entsprechender Befähigung die Unterführerlaufbahn einschlagen wollen, können sich bis zu einer Gesamtdienstzeit von 12 Jahren verpflichten.

'Why did I volunteer for the Waffen-SS and not the Wehrmacht ? The Bolsheviks were seen by me, and by the Waffen-SS, as the principal enemy, against whom I wanted to fight as a member of an elite force.'

RICHARD FUCHS

'I reported to the *Leibstandarte SS Adolf Hitler* in 1934 purely voluntarily, because I wanted to belong to an elite unit. From the 120 of us who volunteered, only 23 were chosen after three intensive medical examinations.'

MATHIEU KLEIN

'Because I was in what was considered a "reserved occupation", I was permitted to complete my apprenticeship before being liable to call up. In the Hitler Youth I had done some glider flying and really wanted to be a pilot. But I was rejected by the Luftwaffe for flying crew because of an old ear infection, and I certainly didn't want to join the ground crews. As I walked down the corridor at the recruiting centre, I saw a poster advertising the Waffen-SS panzer troops, and I thought: "Yes, that's for me!"'

WERNER VÖLKNER

'I completed my six months' compulsory service with the Reichs Arbeits Dienst (Labour Service) in October 1942. During this period we were visited by an SS recruiting official. He talked about how, if we joined the Waffen-SS, not only would we really feel that we had done our bit for the war effort, but, having served in the Waffen-SS at the front, we would enhance our status after the war. This seemed a reasonable suggestion to me.'

FRIEDRICH-KARL WACKER

Political considerations may not have played a conscious part in the decision of many young Germans to volunteer for the Waffen-SS. However, for the foreign nationals who volunteered to wear the field-grey uniform of the Waffen-SS, fervent anti-communism and pan-Europeanism seem to have played a much greater role. Many greatly admired the Germans and sympathised with National Socialism, but were nevertheless fiercely nationalistic. They had no desire to see their own countries absorbed into a greater German Reich as Austria had been, but rather wanted to be partners with Germany in a new 'European Order'.

SS FOREIGN VOLUNTEERS

REMY SCHRIJNEN
SS-UNTERSCHARFÜHRER

SS Freiwilligen Sturmbrigade *Langemarck*

JAN MUNK
SS-STANDARTENOBERJUNKER

SS-Panzergrenadier Regiment *Westland*
5th SS Panzer Division *Wiking*

Right: A recruiting poster for the motorised section of the Sturmbrigade Wallonie *(Walloon spelling). Note that the office was in Brussels.*

'As a Flemish nationalist, with a great admiration for the Germans, and as an anti-communist, I volunteered to work in Germany in early July 1940, to learn more about the country and its people. On the very day that war with the Soviet Union broke out, I reported to the Waffen-SS to offer myself as a "Germanic Volunteer". Unfortunately, because I was only 1.64m [5ft 5in] tall and the minimum height requirement was 1.78m [5ft 10in], I was rejected. This didn't put me off, though. I continued trying to enlist. In the end, in the summer of 1942, I was accepted into the Flemish Volunteer Legion. I served on the northern sector of the Eastern Front, in the swampy terrain around Leningrad, as a company runner.'

REMY SCHRIJNEN

'As a young boy we often visited very good friends of my parents in the east of Holland, near the German border. In 1935 or 1936, we went by car into Germany, as my parents and their friends knew of a restaurant where we could have a delicious dish of trout.

'It was a beautiful summer's day, and when we entered the little German town there was a festival of some sort going on. There were swastika flags, banners, garlands and flowers everywhere, and it looked lovely. I saw groups of Hitler Youth boys and girls marching and singing and they looked so happy that I thought it was wonderful, until my father said to his friend: "Look at all these Nazi children. Isn't it terrible, they will all grow up to be no good." I just couldn't understand this. My family had always been anti-Nazi but not anti-German. When my father made that remark about those youngsters, whose happy singing and marching I thought was so wonderful, that was the moment I became pro-Nazi. The feeling grew, especially as I was always at loggerheads with my father, and culminated in my joining the Waffen-SS. I became the black sheep of the family, but my mother, brother and sisters kept writing to me.'

JAN MUNK

⚡⚡ SOLDIERING AS A CAREER

ERIC BRÖRUP
SS-OBERSTURMFÜHRER

SS-Panzer Aufklärungs Abteilung 5
5th SS Panzer Division *Wiking*

For some, such as Eric Brörup, the chance to carry on soldiering was motive enough for joining the Waffen-SS, and the latter was more than happy to recruit good soldiers.

RIGHT: *Danish volunteer Eric Brörup, seen here in May 1944 as an SS-Untersturmführer. He was promoted to SS-Obersturmführer on 30 January 1945 while serving with the reconnaissance detachment of the elite* Wiking *Division.*

'At school in Denmark, I served in a militia unit named Konigens Livjaeger Korps, which roughly translated would be something like Kings Own Rifles. It had been raised in 1801 to fight the English! When I was called up for national service I chose the cavalry, after seeing the movie *The Bengal Lancers*. I started recruit training on 22 October 1937 in the Gardehusar Regiment. They were household cavalry and a real bunch of snobs. I must have pissed them off somewhat, because at the outbreak of war in September 1939 I didn't get the usual automatic pro-motion to second lieutenant. Then my service was cut short by the arrival of the Germans in April 1940. Our captain explained to us just exactly what the SS-Verfügungstruppe and Waffen-SS were.

'I also learned there was a sub-office of the recruiting department of the Waffen-SS in Copenhagen; they hired soldiers for the SS-Regiment *Nordland*. Having done nothing but soldiering I figured it wouldn't hurt to ask, so I went in, in Sam Browne belt and spurs. They checked me out, found that I wasn't such a bad soldier after all and offered me, for starters, my equivalent rank – SS-Standartenjunker – and a chance to join the next officers' training course at the SS-Junkerschule at Bad Tölz in Bavaria. By 25 April 1941 I had signed my contract.

'When Operation "Barbarossa", the invasion of the Soviet Union, started, all the Danish Nazis wanted to join the glory trail, and they started up the Freikorps *Danmark*. I had already received my marching orders for SS-Junkerschule Tölz, but at the last minute they were changed and I found myself in Freikorps *Danmark*. I didn't mind that so much, but these Danish Nazis really pissed me off. I have never liked politicians – together with pimps and preachers I thought they were the lowest form of life. Whenever I voted, I went for the party which supported the military, otherwise I had no use for them.

'So much for motivation. Basically I went to Germany because they treated soldiers right. I was a professional soldier and I am damned proud of the fact that as a "foreigner" I became an officer in one of the best divisions ever, and I have never rued or regretted what I did.'

In some cases, soldiers were simply posted to the Waffen-SS without consultation because their particular skills were in demand. For those in the police this often meant transfer to the Waffen-SS as members of the Military Police attached to the Waffen-SS divisions or corps. This was not a difficult matter for the Reichsführer-SS, Heinrich Himmler, to arrange. After all, he also held the title of Chief of the German Police, which included the Gestapo, the secret police of the Third Reich.

WAFFEN-SS POLICEMEN

OSKAR LÖSEL
SS-OBERSTURMFÜHRER

SS-Feldgendarmerie Kompanie 17

To many the Waffen-SS is associated solely with soldiers. However, like every organisation, it also needed clerks, drivers and administrators. Oskar Lösel eventually found himself in Russia serving with the Waffen-SS.

RIGHT: *Oskar Lösel, a former career police officer, seen here as an SS-Untersturmführer in the SS-Feldgendarmerie in command of the Military Police troop of the 17th SS Panzergrenadier Division* Götz von Berlichingen.

'I was a police official and at the end of 1941 was sent for training to become an officer. I was commissioned as a lieutenant in the Schutzpolizei and as such was posted to Stettin in early 1942. In the middle of that year I was posted as a platoon commander to I SS Panzer Corps under Paul Hausser. I served with this formation in Russia until the formation of the new 17th SS Panzergrenadier Division *Götz von Berlichingen*. Then I was transferred to become commander of SS-Feldgendarmerie Kompanie 17.'

TRAINING AND INDOCTRINATION

All recruits to the Waffen-SS underwent a brutal training schedule at the various depots throughout the Third Reich. The emphasis was on aggressive battlefield tactics and indoctrination in all the tenets of National Socialism. As the following first-hand accounts indicate, only those with the right mental attitude and fitness levels became black knights.

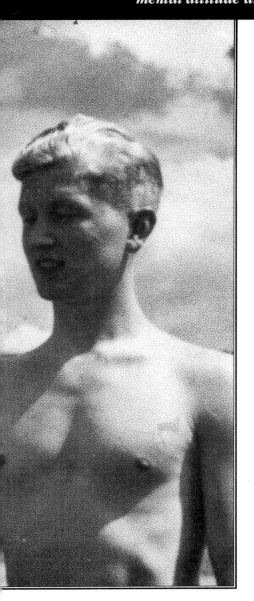

During the early years of the SS-Verfügungstruppe and Waffen-SS, recruitment depended entirely on volunteers. Until around 1940, the SS had to compete with the Wehrmacht for its manpower from among conscripts, and of the three traditional branches of the armed forces the Army had to supply the SS from its own allocation. Unsurprisingly, the Army was more than a little incensed that the SS insisted on taking only what it considered the finest candidates. This poaching led to considerable friction between the Wehrmacht and the SS.

The recruitment service of the Waffen-SS was established in December 1939 under the control of the SS Main Office in Berlin. It was commanded by SS-Gruppenführer Gottlob Berger, a forceful personality and true believer in National Socialism, who would leave no stone unturned in his efforts to expand the armed branch of his revered Himmler's SS.

Initially, there were four main recruiting offices for the SS-Verfügungstruppe, the forerunner of the Waffen-SS. These were in Berlin, Hamburg, Munich and Vienna. At this time, expansion of the armed SS was difficult. Himmler's strict criteria for recruits combined with the Army's intransigence conspired to keep the size of the armed SS within moderate limits. Even the recruitment of *Volksdeutsche* (ethnic Germans) from occupied areas such as the Czech Sudetenland was too low to

Waffen-SS officer recruits in training at Bad Tölz take a breather. Waffen-SS officer training was designed to develop supreme physical fitness and a mental toughness in individuals, which would, the Party hoped, make them the embodiment of Nazi virtues on the battlefield.

ABOVE: Sports and fitness drills played an extremely important part in Waffen-SS training, both to engender a spirit of comradeship and to ensure Waffen-SS formations contained fit men. These are officer cadets at Bad Tölz. Note the SS emblems on the black tracksuits.

swell numbers to any great extent. In any case, the Army continued to oppose any increase in the power and influence of the SS, jealous of its status as sole bearer of arms in the defence of the Reich.

Once, however, the campaign of summer 1940 had seen most of Europe cowed into submission, a potentially huge pool of manpower became available. Hitler agreed to the SS recruiting suitable 'Aryan' volunteers from the occupied lands, as the Army had no first claim on them. The SS maintained its racial criteria, however. Those considered 'non-Aryan', such as the French and Walloons, were passed over to the Army. Soon Danes, Dutchmen, Norwegians, Flemings, Swiss and even a few Swedes were wearing the field-grey uniform of the Waffen-SS.

Following the invasion of the Soviet Union in the summer of 1941, recruitment grew apace as Hitler's much-vaunted 'Crusade against Bolshevism' attracted many anti-communist young men. Not all were particularly pro-German, or anti-British, but they did have a great hatred of everything that communism represented.

As Germany's fortunes waned during 1942, recruitment, not surprisingly, became more difficult in the occupied lands. Surreptitious, and then blatantly forced, conscription into the Waffen-SS became widespread. With the increase in numbers of 'pressed' men came a concomitant general drop in the quality of recruits entering the Waffen-SS.

Many of the Germans who formed the nucleus of the early Waffen-SS divisions were volunteers from the early days of the armed SS and had fulfilled the strictest physical and racial criteria for enlistment. While probably only a minority of Waffen-SS soldiers truly believed in the outlandish racial theories of Himmler, Rosenberg and other Nazi ideologues, even the most dedicated must have felt a twinge of cynicism at the sight of east European Moslem volunteers, complete with traditional fez headdress, kneeling on their prayer mats and making their devotions towards Mecca. This was hardly the master race to which they were supposed to belong and for which they had fought so hard.

As far as recruitment within the Reich was concerned during the later years of the war, many young men still came forward with pride to serve in the uniform of the Waffen-SS, though their numbers were nowhere near enough to replace battlefield casualties. Kriegsmarine personnel without ships and Luftwaffe airmen and ground crew without planes found themselves drafted into the Waffen-SS to make up losses. Wherever they came from, though, unit pride and

a legendary bond of comradeship remained intact for most Waffen-SS soldiers until the bitter end.

Recruitment into the armed SS in the Reich itself was on a broadly geographical basis prior to the outbreak of war.

SS Recruiting Post I was located in the barracks of the *Leibstandarte SS Adolf Hitler* at Berlin Lichterfelde, Finckensteinallee 63, and covered recruitment for those volunteers whose home addresses lay in the areas covered by Military Districts I (Konigsberg), II (Stettin), III (Berlin), IV (Dresden), and VIII (Breslau).

SS Recruiting Post II was located in the Hamburg barracks of the *Germania* Regiment and covered recruitment from Military District VI (Munster), IX (Kassel), X (Hamburg) and XI (Hanover).

BELOW: Cadets at Bad Tölz practice their drill. The young Waffen-SS officers who came from the training depots were responsible for forging the Waffen-SS's reputation, displaying as they did toughness and loyalty and a fanatical belief in their mission.

ABOVE: Paul Hausser, the man who was responsible for shaping the Waffen-SS's training and administration. He introduced many innovative aspects into training, such as officers and men taking part together in athletics.

SS Recruiting Post III was based in the barracks of the *Deutschland* Regiment in Munich to cover recruitment from Military District V (Stuttgart), VII (Munich), XII (Wiesbaden) and XIII (Nuremberg).

SS Recruiting Post IV was located in the Radetsky Kaserne in Vienna, home of the *Der Führer* Regiment, covering recruitment from Military District XVII (Vienna) and XVIII (Salzburg).

Initially, therefore, the regiment into which a recruit would be inducted depended to a considerable degree on his geographical location. The main exception was the *Leibstandarte*, which was entitled to recruit from anywhere in the Reich where recruits could be found who fulfilled its much more stringent entrance requirements.

Within each regiment, the recruit would have been allowed some degree of choice as to which branch of service he wished to serve, i.e. infantry, transport, signals and so on.

Each prospective candidate for the SS-Verfügungstruppe/Waffen-SS had to be between the ages of 17 and 22. Those over 22 were accepted only in exceptional cases, and all had to fulfil the following criteria:

- be a German citizen
- be fit for service in the SS
- have an acceptable political outlook
- provide evidence of an 'Aryan' origin back to 1800
- be unmarried, and not engaged to be married
- have fulfilled all labour service obligations
- have the written permission of a parent or official guardian if at the minimum age of 17
- if undergoing trade training or an apprenticeship, have successfully completed the course, or had the agreement of the relative journeyman as to the course being cut short
- pay for any dental treatment required at the time of acceptance and have it carried out before enlistment
- have normal eyesight without glasses
- have no criminal record, or criminal proceedings pending against him.

Obviously, as the war progressed, these strict criteria were considerably relaxed, then eventually all but dispensed with as the Reich's fortunes worsened.

When recruitment of foreign 'Germanic' volunteers began, the criteria were also altered. Height restrictions were relaxed to a minimum of 1.65m (5ft 5in). 'Aryan' descent had to be proved for just two generations, and the prospective recruit had to be of good character. Recruits could sign on for up to 12 years and receive the same pay and allowances as German SS men. They could also apply for German citizenship at the end of a 12-year period of service.

These men were seen as professional career soldiers, whereas those who later volunteered for the various foreign legions were considered to be temporarily in the service of the Waffen-SS and received less favourable terms. Their contracts were for two years only and they could elect to return home at the end of this term – which many of them did after tasting the rigours of combat on the Eastern Front.

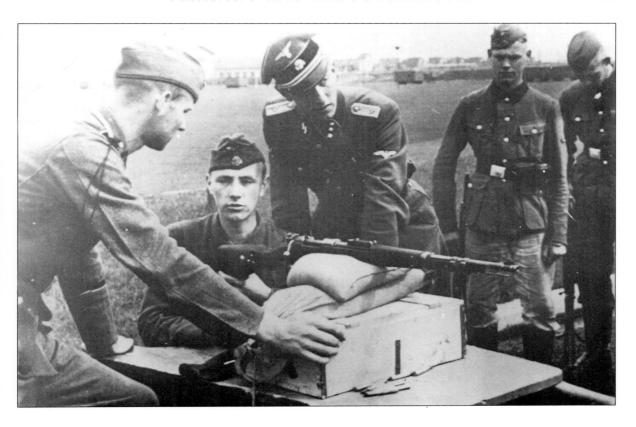

ABOVE: Flemish recruits in the Waffen-SS receive weapons training at Klagenfurt in 1942 from an SS-Unterscharführer and an SS-Untersturmführer. Note the recruits in the background are wearing no collar patches.

Some of the early foreign volunteers received less than sympathetic treatment from their German trainers. This cavalier attitude seems to have been extinguished rapidly once complaints were made, however, and most foreign recruits were treated as well as their German counterparts. And there were always more informal ways to deal with injustices, to which (as in armed forces everywhere) the authorities were capable of ignoring.

Those responsible for training the SS-Verfügungstruppe, and later the Waffen-SS, had learned the lessons of the prolonged, costly and often pointless trench warfare in World War I. The most influential figure in the moulding of the Waffen-SS was SS-Brigadeführer, later SS-Gruppenführer, Paul Hausser. He firmly supported the idea of the highly

mobile, super-fit and well-armed Stosstrupp (shock troop) of World War I (Felix Steiner, one of Hausser's subordinates, had been an officer in such a unit). Therefore, SS soldiers would be given the most up-to-date training possible and, although SS training was based on the traditional methods of the Army, a much greater emphasis was given to sport, physical fitness and, above all, fieldcraft.

Initial training was undertaken in depots outside each unit's home town. Those selected as being capable of earning a commission were sent to the officer training schools at Bad Tölz and Brunswick.

All recruits had to be able to complete a 3km (2-mile) battle march in full combat order with 100kg (220lb) of kit in just 20 minutes. Exercises were held under realistic battle conditions under live artillery and small-arms fire. Fatalities among recruits undergoing this type of training were not uncommon. Considerable emphasis was given to hand-to-hand combat and close quarter battle with grenades, machine guns and automatic pistols. The Waffen-SS also pioneered the use of disruptive pattern camouflage clothing, which was so successful that very similar patterns are still in use today with the Bundeswehr.

Many apocryphal stories circulate about training in the Waffen-SS. One particular favourite is that SS recruits were expected to balance a hand grenade on their steel helmet and test their nerve by standing to attention while it went off. If their nerve held, the blast would (in theory) be deflected upwards and away from them, supposedly leaving them with nothing worse than a severe headache. If their nerve failed, and they shook, the grenade would drop off their helmet to the ground, explode, and kill the recruit. Such harebrained ideas actually had no part in Waffen-SS training, since anyone trying this trick would most likely be killed either way. Certainly the author found not one single former Waffen-SS soldier who had seen such a thing or who had even heard of it being done.

The story may, however, have a different significance – as an impression of the unquestioning obedience that was instilled into Waffen-SS recruits. The results of this training had drawbacks as well as advantages. Waffen-SS units probably took the high casualties they did because they took their orders literally, fighting for an objective to the last man and rarely looking for opportunities for tactical withdrawal. On the other hand, it is in the nature of elite troops to have a 'short life expectancy', as General Montgomery said when recommending the formation of British paratroop units. A battlefield is no place for democratic debate at the best of times, but for soldiers intended to carry on where even the best of others might falter, iron discipline and instant obedience are absolute necessities.

Although all the contributors to this book agree that Waffen-SS training was tough, none considered it unreasonably hard. Methods of testing the recruits' grit were often inventive, but – again, as in most armies – insistence on rigid discipline for its own sake was sometimes inappropriately applied, and the soldiers found their own ways to deal with this. The effect seems to have been to increase their solidarity and their respect for their superiors. This was no doubt intended, since every one of their instructors must have suffered the same routines, and found ways round them, during their own training.

What of indoctrination? Recruits were often encouraged, but by no means forced, to revoke their membership of any particular religion they adhered to. Membership of any specific church was not recommended by the authorities (although many high-ranking figures of the time retained their full church membership), who preferred that soldiers adopt the rather nebulous status of *Gottgläubigkeit*, a rather vague statement that the soldier believed in God but by implication was not a Christian.

Although many of the recruits into the Waffen-SS were already firm supporters of Hitler and National Socialism, having in the main already served in the Hitler Youth, much of the subsequent effort to indoctrinate them further seems to have been wasted. Sometimes, these attempts ran aground on foreign volunteers' own nationalism.

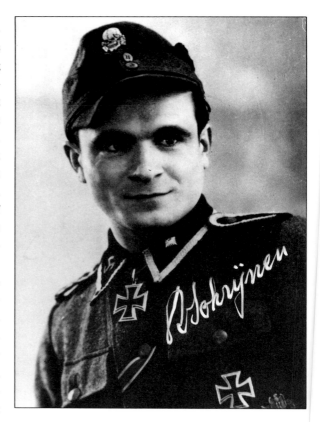

ABOVE: SS-Unterscharführer Remy Schrijnen. The three-legged 'Trifos' sunwheel-type swastika of the Sturmbrigade Langemarck can be seen on the right-hand collar.

In general, as fit, active young men, the recruits preferred military training or sporting activity to sitting in a classroom listening to debates on *Mein Kampf* or to some of the madder racial theories promulgated by Nazi 'experts'. So

little impact did this aspect of their training have on most soldiers of the Waffen-SS that few can recall much about it, apart from their difficulty in following much of the debate, which counters the popular image of the Waffen-SS.

⚡⚡ THE FORGING OF AN ELITE

ERIC BRÖRUP
SS-OBERSTURMFÜHRER

SS-Panzer Aufklärungs Abteilung 5
5th SS Panzer Division *Wiking*

REMY SCHRIJNEN
SS-UNTERSCHARFÜHRER

SS Freiwilligen Sturmbrigade *Langemarck*

HEINZ KÖHNE
SS-OBERSCHARFÜHRER

1st SS Panzer Division *Leibstandarte SS Adolf Hitler*

HANS-GERHARD STARCK
SS-OBERSCHARFÜHRER

1st SS Panzer Division *Leibstandarte SS Adolf Hitler*

RIGHT: A Knights Cross-bearing SS-Hauptsturmführer from the Das Reich *Division provides instruction in the use of the MG42 machine gun.*

'I wasn't personally subjected to any form of demeaning or degrading treatment because I was a Dane. I went through officers' school where there was respect for every individual, not like the usual senseless bullshit you normally find – the US Military Academy at West Point being a case in point.

'How hard was it? I can state quite categorically that the training I went through in the Danish Cavalry was tougher than anything I later encountered in the Waffen-SS.

'Manoeuvres were very realistic, with live ammunition being used on certain exercises, but not before every man knew his weapon and how to take cover. By the way, similar "shoots" were also used in the Danish forces.'

ERIC BRÖRUP

'The training in the Waffen-SS was very hard and among other things included learning the Parademarsch (Goose Step), training for combat at the front, and of course lots of sporting activity. As a recruit I thought the training was very good and covered everything one needed to know. Our instructors were all specialists with years of experience. They treated us just like they treated the German recruits.'

REMY SCHRIJNEN

'It is true that training in the Waffen-SS was very hard indeed. Otherwise when we went into action we would not have been so steadfast. The comradeship of the Waffen-SS was based on the tenet of "all for one and one for all". Throughout the training great emphasis was put on this.'

HEINZ KÖHNE

'The days spent in training were long and hard. The training was always intense and repetitive, and very realistic. It was repeated until everything was done almost automatically, but I think this helped save many lives when we were in combat. We were all good at sports, but the instructors always pushed us to the limits of our endurance and gave us tasks to prove our steadfastness. One day, for example, we were taken on a march carrying full kit and wearing gas masks. We reached the Dutzend-Teich, a large pond or pool with water around 150–180cm [5–6ft] deep. We averaged 177cm [5ft 9.7in] tall. We were ordered to march on, straight into the water, singing all the while. Nobody faltered. Then, at last, we were ordered to turn back when the water reached our necks. We returned to the barracks, soaking wet, at the double.'

HANS-GERHARD STARCK

ᛋᛋ MATCHSTICK BURIAL DUTY

JAN MUNK
SS-STANDARTENOBERJUNKER

SS-Panzergrenadier Regiment *Westland*
5th SS Panzer Division *Wiking*

Munk remembers the difficulties faced by foreign recruits to the Waffen-SS, such as getting to grips with the tenets of National Socialism in a different language.

RIGHT: Jan Munk in the uniform of an SS-Oberjunker while attending the SS-Junkerschule at Bad Tölz.

'We liked the great majority of our superiors, the squad leader, the platoon commander and the company commander, and not just liked but respected them. If we were wet, cold and tired we knew they would be as well. I only know of one case of an NCO being disliked, a corporal, because of his treatment of the Flemish in particular. One Christmas night, when he was stoned out of his mind, we wrapped him in a blanket, dragged him feet-first down the stairs into the cellar, threw him into one of the long washing troughs and turned on the cold water. He got a sound beating, his colleagues turning a blind eye. He behaved much better afterwards.

'The training concentrated mainly on discipline. It was rammed home to us that an order from a superior had to be

nach IV. Aktiver	Wehrdienst
Ausbildung (auch im Kriege)	Ausbildung (auch im Kriege)

ABOVE: A section from the Wehrpass of a Waffen-SS soldier showing the way in which training was recorded. The left-hand page shows the weapons in which instruction was given, such as the MG34 machine gun. The right-hand page shows the training institutions attended.

obeyed. If that person was, for example, just an Ober-schutze (Private First Class) and just slightly higher in rank than you, it made no difference, he was still your superior and you had to obey his order. We were never, however, ordered to do anything unreasonable, such as jumping from a window without checking to see how high it was and things like that. However, they did excel in making you obey an order to take cover in a water-filled ditch, or a bramble bush, or slushy melting snow. But of course such training could later save your life.

'It was really just a battle of wills. This does not mean that our spirits were broken, not at all, it merely meant that when an order was given it was carried out. We once had exercises on a field that had been flooded and frozen then partly thawed out, ideal for their "take-cover" drill. At first everyone tried to keep dry by supporting themselves on their toes and hands, then, as they got more tired, their elbows and knees. Eventually we realised how futile it was not to obey the order properly. We began throwing ourselves completely down. We even began to enjoy ourselves, aiming for the NCO every time we had to dive for cover and try to topple him. With luck we would succeed, and the other NCOs who had kept dry would be grinning.

'Cleaning things was something special. If they told you that your room, your rifle or your uniform had to be clean, they meant *clean*. On a Saturday morning we usually had our major cleaning exercise. It started with all the lads on hands and knees scrubbing the long stone corridors and stairs. That done (and to get it to their satisfaction could mean doing it two or three times over) we started on our

own rooms. Moving beds and wardrobes, scrubbing the floor and dusting every ledge or shelf. The windows were polished with damp newspapers. After that – the inspection.

'Our weekend pass depended on the outcome. Not only were the rooms inspected, but also each soldier, his bed, bedding and wardrobe contents. The only item not checked was one's personal haversack, in which we kept private items, such as writing paper, photos, letters from home and so on. I soon found it was easier to keep two sets of some items, such as toothbrush, comb, safety razor, handkerchief and socks. Brand new ones could be kept in the wardrobe ready for surprise inspections and used ones could be stuffed into the haversack.

'Once, during an inspection, a matchstick was found down behind the leg of a wardrobe. Nothing was said at the time, but that night at about 2300 hours when we were all

fast asleep, there was a call-out with full pack. We were ordered to bring one blanket as well. When we were assembled and ready, four men were ordered to carry the blanket, one at each corner, with the match in the centre. We then marched for about an hour, and then had to dig a hole exactly one metre by one metre by one metre [3ft by 3ft by 3ft] and bury the match. Next morning it was back to normal as if nothing had happened.

'At Bad Tölz, we had passed the first course and become Standartenoberjunkers [officer cadets, with substantive rank of warrant officer]. Somehow one of the instructors had a heated argument with one of our Danish comrades. The discussion was over the forced union of European countries with Germany. The argument developed into something more serious than just a difference of opinion between two persons. We all became involved. It was clear that a lot of "Germanic volunteers" felt that in no way should their countries be taken over by Germany. Feelings were running high and a gesture was deemed necessary. That same evening nearly all of the foreign officer cadets had sewn their country's national arm badge on their lower left sleeve. Normally only a few wore their country's badge. Most wore nothing, or just the regimental arm band.

'The following day there was no reaction from our instructors or staff. No one complained, no one enquired or questioned us, but a few days later the officer who had had the argument was transferred to a frontline unit.

'When it comes to political indoctrination, yes I certainly remember that! We were told to study certain passages from Hitler's *Mein Kampf* as we would be questioned about them in the next session. We all disliked this very much. We had to spend a lot of our free time reading something that we were not very interested in. Another important factor was the language difficulty. For most of us it was extremely hard to explain in our own language what we had read in such a book. But in German, we did not even know everyday words or simple expressions. We could understand commands, we knew all the German names for all the bits and pieces of our weapons, uniform and so on, and we had no trouble when, in town, we wanted to order a beer, a meal or start a conversation with a civilian. But our vocabulary literally did not stretch to political arguments.

'At Bad Tölz this *Weltanschauung* – philosophy of life, or political schooling – was of course also carried out. Our instructor was called Weidemann. He too used *Mein Kampf*, but went much deeper into it. Again we didn't like it much but it did provide some lighter moments. In our room of eight Junkers [officer cadets], we had a Dutchman from Nijmegen called Frans Goedhart. He was already an SS staff sergeant and had the Deutsches Kreuz [German Cross] in gold. We never knew exactly what he had done to earn it. Every evening when we were having to do our homework, he would manage to go out on the town. Always just at the last minute he would return, ask what had to be done for the next day, then just read through his notes and go to bed. Next day he was never lost for the correct answer.

Our instructor would assign one of us to represent an enemy, a communist for example, while he was the NSDAP [Nazi Party] member, ready to defend the Party and the Fatherland. Normally he would argue us into a quick defeat. However, one day he told Goedhart to be an English newspaper reporter. The debate was won hands down by Goedhart and Weidemann almost completely lost his temper and made a proper fool of himself.'

⚡⚡ TRAINING IN FRANCE

ERHARD KINSCHER
SS-STURMMANN

SS-Panzergrenadier Regiment 25
12th SS Panzer Division *Hitlerjugend*

For young men such as Kinscher, who possessed skills that were much in demand, a series of postings and transfers became the norm.

RIGHT: Erhard Kinscher as an SS-Schütze in the 12th SS Panzer Division Hitlerjugend. He is wearing the typical M43 service dress.

'After completing my Labour Service in July 1943, I was posted, on 30 August, to the Transport Reserve Depot at Weimar-Buchenwald [Waffen-SS uniforms were processed through distribution centres that were co-located with concentration camps, such as Buchenwald, Ravensbruck and Dachau; both free and camp labour was used for the manufacture of uniforms and insignia] and was kitted out there. After three weeks or so we were sent to Beverloo in Belgium, where some of us were allocated to the pioneer [combat engineer] battalion. I was posted to 11 Company, III Battalion, SS-Panzergrenadier Regiment 25. After a short period I was transferred to 9 Company. As they needed instructors – I was a former Hitler Youth leader and had completed my Labour Service – I was made leader and instructor for 3 Squad. At the end of October, 9 Company was amalgamated with 16 Company, with

only around 30 men left over to form a nucleus for 14 Company. It was soon brought up to nominal strength and I came to the company staff as a despatch rider. As soon as training began, I received training on 20mm guns, which were not towed by vehicles but moved by manpower or by dismantling them. As well as training on the gun, we got instruction on how to use the rifle, pistol, machine pistol and, especially for us despatch riders, the map and compass. During this time we also took our oath.

'After the arrival of our vehicles, driver training started, which we were put through as quickly as feasible. Then, in January 1944, we took part in motorised exercises with SS-Panzergrenadier Regiment 26, but only one platoon from my company took part. After that, the company was equipped with half-tracks mounting 20mm guns.

'A second great motorised training exercise was inspected by Field Marshal von Rundstedt. The entire company took part. It included tanks, artillery, grenadiers and so on. Afterwards, "Panzermeyer" [Kurt Meyer], our regimental commander, fell in the company and congratulated us on

BELOW: Waffen-SS soldiers at the Wildflecken troop training grounds, March 1942. Within days of this photo being taken they were serving with the Nord *Division in Russia.*

our first symbolic victory. A Fieseler Storch [a single-engined light transport aircraft] had been hit by the wad from a 20mm practice round and was damaged! Thereafter we moved to Espenay, France, for training in anti-aircraft

tactics. The shooting was excellent and we were often congratulated by the Luftwaffe. After this it was back to Beverloo where, after a couple of weeks, I was finally posted as a despatch rider to the regimental headquarters staff.'

⚡⚡ INVITATION TO THE BALL

WERNER VÖLKNER
SS-ROTTENFÜHRER

Flak Abteilung
3rd SS Panzer Division *Totenkopf*

For men who wished to be elite troops, days spent in hard training were accepted as necessary. However, Völkner remembers other methods used to weld individuals into cohesive units.

RIGHT: *Cadets training at Bad Tölz. Waffen-SS officers could be harsh and ruthless, but they led by example.*

'The training was very hard but quite short for me as I had already done my pre-military training. We had gun training, long-distance marches, eight weeks of basic infantry training, specialised training for gun crews, weapons drills and so on. There was so much to do, we hardly found time to sleep.

'One of our room mates went down with diphtheria and had to be hospitalised. Our room was made out of bounds – we were all in quarantine. One day, the duty NCO came and inspected our room. It was in a real shambles. He went crazy and wanted to chase us right out into the barrack square but couldn't, of course, because of the quarantine. In a fit of temper, he emptied out all of our lockers and threw everything out of the window – steel helmets, the lot, shouting that he'd show us how to clear up a room. Of course, he'd completely forgotten about the quarantine. We

couldn't leave the room so he had to go and get someone else to go and pick it all up.

'One of the trainers' favourite methods of keeping us occupied was the "Masked Ball". This would always happen in the middle of the night. The squad, platoon or even the whole company would be called out and then told we had three minutes to report back in sports kit. The first three to get back would be dismissed and be allowed to return to bed. The remainder would then be told they had six minutes to get changed into full battle dress and report back. Again, the first three back would be allowed to return to their beds. Some tried to cheat, and didn't change properly but just put their battle dress on over their sports kit. But, whoever was in the group of three being dismissed to return to their beds would always be checked. Woe betide anyone who had been caught cheating. As we had maybe five or six forms of dress – battle dress, walking out dress, parade dress and so on – they could keep us at this all night long. Of course it did create a spirit of competition and

hardened us, making us determined not to let the instructors break our spirit, so in the end I suppose it really was a useful exercise.'

SS GUARDING THE REICH

GERD ROMMEL
SS-ROTTENFÜHRER

SS-Panzer Aufklarüngs Abteilung 10
10th SS Panzer Division *Frundsberg*

FRIEDRICH-KARL WACKER
SS-STURMMANN

16th SS Panzergrenadier Division *Reichsführer-SS*

KARL-HEINZ DECKER
SS-STURMMANN
(UNTERFÜHRERANWARTER)

SS-Panzergrenadier Regiment 25
12th SS Panzer Division *Hitlerjugend*

RIGHT: SS-Schütze Gerd Rommel. This photograph was taken in 1942 when he was 18 years old.

'Our training was indeed hard, especially in the divisions that were formed later in the war, such as the 9th SS Panzer Division *Hohenstaufen*, 10th SS Panzer Division *Frundsberg* and 12th SS Panzer Division *Hitlerjugend*. These were the last divisions that were able to make use of relative peace in the West for their training, before the D-Day invasion in June 1944. However, it was very intensive. They all received the most up-to-date and modern equipment but, because they were so well equipped, a great deal was expected of them when they went into action.'

GERD ROMMEL

'Most of 1943 I spent in training. I did different courses, such as a sniper's course, anti-tank training with infantry weapons, magnetic mines and so on. The training was done with real Russian T-34 tanks. Most important to me was the Unterführer Lehrgang [NCOs' training course] in November 1943. We did, however, take part in some anti-partisan operations in Poland during this period, and were also involved in the occupation of Hungary.'

FRIEDRICH-KARL WACKER

'At NCO preparatory school, we had the same basic training as every other soldier, but also learned how to become an NCO. That meant lectures in tactics and infantry weapons,

ABOVE: Staff officers at Bad Tölz. Of particular interest is the range of collar patches worn: (from left to right) the rare mirror image SS runes patches; the death's head collar patch with rank patch; the SS runes collar patch with rank patch; the SST collar patch of the SS Junkerschule Tölz (worn by the diminuitive figure); the SS runes collar patch with rank patch; the polizei-style collar patches of the SS-Polizei Division; the death's head collar patches on both sides; and SS runes with rank patch.

LEFT: SS-Sturmmann Karl-Heinz Decker as an NCO candidate with the SS-Panzergrenadier Regiment 25, Hitlerjugend Division.

both in theory and in the field, so that we were able to teach and train other recruits and set an example. Because we were all very young and found the training to be extremely hard, we were ordered to take a rest period of one hour every day. The NCO or officer on duty made sure that this order was carried out. Where other soldiers would be given cigarettes or beer, we were given chocolates and sweets.'

KARL-HEINZ DECKER

BROTHERS IN ARMS

From the beginning the Waffen-SS was different, a brotherhood apart from the Wehrmacht. Its members saw themselves as fitter, better and more motivated than their Army counterparts: in short, an elite. On and off the battlefield they were a self-contained order, knowing that their strength lay in their loyalty to each other. This bond endures still.

From the very first days of his training, the fact that he was a member of a very select force was impressed upon the Waffen-SS recruit. This status brought with it considerable responsibilities, however. Nothing less than unflinching obedience, honesty and dedication to duty was deemed acceptable. And each soldier, confident in his own adherence to these principles, also expected each and every one of his comrades to be as obedient, honest and dedicated as himself. This chapter examines the unique Waffen-SS creed.

The Waffen-SS instilled this combination of self-confidence and confidence in the trustworthiness of others into its members only partly through hard training and discipline. Surviving veterans almost invariably mention the intense and quite deliberately fostered sense of comradeship and equality as fighting men that existed between all ranks in the Waffen SS. This is a common feature of elite units in today's armies, but in those days was highly unusual – especially in the German military, where traditional Prussian discipline had always acted to reinforce the very rigid formal barriers that already existed between officers and other ranks.

As the contributors below make clear, one of the particular aspects of Waffen-SS training was the total lack of a 'them and us' class system separating officers and other ranks. Officers were expected to earn the respect of their men and not

Waffen-SS soldiers on the Eastern Front in 1942. The sense of comradeship among those who wore the SS runes manifested itself in Waffen-SS units making superhuman efforts to rescue encircled SS formations, and sometimes fighting to the last man to hold positions.

assume it merely because of their rank. Indeed, potential officers in the Waffen-SS were expected to serve at least two years in the ranks before going forward for their commissions, a fact that certainly helped engender an affinity between officers and their men. Soldiers were not expected to call their officers 'sir', but were to address them by their military rank. Officers in turn often took their meals with their men, or shared a drink with them off duty. This sense of comradeship, still as strong today after 50 years or more, is, for many veterans, probably the single most memorable aspect of service in the Waffen-SS.

An unshakeable faith in one's commanders to the bitter end

Many Waffen-SS officers were much younger than their counterparts in the regular armed forces. Because so many Waffen-SS officers were prone to 'lead from the front' there was a constant need to replace battlefield casualties. The replacements usually came from experienced NCOs, themselves comparatively young. As these young officers progressed through the ranks, they retained their regard for, and comradeship with, their lower-ranking fellow soldiers. Even senior corps or divisional commanders shared this trait. SS-Oberstgruppenführer Josef 'Sepp' Dietrich was a committed Nazi, a major protagonist in the 'Night of the Long Knives' in 1934 (the purging of the SA), who could at times be ruthless. But his troops were devoted to him, and he would exhort his regimental commanders, when sending them into battle, to 'bring my boys back safely'.

The sense of comradeship engendered during training undoubtedly contributed to the Waffen-SS's success on the battlefield. Soldiers had great respect and confidence in their officers and would obey them without question, sure in the knowledge that no officer would ask them to do anything he was not fully prepared to do himself.

In the latter part of the war most Waffen-SS soldiers had become hardened and cynical after seeing so many of their comrades fall on the field of battle. Most realised that the war was probably lost and they had little respect left for the leadership of the regime. What remained, however, was an unshaken faith in, and loyalty to, their own extremely popular commanders and to their own comrades. Even today, veterans talk with reverence of their former commanders, referring to Dietrich as 'our' 'Sepp' or Kurt Meyer as 'our' 'Panzermeyer'.

On the whole, it seems clear that for most Waffen-SS soldiers the comradeship they experienced was a major factor in maintaining their high morale. Even those who never met during the war may form an instant bond on discovering they both served in the Waffen-SS. And for most of the Waffen-SS veterans consulted in the preparation of this book, thoughts of loyalty, comradeship and obedience bring back positive memories. For example, many of the battle-hardened NCOs in Waffen-SS units took a very strong, fatherly interest in the younger grenadiers under them. It was not uncommon for such men to go to great lengths to avoid being separated from their men, even when they themselves were seriously wounded.

Instant and unquestioning obedience to orders also had its negative side, though. The young grenadiers of the Waffen-SS may have been superbly fit, tough and dedicated, but many went to war when still extremely young, with little experience of life and without the psychological and emotional maturity to handle some of the situations in which they were sometimes placed. That is true of most soldiers in modern wars, but most of those who joined the Waffen-SS in the later stages of the war had, also, hardly known any political or social system beyond the regimentations and orchestrated hatred of the Third Reich. Thus it was fatally easy for them to assume that all instructions were justified. And so when a fanatical officer ordered his men to shoot Canadian prisoners at the Ardenne Abbey in Normandy, his order was obeyed without question.

There was also another, literally fatal, drawback to the Waffen-SS's culture of obedience. Unlike the training given to modern special forces, it did not encourage initiative on the battlefield. Without their unhesitating response to orders that would have daunted lesser men, the men of the Waffen-SS would surely never have achieved what they did. But as a result they almost certainly took more casualties than they might have given more imaginative training. Waffen-SS losses were high. From an estimated total strength during World War II of some 12 million, for example, the Wehrmacht suffered losses of around 2.9 million killed, a casualty rate just under 25 percent. For the Waffen-SS, out of a total strength of around one million, some 253,000 were lost, a casualty rate of just over 25 percent. Thus the casualty rate for the Waffen-SS is marginally higher. It should also be pointed out that Waffen-SS surrendered personnel percentages are much lower than the Wehrmacht's, indicating, perhaps, a higher degree of motivation.

The mutual loyalty among Waffen-SS soldiers was such that misdemeanours, and sometimes even fairly serious crimes, would be overlooked if it was considered that there were extenuating circumstances. But if it was considered that a Waffen-SS soldier had acted dishonourably in committing an offence, punishment would be severe in the extreme, as the accounts below illustrate. For example, veterans most often quote the rule that on no account were personal lockers to be secured. To padlock one's locker implied a distrust of one's comrades, which was considered unworthy and counter to the Waffen-SS creed. And woe betide anyone who did steal from their comrades and was caught.

The comradeship of the war years endures still

This sense of comradeship, born of belonging to a military elite and nurtured through hardship and sacrifice in battle, was the cornerstone on which the great combat achievements and reputation for dependability and fortitude of the Waffen-SS was built. This sense of belonging also helped many to survive the hardships of post-war imprisonment, which for many meant years of suffering in Stalin's gulags.

After the war, former Waffen-SS soldiers became, for many, the 'alibi of a nation'. Attempts were made to lay the

responsibility for virtually every crime committed by the Nazi regime at the feet of the SS. But no attempt was made to differentiate between the frontline combat troops of the Waffen-SS and the personnel who staffed the concentration camps, the Gestapo, or the death squads of the Einsatzgruppen (Special Action Groups). As a result, the comradeship that saw them through long years of war re-emerged stronger than ever. Seen as outcasts from society, Waffen-SS veterans turned to each other for help and support, and so the HIAG (Hilfsgemeinschaft auf Gegenseitigkeit der Soldaten der ehemaligen Waffen-SS – Mutual Aid Association for Soldiers of the former Waffen-SS) was formed.

The sense of equal respect between leaders and those who they led in battle, the admiration for professionalism and gallantry, and a history of common suffering and survival created a mutual pride and loyalty among Waffen-SS soldiers, irrespective of rank or even nationality, that remains to this day.

RIGHT: No matter what the circumstances or the theatre of war, every effort was made to give Waffen-SS dead a proper burial. Here, SS-Standartenführer Joachim Peiper (an SS-Sturmbannführer at the time this photograph was taken) presides at a solemn interment ceremony of one of his fallen grenadiers.

⚡⚡ UNSURPASSED UNIT PRIDE

FRIEDRICH-KARL WACKER
SS-STURMMANN
16th SS Panzergrenadier Division *Reichsführer-SS*

ERIC BRÖRUP
SS-OBERSTURMFÜHRER
SS-Panzer Aufklärungs Abteilung 5
5th SS Panzer Division *Wiking*

ERHARD KINSCHER
SS-STURMMANN
SS-Panzergrenadier Regiment 25
12th SS Panzer Division *Hitlerjugend*

RIGHT: Friedrich-Karl Wacker, seen here as an NCO candidate in the Totenkopf *Division.*

'Our confidence was overwhelming. We had an arrogant pride in ourselves, an immense *esprit de corps.* I always felt better than any Wehrmacht soldier. I wasn't, of course, but I felt that I was.

'So much is said about the special comradely relationship between officers and men in the Waffen-SS, but I have to say that it wasn't always so. In the *Reichsführer-SS* Division, for example, I didn't even know that SS-Gruppenführer Max Simon was my divisional commander until after the war had ended. Sometimes we didn't even know who our company commander was. And old allegiances died hard. In France, for example, some of the NCOs who had come from the *Totenkopf* Division built themselves a mess with a bar. They made it abundantly clear that we young soldiers were not welcome there.

'Nevertheless, we were all united when it came to our creed. I remember one time, a corporal had deserted. He was recaptured and sentenced to death. They called for vol-unteers for the firing squad, but only accepted volunteers from the older soldiers in the unit. We younger ones were rejected. I can remember that we were very disappointed at not being chosen.'

FRIEDRICH-KARL WACKER

'An absolute No-No was to curse or call anyone by insulting names and the like. The honour and dignity of any man, officer or other rank, was not to be violated. This has a lot to do with the great sense of comradeship which was instilled into the Waffen-SS. A mutual respect existed. Many commanders radiated a certain charisma and their troops would follow them to hell and back.'

ERIC BRÖRUP

'In the fighting around Caen, France, after the Allied D-Day landings in June 1944, my platoon was attached to I Battalion, and the other three platoons were used to help stabilise the front near Caen. They were dug in, without infantry support [the crews of the armoured personnel carriers and their gunners], between III Battalion and 16 Company, together with the command post. Behind the 20mm guns, the bigger 88mm guns were dug in to fulfil a ground combat role. On the evening of 7 July, heavy artillery fire began to fall on us. On 8 July I could only find one man from these three platoons who had made it back alive. Among other things he told me that SS-Hauptscharführer Grabsch re-ceived a bullet wound in the chest, but just bandaged it himself and refused to be taken to the rear for treatment. He insisted: "I'm staying with my lads." He was the oldest in the company. A little later he was shot dead.

'Earlier, on 5 June 1944, a deserter was shot in front of our whole battalion. "Panzermeyer" said: "German mothers bore their sons to fight, not to betray the Fatherland."'

ERHARD KINSCHER

ON YOUR HONOUR

HEINZ KÖHNE
SS-OBERSCHARFÜHRER

1st SS Panzer Division *Leibstandarte SS Adolf Hitler*

KARL-HEINZ DECKER
SS-STURMMANN
(UNTERFÜHRERANWARTER)

SS-Panzergrenadier Regiment 25
12th SS Panzer Division *Hitlerjugend*

HANS-GERHARD STARCK
SS-OBERSCHARFÜHRER

1st SS Panzer Division *Leibstandarte SS Adolf Hitler*

RIGHT: A gilded SS eagle bearing the motto of the Waffen SS, 'Loyalty is my Honour', in German.

'In the Wehrmacht one had to keep one's locker secured. In the Waffen-SS they had to be left un-locked. There was no theft in the Waffen-SS. If any Waffen-SS man was caught stealing from his comrades, the punishment would be extremely severe. For that reason every soldier had to make sure never to allow himself to feel any temptation to take any man's property.

'The comradeship of the Waffen-SS was based on the tenet of "all for one and one for all". Throughout the train-ing great emphasis was put on this to ensure this principle would be adhered to.'

HEINZ KÖHNE

'In the Waffen-SS, we had to leave our lockers open all the time. Stealing from your comrades was an offence that would be very heavily punished, so you had to learn to trust, to depend on your comrades, and to share. This all contributed to the formation of the legendary sense of intense comradeship which permeated the Waffen-SS.'

KARL-HEINZ DECKER

'In our regiment, and also in our own company, there were two soldiers who were caught stealing from their com-

rades. Both were sentenced to death and were subsequently shot, and afterwards the entire company marched and trampled over their graves. That was the price one paid for stealing from one's comrades.'

HANS-GERHARD STARCK

UNIT CAMARADERIE

JAN MUNK
SS-STANDARTENOBERJUNKER

SS-Panzergrenadier Regiment *Westland*
5th SS Panzer Division *Wiking*

Unit solidarity in the Waffen-SS was second to none, and Munk remembers with amusement the games different companies played in an effort to outdo one another.

RIGHT: SS-Standartenführer Kurt Meyer – 'Panzer-meyer' – takes a fatherly interest in one of his young charges of the Hitlerjugend Division. The Waffen-SS had an intense unit camaraderie.

'I had arrived at Ellwangen from a hospital in Krakow on 4 June 1944. I think my period in Ellwangen was among the best of my times in the Waffen-SS because of the company I was in. I landed in 3 Company, SS-Panzergrenadier Training and Replacement Battalion 5.

'It really is a great feeling to march en bloc'

'Our company commander was feared by all his fellow commanding officers. If he had a bone to pick with any of them he would wait until a Saturday night. That was cinema night in town. He would make sure we left the cinema behind the company whose commander had annoyed him. We

waited a while then followed. Everyone would be singing as they marched. The moment we started to overtake the other company, marching quicker and singing a different song, louder than the other lot, they just folded up. They went out of step and lost their tune, which meant their commanding officer would be held responsible for their performance.

'Most of the time this was done as a challenge between the various commanding officers and their companies. It therefore had a positive side to it. The other company would then train more, improve their marching and singing, but no other unit was able to beat my company. It really is a great feeling to march *en bloc*, as one man, and to have good parade ground drill, where movements were done in such perfect time that it sounded like one sharp crack.'

SS THE ENDURING BOND

RUDY SPLINTER

SS-STURMMANN

10th SS Panzer Division *Frundsberg*

GERD ROMMEL

SS-ROTTENFÜHRER

SS-Panzer Aufklarüngs Abteilung 10
10th SS Panzer Division *Frundsberg*

RIGHT: Newly trained Waffen-SS soldiers, who would forever remain comrades in arms.

'While on holiday with my family in Germany, I passed the house of former SS-Brigadeführer Heinz Harmel, my old divisional commander. I decided to pay a courtesy call. Harmel welcomed me enthusiastically, asked what I was doing in that part of Germany and insisted I stay there with him as his guest. I respectfully declined, saying that I couldn't possibly impose on him as I had my whole family with me. He had an index system with the names of every single soldier who had served in the *Frundsberg* Division. He confirmed my name was on it and we had an interesting chat about old times.

'I told him about one occasion, when he was newly posted to take command of the division. The lads were asking what the new commander looked like. Some of the old salts said: "If you see a guy with a bottle of good brandy in one pocket, a big box of cigars in the other, and the Knights Cross sparkling at his neck, that's him." Of course we thought this was a wind-up. Then, some time later, during the fighting in Normandy, a captured American jeep arrived at our location. Out got this big chap, a bottle of brandy sticking out of one pocket, a big box of cigars sticking out of the other, and a Knights Cross at his neck. He wasn't dressed in a general's finery, no riding breeches or polished jackboots, just baggy trousers and hob-nailed ankle boots.

'That was Harmel. A real soldier's soldier, no airs and graces, and he would do anything for his men. It's no wonder they would follow him anywhere and do anything he asked, even today, 50 years or so later.'

RUDY SPLINTER

'My most enduring memory of the Waffen-SS was the spirit with which we were all filled. We were all just around 18 years old, and our officers just 20 to 30 years old. Our divisional commander, SS-Brigadeführer Heinz Harmel, was then just 38 years old. The troops never addressed him as "Herr General", just as "Brigadeführer". It was this spirit of equality which made us all feel so proud.

'But you know, the best example I can give of the comradeship in the Waffen-SS in fact occurred just recently. My telephone rang and at the other end of the line was my old chief, General Heinz Harmel, recently turned 88 years old. He had heard that I was about to go into hospital for a heart operation. Now, I ask you, how many former soldiers get their old commanding general telephoning to ask how things are? Doesn't that say everything about our comradeship? In the old days I was just a corporal and the driver of a command tank which Harmel occasionally used.'

GERD ROMMEL

THE EASTERN FRONT I: BLOODY ADVANCES

F or the Waffen-SS, the war on the Eastern Front was a struggle of ideologies. As the standard bearer of Nazism, the SS organisation as a whole viewed the Soviet Union and its Slav inhabitants with utter contempt, to be conquered and reduced to slave status in the quest for German *Lebensraum*. For the ideologically indoctrinated Waffen-SS, the war against Russia took on the nature of a crusade – a crusade against Bolshevism.

When two ideologies such as National Socialism and Bolshevism clashed, it would have been inevitable that the subsequent conflict would be savage. For the Nazi Party's military elite, the war on the Eastern Front was ruthless, fanatical and unrelenting. It was in Russia that Himmler's legions fought their most brutal battles and incurred their most horrendous losses, for in a war where retreat in the face of the enemy was unthinkable and capture meant almost certain torture and death (Himmler himself had forbidden any Waffen-SS soldier to surrender), some Waffen-SS units were literally wiped out in clashes with the Red Army.

From the beginning, therefore, it was obvious that the war in East was going to different in character to the campaigns of 1939-40. Both sides executed prisoners and committed atrocities, and disregard for the conventions of war regarding prisoners and civilians became the norm. Yet amid the horrors the

The spoils of war. Waffen-SS troops with a captured Soviet banner in the summer of 1941. Himmler ordered his commanders in Russia to 'instruct your men again and again in our ideological beliefs... and do not let them go before they are really saturated with our spirit.'

ABOVE: *Imbued with an almost religious zeal, the soldiers of the Waffen-SS fought with unmatched enthusiasm during Operation 'Barbarossa', eager to get to grips with the ideological enemy. These men are from the* Das Reich *Division, which in early August 1941 helped hold off some 11 Red Army divisions in southern Russia.*

Waffen-SS achieved some spectacular results and achieved an influence out of all proportion to its size.

The enormous force for Operation 'Barbarossa' – 140 divisions including over three million men, 7100 guns, 3300 tanks, 2770 aircraft and a further 500,000 troops from allied countries – crossed its start line at 0300 on 22 June 1941. They were three army groups: North, which aimed at the Baltic states and Leningrad; Centre, which headed across Soviet-occupied Poland for Smolensk and then to Moscow; and South, which struck across southern Poland at the Ukraine, the oilfields of the Caucasus and the Crimea. The Waffen-SS divisions were spread throughout the army

groups: the *Totenkopf* and *Polizei* Divisions with Field Marshal von Leeb in Army Group North; the *Das Reich* Division under Field Marshal von Bock in Army Group Centre; the *Leibstandarte* and *Wiking* Divisions with Field Marshal von Rundstedt in Army Group South; and Kampfgruppe (Battlegroup) *Nord* in Finland with General von Falkenhorst.

In the first few weeks of the campaign, everything appeared to go the Germans' way. The Red Army in Poland was scattered, uncoordinated, and without a strategy for dealing with the assault – a situation aggravated by Stalin's refusal to heed diplomatic and intelligence warnings that an invasion was imminent. In the initial attack 4000 Soviet aircraft were destroyed, many on the ground, and by the end of September Axis forces had surrounded Leningrad, were within 320km (200 miles) of Moscow, and had broken the Soviet front south of Kiev. Over half a million prisoners had been taken as the defenders were encircled.

The Waffen-SS had notched up an impressive list of victories during the advance. The *Totenkopf* Division fought its way through Dvinsk and Opochka in the face of deter-mined opposition, before digging in around Leningrad. In the centre, *Das Reich* helped take Gorki, secured the left bank of the River Yelnya, and was then involved in helping to blunt an attack by 11 Soviet divisions. In September the division took Sosnitza, and then assisted in the German cap-ture of Kiev. It was then assigned to Operation 'Typhoon', the assault on Moscow. In the face of fanatical resistance and bitter weather, *Das Reich* fought to within 20km (11 miles) west of the outskirts of the Soviet capital.

In the south, the *Leibstandarte* Division was not commit-ted to battle until 27 June. In combat it proved itself unstop-pable in the attack, taking Moszkov, Miropol, Shepovka, Zhitomir and Cherson (after bitter house-to-house fighting),

BELOW: A Waffen-SS officer interrogates a captured Russian during the German advances of 1941. In the racial and ideological battle that the war in Russia was for the Waffen-SS, the conflict soon reached a level of brutalisation not previously seen.

before being given a spell of well-earned rest in late August. It was a brief respite, though, for between September and November the division was involved in savage fighting as it once again assisted in the German advance.

The *Wiking* Division also achieved some notable suc-cesses, taking part in the encirclement of Soviet forces at Uman and overcoming fanatical resistance at Dniepropetro-vsk, before digging in to await the anticipated Soviet counteroffensive.

By the end of 1941, though, the Soviet Union had not been brought to its knees. Worse for the Germans, their units at the front were at the end of their supply lines and were ill-equipped for the Russian winter. For the Waffen-SS, losses had been horrendous. Its total strength at the begin-ning of the campaign (including reserve units, training cadres and concentration camp detachments) was 160,405. By the end of 1941 it had suffered 407 officers and 7930 men killed, 816 officers and 26,299 men wounded, 13 offi-cers and 923 men missing, and four officers and 125 men killed in accidents. Nevertheless, it had established for itself

a legendary reputation among friend and foe alike, a reputation that would be enhanced over the next four years.

On 6 December 1941 came the first massive Soviet counterattack in the centre before Moscow. A month later came the counterattack in the north, during which the German 16th Army was encircled. The ferocity of the Soviet reaction may be judged from the fate of the 3rd SS Panzer Division *Totenkopf*, which escaped the notorious Demyansk Pocket having lost 12,600 killed or wounded of the original 17,000 men with which it had started the campaign.

By March 1942, the Germans had been driven back along the whole of the front. To regain the initiative, Hitler decided to concentrate on the drive south across the oil-rich Caucasus to the Caspian Sea. This succeeded to the extent that by the beginning of May the Crimea was taken, and the great oil centre at Maikop was taken in early August – although the oil installations themselves had been destroyed. At this point the southern drive literally ran out of energy, as the Germans ran out of fuel. Meanwhile, the Red Army was being pushed slowly east out of the great bend in the River Don; by the end of August the Germans were within 25km (16 miles) of Stalingrad.

The epic of Stalingrad ended on 2 February 1943, when the remains of the German forces in Stalingrad surrendered, having lost 147,000 men of an original 280,000 to cold, starvation and battle. While their resistance had allowed the armies in the Caucasus to retreat safely, the defeat had a devastating psychological effect on the German public and the German armies in the East; but it made Hitler even more contemptuous of his generals.

The expansion of the Waffen-SS

For the Waffen-SS, 1942 was a tale of defensive battles. In addition to the *Totenkopf*'s endeavours in the Demyansk Pocket, the *Das Reich* Division suffered 400 casualties between January and March fighting Marshal Zhukov's counteroffensive before Moscow. It was subsequently withdrawn to France for a refit in March, upgraded to a panzergrenadier division, and returned to Russia in January 1943.

The *Leibstandarte* was engaged against the Red Army around Dniepropetrovsk and Stalino, before being moved

ABOVE: A Das Reich *officer, a photograph that amply conveys that mentality of the Waffen-SS during the early stages of the war in Russia: fit, cocky and supremely confident of attaining ultimate victory.*

to France to pre-empt an anticipated Allied invasion – it stayed for the rest of the year. The *Wiking* Division stayed the whole year in Russia, and took part in some heavy fighting in the Caucasus.

The increasing demands of the Eastern Front resulted in more Waffen-SS divisions. Two new divisions were formed: the 7th SS Freiwilligen-Gebirgs Division *Prinz Eugen* and the 8th SS Kavallerie Division *Florian Geyer*. In addition, despite a poor fighting record, Kampfgruppe *Nord* became the 6th SS Gebirgs Division *Nord*.

The beginning of 1943 was a time of crisis for the German Army in Russia, as Army Group A pulled back from the Caucasus to prevent its annihilation. In an effort to help to stabilise the front, the *Leibstandarte, Das Reich* and *Totenkopf* Divisions were formed into I SS Panzer Corps and despatched to southern Russia. This corps was soon engaged in heavy fighting in an effort to stem the Red Army. The corps commander, SS-Obergruppenführer Paul Hausser,

BELOW: 'If you answer the call of the Waffen-SS... you will belong to a corps which from the beginning has been associated with outstanding achievements.' (Waffen-SS recruiting pamphlet). A column of Das Reich *Division vehicles during the advance in southern Russia, 1941.*

disregarded Hitler's orders to hold Kharkov at all costs and abandoned the city in February 1943.

The Red Army by this time was exhausted and had outstretched its supply lines, and so Field Marshal von Manstein launched a devastating counterattack, of which I SS Panzer Corps formed the northern spearhead. Hausser retook Kharkov in a spectacular action, though he lost 11,500 killed, wounded or missing in the process.

In the wake of Kharkov, Hitler, intoxicated by the fighting prowess of the Waffen-SS, agreed to the formation of two more SS corps. I SS Panzer Corps would consist of the

ABOVE: Though the door had been kicked in at Minsk, Kiev and Smolensk, 'Barbarossa' failed to knock the Soviet Union out of the war. As summer gave way to autumn, the German advance slowed. Then it started to snow.

Leibstandarte and the not-yet-formed 12th SS Panzer Division *Hitlerjugend*; II SS Panzer Corps would consist of the *Das Reich* and *Totenkopf* Divisions; while III SS Panzer Corps would be made up of the *Wiking* Division and the new 11th SS Freiwilligen-Panzergrenadier Division *Nordland*. In addition, two other SS divisions were in the process of being formed: the 9th SS Panzer Division *Hohenstaufen* and 10th SS Panzer Division *Frundsberg*.

But the successes around Kharkov were tactical, not strategic – and the last major successes for the Germans in the East. Their armies had lost about a million men since the previous November, and they could no longer contain any encirclement they achieved. As the spring thaw set in, bogging the battle down along the whole front, the Soviets grad-

ually prevailed. By April the southern German armies were 480km (300 miles) from Stalingrad, stretched from Taganrog to Belgorod on the Donetz. Farther north there were huge Soviet salients around Kursk and toward Nevel, and the siege of Leningrad had been broken by the Red Army.

To Hitler the key to the campaign now seemed to lie in the Kursk salient. He did not consider the virtue of waiting for the Red Army itself to break out and expose its flanks, yet it was July before he had sufficient forces - 17 divisions - and the latest equipment, notably Tiger and Panther tanks, in place to begin the assault (Manstein had 900,000 men, 2700 tanks, 10,000 artillery pieces and 2000 aircraft for the attack). By then the Soviets had had time to withdraw from the most threatened positions, sow vast minefields, and assemble a gigantic defensive force. More than two million men, 6000 tanks and 5000 aircraft joined in combat on 5 July 1943. II SS Panzer Corps, consisting of the *Leibstandarte*, *Das Reich* and *Totenkopf* Divisions (see Appendix 1), was assigned to the 4th Panzer Army.

This, the greatest tank battle ever fought, raged on for a week. By the fourth day the German assault was breaking up into local actions, and came to halt next day as fresh Soviet tanks poured into the fight. By now the battlefield was so obscured with dust and smoke that artillery became useless. The Germans, despite enormous efforts, could not break through the seemingly endless stream of Soviet reinforcements. On 12 July the Red Army increased the relentless pressure by opening a counteroffensive in the north, and Hitler ordered a fighting withdrawal. Hausser's command, which had started with over 700 tanks, emerged from the offensive with 280 still intact.

For all the individual heroism there was in the fighting around Kursk, the battle showed that the depleted and exhausted German armies could muster their strength only for limited engagements: Kursk had called on all their available armour, and reduced it still further. The eventual collapse of the front was inevitable, and the strategic initiative passed to the Red Army.

The nature of war in the East

The dire situation again aided the Waffen-SS, as more divisions were created to bolster the Eastern Front, though many were of variable quality. The end of 1943 saw the birth of the 13th Waffen-Gebirgs Division der SS *Handschar*, 14th and 15th Waffen-Grenadier Divisions der SS, 16th SS Panzergrenadier Division *Reichsführer-SS* and 17th SS Panzergrenadier Division *Götz von Berlichingen*.

The experiences of those Waffen-SS soldiers who took part in the fighting in Russia up to Kursk illustrate vividly the peculiarities of the war on the Eastern Front: the vastness of the theatre of operations, the disorganisation that even elite units suffered, the breakdown of supply systems, the appalling living conditions, and the ferocity of the fighting (which may be judged by the number of contributors who were wounded while fighting in Russia).

BELOW: The failure of the German offensive to take Moscow – 'Typhoon' – signalled the start of a long war in the East for the Wehrmacht and Waffen-SS. Here, Waffen-SS SdKfz 250 half-tracks struggle through the snow.

⚡⚡ OPERATION 'BARBAROSSA'

ERWIN BARTMANN
SS-UNTERSCHARFÜHRER

1st SS Panzer Division *Leibstandarte SS Adolf Hitler*

Bartmann remembers the staggering advances made by his division during Operation 'Barbarossa', but he also recounts the bitter fighting he and his comrades were engaged in against the Russians.

RIGHT: Erwin Bartmann as an SS-Sturmmann. Note the black cloth slip-on shoulder strap mounts bearing the monogram of the Leibstandarte SS Adolf Hitler. *The Infantry Assault Badge can just be seen on the left-hand breast pocket of his standard M43 field blouse.*

'As the advance eastwards continued, we moved towards Cherson [east of Odessa on the River Dnieper], where the fighting lasted from 19-22 August 1941. Our I Battalion attacked the village of Znigerovka. The Russians fled, leaving behind huge amounts of weapons and munitions. We then moved on through the Caucasus, taking Berdansk, Mariupol and Taganrog, which fell to us on 17 October.

'As we advanced between Mariupol and Taganrog, we halted our vehicles along the roadside to take a rest. A recce patrol was sent out and soon spotted Russian troops moving past us, heading west. Perhaps they hadn't realised we had already overrun their positions, or were trying to get around behind us and attack from the rear, though I don't think this was the case. We set up our machine guns on a railway embankment, and our mortars on the road. The subsequent action was swift. Thanks be to God we didn't suffer any casualties, but the Russians lost all their weapons and supplies. As we progressed farther towards Taganrog, we passed an airfield. Once again we had to disembark from

our trucks and take the airfield, even as planes were still landing and taking off.

'When we eventually reached Taganrog, our task was to capture the harbour and harbour installations, together with the radio station which was on a higher area of ground near the harbour. We stormed the installations. As we burst in through the door, the Russians ran out the back. They had destroyed the radio antenna, and the floor was awash with mercury from the smashed equipment. A large ship was trying to leave the port but was sunk by our 88mm flak guns. I can remember seeing it still lying there in the shallows in 1942, just before we returned to France.

'From Taganrog we moved farther east before halting and digging in. We lay there for about three weeks. We were widely dispersed (we had a large plain to defend). I lay with my telephone equipment between the company command post and the third platoon. It rained constantly and the enemy bombarded us with artillery every day. We always anticipated an enemy assault, but it seemed it would never come. Then one day a shell landed right on the edge of my foxhole and blew my telephone and my hand grenades into the air. Because of the blast and the impact I could hear nothing. I began to wonder if I had been killed, but I was only stunned. My telephone was no more, but I was still alive, which was the main thing. Our losses had been rising steadily and we needed every man. After this artillery barrage came the enemy infantry. Our ammunition was running low and we had to make every shot count.

'We lay there with bayonets fixed, waiting for the enemy. Then suddenly they appeared, but they were holding their hands up high, surrendering, not attacking, and shouting to us not to shoot. They had had enough. We could see their political commissars behind them, running away. We fired at them but they were too quick. I think on that day both sides were just happy to have survived.

'By 17 November 1941, we were ready for the attack on Rostov. The attack began early in the morning of 20 November. It was originally intended that the assault would begin at 0500 hours, but the fog was so dense it had to be postponed. At 1100 hours, the reconnaissance section went off first, then about 20 minutes later the infantry, supported by tanks from the Army. They said later that they had never seen an attack like this. Usually when the tanks stop the infantry dig in. When these tanks stopped, at the anti-tank ditches at Rostov, we just kept on advancing!

'Suddenly our flak opened up'

'As we advanced our ammunition trucks followed us – the pioneers had made sure they were able to cross the anti-tank ditches. By the next day we had penetrated into Rostov itself. As we advanced we had to cross the area around the railway station. Our task was to capture the railway bridge over the river. This was also the task of SS-Hauptsturmführer Springer and his company. As we came to the railhead, we could see an armoured train, with two locomotives, just about to depart. I got to the railhead just as the train pulled out. Suddenly our flak opened up and destroyed both locomotives. It turned out that the train was full of political commissars and their families who were about to flee, but things didn't turn out quite as these gentlemen had intended. In the station our company went into position and I was sent

to the battalion as signaller and telephonist. As I was reporting to SS-Sturmbannführer Fritz Witt, 3 Company was already over the bridge. Eventually I was given an order to lay a telephone line over to the other side of the bridge, but only got so far before being called back. The Russians were attacking the other side, but they couldn't break through and we held the bridgehead.

'On 2 December we had to evacuate Rostov again, the enemy being too strong for us. We had little or no supplies – our advance had been too fast and we had outran our replenishment vehicles. When we took Rostov, we had no radio communications with our supply troops or with Army HQ. We were on our own. It was very cold and we had no winter clothing, only what we were wearing, and that wasn't much. It was a wild retreat – we had to get out as soon as possible.

'The fuel tanks in our diesel trucks were frozen so we had to feed the engines directly. One man was in the cab with a can full of diesel fuel while another fed the fuel directly into the engine with his drinking cup, and this is what we had to do all the way back over the Zambeck until we reached our new positions.

'Our comrades from the Wehrmacht were already there – they hadn't followed us into Rostov. There, in our frozen holes in the ground, we brought in Christmas and the New Year. We made our subterranean hell as habitable as possible, making lanterns from small tins filled with diesel and a wick. In January 1942 we were moved into the village and built our shelters and machine-gun bunkers in the houses. To us it was luxury. In front of us, down by the river, lay the rifle company, widely scattered, with few men. Our condition was not much better. We had had considerable losses and no replacements. I can remember we were four hours on watch, four hours off. It must have been worse for the rifle company, as they were in the frontline and had to drive off any enemy attacks. For us it was a little better because we lay behind some cover in our bunkers with our heavy machine guns.

'We often had to give fire support to our comrades to beat off enemy attacks. As the weather became warmer the results of our handiwork became evident. As the snow melted the bodies were exposed and began to rot. The stink was terrible. Then we were withdrawn from our positions and replaced by polizei troops. We were only halfway back to Taganrog when we heard that the Russians had overrun our old positions and we had to go back and throw them out

again. The Russian propaganda loudspeakers wished us a pleasant stay in France. This was how we first learned that we were to be withdrawn from the Russian Front and transferred to France for refitting and reorganisation.'

⚡⚡ THE DEMYANSK POCKET

WERNER VÖLKNER
SS-ROTTENFÜHRER

Flak Abteilung
3rd SS Panzer Division *Totenkopf*

When the Soviets launched their winter offensive in northern Russia in January 1942, the* Totenkopf *Division was cut off in the Demyansk Pocket. Völkner and his comrades endured 73 days of isolation.

RIGHT: SS-Rottenführer Werner Völkner as a member of 4 Kompanie, SS Flak Abteilung 3, Totenkopf *Division, in a photograph taken in Russia in 1944. He remembers the brutalities committed by the Soviets against his comrades.*

'On the morning of 26 February 1942, we were warned that the Russians had broken through our lines and were attacking the supplies. We were sent to help, but when we arrived at the scene we found the Ivans had already been there. Trucks lay abandoned in the snow, their contents scattered all around. It was a scene of utter devastation. The drivers had been dragged from their cabs and either clubbed to death with rifle butts, had their throats cut, or been bayonetted. It was a really sickening sight.

'We heard later that the Russians had broken out of an encirclement we had them in - there wasn't enough of our infantry to hold them - and had attacked our supply column, stolen all our food and disappeared. We were tasked with finding them in our half-tracks.

'It was a short, sharp engagement. We took a direct hit in the engine. Stuck there, unable to move, we were sitting ducks. The number one on the gun was hit in the head by a bullet that went straight through his steel helmet. The loader was hit in the hand, and then our sergeant was peppered with shrapnel. We had to get out quick. We jumped off the vehicle into the deep snow, which, being a metre thick, made for a soft landing, though subsequent movement was difficult. I went to get my rifle from the rack on the vehicle. Now, our regulations stated that when they were secured on the rack the slings had to be tightened up against the stock. One of my comrades had been careless, though, and had left it loose. His carelessness saved my life, for the loose sling got tangled with my rifle and held me up for a couple of seconds. Just then a Russian bullet hit the vehicle right next to me. If the tangled sling hadn't have held me back for just that second or so the bullet would have hit me.

'I took two rifles and, holding them at the muzzle end, used them as a pair of skis to propel myself through the snow. I had only gone 10 metres or so when I came under fire. I couldn't see the enemy, and in any case I only had five rounds in each rifle. I began firing in the direction of the muzzle flashes, but it would be only a matter of time before I would be hit. Fortunately, a half-track from the pioneer section arrived on the scene and rescued us.

'The next day we went back to recover the vehicle. The body of the number one on the gun crew had been badly mutilated by the Russians. He was dead, of course, and wouldn't have felt anything, but why did they have to mutilate his body like that?

BELOW: Totenkopf personnel await a Red Army assault while isolated in the Demyansk Pocket. The division had started the campaign in Russia with a strength of 17,000 men. By the time it had been rescued from the pocket, this number was down to 6700 personnel.

'As the supply problem got worse we had to "live off the land" to supplement our meagre rations. We would try to exchange our cigarettes with the local civilians for bread or some eggs. Of course, there were some who had no hesitation in just helping themselves. One day, for example, a local complained that some soldiers had stolen one of his pigs. Our commanding officer ordered us to line up in full battle order for an identity parade. Lined up in camouflaged smocks and the rest of our gear we all looked exactly the same to the poor peasant, and he couldn't identify the one who had taken his pig.

'Then we had to dig foxholes'

'On occasion we were paraded to check that no one had eaten their iron rations [hard tack biscuits and tins of cooked meat], which could only be used in an emergency, and only then if authorised by an officer or NCO. Our commanding officer ordered any man who had eaten his iron rations to take three steps forwards. Well, we all looked sideways at one other, then the whole company took three steps forward. Normally this would mean three days' pun-

ishment, but of course they couldn't jail the entire company. However, as a punishment we were made to dig trenches large enough for our vehicles to be driven into, to protect them from shrapnel. The hole that can accommodate an eight-tonne half-track is big, I can tell you! Then we had to dig foxholes for ourselves. It was punishment, of course, but at least we could use the trenches as cover during enemy attacks.

'When the fighting in the pocket had ended I was summoned to see the commanding officer, though I couldn't think of anything I'd done wrong to get into trouble. We had already been punished for eating our iron rations. When I got there he asked: "Völkner, when did you last have some leave?" I replied that I hadn't had any leave yet. It wasn't punishment at all, far from it, I was going home on leave. It all happened so fast I didn't have time to write and tell my parents, so they got quite a surprise when I turned up. My mother was also quite excited about my ration cards, and suggested that we go out straight away and find a butcher to buy some pork. Pork! I wouldn't have cared if I'd never seen pork again – I had been one of those who had scoffed all the pork from that stolen pig!'

✠ ONE MAN AND HIS DOG

ERICH HELLER
SS-UNTERSTURMFÜHRER

2nd SS Panzer Division *Das Reich*

Heller's account of his travels in Russia gives the reader an indiction of the vast distances involved in Russia, as well illustrating that a semi-normal lifestyle could be maintained away from the front and the fighting.

RIGHT: Erich Heller is photographed here as an SS-Oberjunker, but he was later commissioned as an SS-Untersturmführer. He wears the General Assault Badge and Wound Badge (in black) on his breast pocket, while in his tunic buttonhole can be seen the ribbon of the Eastern Front Campaign Medal.

'The workshop supervisor had a German Shepherd dog, which sat at his desk and never took its eyes off me or the BMW motorcycle. He had turned up just two days after the brigade had moved out. Then I remembered that someone on the brigade staff had such a dog, so I asked the senior doctor if I could take the dog, called Rex, along with me. He agreed and so, on 15 August, I set off behind a truck towards Latnaya and the railway station. There, the motorcycle combination was loaded onto a flatcar behind an assault gun.

'On 18 August [1942] our train finally reached Kursk. My vehicle was unloaded and at the commandant's office I was told that I should get a train to Kiev next, but the next one wouldn't be for a couple of days. First I had to report to the movements office and have my papers stamped. There I heard to my astonishment that I would have to have travel papers for the dog also, so that I could draw rations for him. After much toing and froing an elderly hauptmann, who wore the Iron Cross from World War I, got everything in order for me. In the evening I went with him and a lieutenant to visit the Kursk State Theatre. That was a real lark. There were many pretty ladies, elegantly attired, some with children in the boxes with them, but all of them were escorted by members of the Wehrmacht.

'Around midnight our train left, heading for Kiev, where we arrived next morning. I unloaded my vehicle and reported to the movements office. Here my travel papers were stamped for Minsk and I drew rations for myself and Rex, and received pay and ration coupons. I must say, the German administration system worked perfectly. As I had two days before the next leg of my journey, I went sightseeing around Kiev, which we had captured during the previous year.

'I was eventually able to get on an empty Italian train heading towards Gomel. There I was able to exchange some bread with the Italian escort personnel for some tomatoes. I remember the only warm food available was spaghetti. After two days the train reached Minsk. I reported to the movements office and was told that I should report to the assembly point for the brigade. This I found right away, in a village near Borissow, where I was ordered to report to the 10th Regiment.

'It was already beginning to get dark as I made my way there; fortunately the roads were in good order, which made the journey bearable. Suddenly, from the woods on my right came rifle fire. Two or three bullets hit the bike, though fortunately not the fuel tank, and another bullet hit my lower left arm. Rex remained unharmed, always crouching down low in the sidecar. I immediately opened up the throttle and sped away. At the regimental command post a doctor bandaged my arm and gave me a tetanus shot. My attackers had been partisans, who were active in the area and were threatening the road and rail lines. I reported that I was ready for further orders, but the doctor ordered that I was to have two days' rest.

'Then came the order to move once again. The regiment moved from Brisov towards Gschatzk and then turned northwards. Shortly before reaching Rakov, the gear lever on the bike broke. A Russian helped me to push the bike into a village where there was a blacksmith. He welded up a new gear lever, which was so perfect that even today it astonishes me what that man could do. By then it was dark and I could not risk travelling farther because of the ever-present threat from partisans. I gave the blacksmith bread and tobacco as payment. His wife wouldn't take me into their house as their younger sister lived with them. She could have thought I would molest the girl, or it might have been the lice I was infested with (we had to smear ourselves with zinc ointment to get rid of these little pests).

'Next morning I joined a column travelling to Ivieniez. There I met our liaison officer, who said the positions of 10 Regiment had changed, and we were to report once again to the brigade. They were very pleased by our sudden appearance. Rex and his master, an orderly officer, greeted each other with great excitement, and I was given a flask of cognac and some cigarettes for looking after him. Strangely enough, though, over the following days the dog would travel only with me.

'There we stood, the dog and I, not knowing what to do'

'In the first half of September 1942, while driving the combination through a wood, the cable to the battery broke. There we stood, the dog and I, not knowing what to do. After a few minutes I heard children's voices and then a group of young boys and girls appeared and stood staring at us. I realised there must have been a village in the area and asked the group to give us a push to the settlement. That was great fun, and the adults in the village didn't seem the least perturbed to see a motorcycle and sidecar with an SS-Sturmmann steering, the children all pushing, and a German Shepherd dog sitting in the sidecar. The burgermeister had been summoned and appeared, an elderly man, to greet me with the words: "Guten Tag, lieber Mensch."

'No one was more surprised than I. I got off the bike, shook his hands and asked him how he came to speak German. He laughed and told me that he could speak German, Polish and Russian. In 1914 he had taken part in the Battle of Tannenberg and was captured [the Battle of Tannenberg took place in August 1914, during the opening stages of World War I. The Russians, with 300,000 men, attacked a German force of similar size. However, the Russians were caught in a massive double envelopment on both flanks and suffered accordingly, losing 30,000 killed or wounded, 92,000 taken prisoner and 400 out of their 600 artillery

BELOW: Motorcycles and sidecars of the Das Reich *Division in Russia. It was in such a combination that Heller and his canine companion had their adventure. Note the wooded terrain, which gave excellent cover to partisans.*

pieces]. He ended up working on a farm in the Saarland for five years and said that he was treated well during his enforced stay. He ordered a young man to load my bike on to a cart and took me into his house. There, using chalk, he sketched out the position of his village and a small town that, according to him, was just 10km (six miles) away and contained a German unit. First, however, he insisted we eat.

'A pan of ham and eggs was produced'

'A huge pan of ham and eggs and some vodka was produced. I saw some of the men begin to roll cigarettes using newspaper and Makhorka tobacco. I beckoned them over and lay a pack of tobacco and cigarette papers on the table and indicated that they should help themselves. I ate and drank my fill. I asked the burgermeister if there were any

partisans in the area. He said that there would be no partisans so long as he was there. Only long afterwards did the ambiguity of his words strike me.

'The younger men took me to the larger village where the German unit was. It was a company of schutzpolizei. They repaired my bike while I slept off my intoxication, and then I joined a column heading towards Rakov. When I arrived there, the commandant's office did not know where the brigade was and said that I should wait. I was given food for myself and the dog, and then did what most soldiers have to do – wait!

'Next morning I joined a supply column heading for a village about 30 km (19 miles) from the Sluzker Forest. There I was told I would have to wait until the next morning before I could proceed. Because of the danger from partisans, movement was allowed only during the day and in columns with sufficient firepower.

'The skies suddenly darkened and then came a cloudburst'

'I was quartered with two ladies in their forties. One was always smiling, to show off her wonderful gold teeth. I was just 19, however, and didn't find ladies in their forties particularly attractive. More and more ladies arrived, then German junior NCOs and sergeants. A gramophone was produced and a real party started. As I had drank plenty of vodka, I went to sleep, as ever, with the dog by my side.

'Next morning I travelled up to Sluzk. There, I went to the Soldatenheim for a wonderful midday meal. I remember it well: spaghetti with goulash. As no other columns were travelling farther, I would have to go on alone. In the meantime, I had armed myself well. I had my pistol, my rifle and also a wonderful Finnish machine pistol, a superb weapon. I also had some egg grenades and stick grenades, stowed away so that they could not be hit by any stray bullets – I was a travelling arsenal.

'After travelling a few kilometres along good roads, the skies suddenly darkened and then came a great cloudburst. I really could not continue. I turned off the road at the next farmhouse and drove right up to the door. The dog and I

stood in the porch, soaking wet. I knocked on the door and it was opened by the most beautiful Russian girl I have ever seen. She burst out laughing – the dog and I must have made quite a sight. She gave me hot milk, and I was able to dry my wet clothes. I gave her some bread and sausage paste, for which she was very grateful. She spoke a little German and I gathered there had been a German signals unit quartered in the house and that it was now in Sluzk. She had a photograph of all the unit's NCOs which the men had given her. She gave it to me as I stood in front of the oven drying myself. When I took a closer look at it I got such a surprise I nearly fell in!

'I had found an old boyhood friend in the vastness of Russia'

'There, in the front row, stood my old friend Heini Schmidt from Cologne, who had led the Hitler Youth when I led the German Young People's troop. That was a real joy, and the girl also seemed genuinely delighted that I had found an old boyhood friend here in the vastness of Russia. I said my goodbyes and was on my way in a few minutes, promising that I would call in again if I passed by.

'Within a few minutes I was at the barracks in Sluzk where the signals company was based. I got directions to the room that Schmidt shared with two other NCOs. His face was quite a sight when he saw me. We had plenty to eat and drink. It was an amazing coincidence that that cloudburst had happened outside that particular house.

'Next day, I stopped off at the girl's house to tell her my news. As it was beginning to get late, I stayed the night. We were like brother and sister. She boiled and cleaned all my underwear, which was full of lice. I put on zinc cream to combat the lice and re-bandaged my wound, which was beginning to suppurate.

'Next morning I joined a column and eventually got back to my brigade. Because of the lice and my wound I was immediately sent to hospital. I was in a very poor state. Things improved a bit after that, though. At the end of October 1942, after recovering, I managed to get some recuperation leave.'

FOREST FIGHTING

ERIC BRÖRUP

SS-OBERSTURMFÜHRER

SS-Panzer Aufklärungs Abteilung 5

5th SS Panzer Division *Wiking*

The failure of the German offensive in the summer of 1942 resulted in Wehrmacht forces being hard pressed as the year drew to a close. For the Waffen-SS divisions in the East, a long, hard winter lay ahead.

RIGHT: Waffen-SS troops move out to engage Red Army units during the winter of 1942. The Wiking *Division was located in the Caucasus at the end of 1942, a region that suffers less severe winters than northern Russia.*

'With the onset of winter in November 1942, I was transferred to Aufklärungs Abteilung 8 as a platoon commander. The recce battalion was now a ski-troop outfit and an interesting form of warfare began for us. It was similar in content to the way the Finnish ski-troops operated. Fighting in trees is a little different from a traditional battle, where you usually have all kinds of fireworks – artillery, mortars, rockets, machine guns – and all kinds of other hardware to back you up. In the trees you are on your own. The weapons we used for forest fighting were just rifles, machine pistols and grenades. It is also very sneaky. You work in circles around each other in a kind of deadly "hide and seek".

[The German Army produced a 372-page book on winter warfare in 1942, the object of which was to convince German soldiers that they could easily adapt to the conditions in Russia during the winter months and could even use the weather and climate to their advantage. This publication went some way to restoring the drop in morale that had occurred as a result of the Wehrmacht's first winter on the Eastern Front. In addition, it is a myth that all German units had been unprepared for the Russian winter. Some units, for example, had access to large amounts of winter clothing. For example, when the *Totenkopf* Division had been trapped in the Demyansk Pocket at the beginning of 1942, the Luftwaffe had been able to drop ample quantities of warm clothing to the Waffen-SS soldiers.]

'I got the Iron Cross Second Class on 1 December 1942 for a raid into a forest when we ran into a Russian battalion. My job was to establish how far the Russians had penetrated into the forest. We killed some of them, lost one man, and brought back six prisoners, two of them NCOs.'

SS IN SOUTHERN RUSSIA

RICHARD FUCHS
SS-UNTERSCHARFÜHRER

SS-Panzerjäger Abteilung 5

5th SS Panzer Division *Wiking*

Fighting on the Eastern Front in winter presented both advantages and drawbacks to Waffen-SS armoured and self-propelled gun units. On the one hand, the rock-hard surface greatly facilitated movement, and made terrain that was impassable in warmer weather negotiable. However, the freezing conditions also jammed machinery and weapons, as Richard Fuchs found out...

RIGHT: SS-Unterscharführer Richard Fuchs of the Wiking *Division. In this photograph Fuchs is wearing the special field-grey version of the panzer-style clothing designed for crews of self-propelled guns and other armoured vehicles.*

'My unit was the Panzerjäger Abteilung of the *Wiking* Division, which was initially equipped with 37mm and 50mm anti-tank guns. Then we received the self-propelled 7.62cm anti-tank guns mounted on Panzer II chassis [the 7.62cm PaK(r) auf Fgst Pz Kpfw II (SF) were issued to the tank-hunter detachments of the panzer and panzergrenadier divisions from April 1942, to units mainly on the Eastern Front. Fielded mainly as a stop-gap until better designs could be deployed, they fought on until early 1944]. Later we received the 75mm cannon mounted on the chassis of the Czech Panzerkampfwagen 38(t).

'In January 1943 I was the driver of one of the company's radio and command half-tracks, which was armed with only a MG34 machine gun. We were patrolling near a village called Metschidinskaja in the Kalmuk Steppes. The weather was freezing, and though the six 75mm guns were in working order, all the Czech machine guns were frozen solid and totally useless.

'Suddenly we were attacked by a Russian infantry battalion. Our cannons opened fire, but the machine guns were out of action because of the cold. Fortunately I had a German MG34 mounted on my vehicle, which worked perfectly well, and I quickly brought it to bear on the enemy. The intensity and accuracy of our firing broke up the attack, and soon the Russians were streaming back in disarray. I received a commendation from my company commander for my part in the battle, and some time later was awarded the Iron Cross. Including this action, by this time I had taken part in 25 combat actions.'

⚡⚡ RETAKING KHARKOV

ERWIN BARTMANN
SS-UNTERSCHARFÜHRER

1st SS Panzer Division

Leibstandarte SS Adolf Hitler

The recapture of Kharkov by I SS Panzer Corps in March 1943 was one of the greatest Waffen-SS victories on the Eastern Front. For those who took part, the action was characterised by heavy and confusing close-quarter fighting.

RIGHT: SS-Unterscharführer Erwin Bartmann. He is wearing the M36 field blouse with dark green contrasting collar. The piping on his shoulder straps is white, indicating he is an infantryman. His peaked cap, though, is piped black, indicating the pioneers. The explanation is simple: he borrowed the cap from a pioneer.

'I rejoined my own unit as we were preparing to go into action at Kharkov. We had taken one area after heavy combat. Then it was re-taken by the Russians, then we pushed them out again. There seemed to be no end to the fighting. We had to take this ground three times, hoping on the last time that we had secured it for good. However, our guards were surprised by the enemy in the night and the positions overrun. My section's escape was quite cunning. We had watched the Russians approach from the house we were in, and decided to try to outwit them rather than outfight them. We had an interpreter with us, and he shouted out an order to us in Russian, whereupon we opened the window, leapt through it and ran off. I think the Russians were very surprised as we came through the window and ran past them. Luckily it was just one solitary Russian unit. Although we were unfortunately pushed out of this village, we only suffered a few minor casualties.

'Then we went into our preparatory positions for the assault on Kharkov. To me it seemed as if everything was going quite well, but that was not the case and we were forced to withdraw with heavy losses – the High Command was not prepared to let happen at Kharkov what had occurred at Stalingrad. The renewed attack on Kharkov started on 18 February and ended on 18 March 1943. The *Leibstandarte* and *Das Reich* Divisions made their attack on the city itself on 6 March, and within a couple of days we had penetrated the outer defences of the city. The Russian resistance stiffened, however, and we were involved in heavy street fighting.

'As we entered the suburbs, I was sent back as a messenger to request more ammunition supplies. As I made my way back, I came to a fork in the road. I had to make a decision which way to take, left or right. After a moment's hesitation, I took the right fork. I went along this road for a couple of minutes and then hesitated when I saw soldiers in the distance who didn't look German. They also halted. They waved at me to come over to them and that made my mind up – they were Russians. I took off as fast as I could and made my way back to the fork in the road. I eventually reached the supply unit and reported to the *Spiess* [slang: sergeant-major]. I told him I had seen some Russians. This caused quite a stir – they were only a few kilometres away from our supply units. I returned to my unit in the evening along with the ammunition supplies and a driver.

'By the time I got back, my unit was involved in heavy house-to-house fighting. I recall one block of houses we had to clear. An SS-Oberscharführer was in front of me as we

BELOW: Early 1943 was a successful period for the Waffen-SS on the Eastern Front. Here, members of SS-Panzerjäger Abteilung 5, Wiking Division, pose beside a lend-lease British Churchill tank they have just knocked out. One of the book's contributors, Richard Fuchs, stands far right.

sprinted up the stairs. He disappeared through a door. When we caught up to where he had been the door was shut and there was no sign of him. We cleared the block but he had completely vanished. He was probably captured by the Russians – we never saw him again.

'The Russians opened fire'

After Kharkov had fallen, we moved to Olkani. After a few days we were allowed back into Kharkov to the Soldatenheim, where we could be deloused and have a good wash. After a fine meal we could go to the cinema or the opera. I went to see *Boris Gudenov*.

'The advance continued towards Belgorod. I can remember one incident as if it were yesterday. We were on a reconnaissance mission and all was going well until we advanced up a hill and found a Russian artillery piece at the top. The crew were not at their gun and so we scarpered quickly before they had time to fire at us. I was in a motor-

ABOVE: Panzer crews of the Das Reich *Division grab some food before rolling into Kharkov. I SS Panzer Corps' victory had a marked effect upon Hitler, who insisted that the Waffen-SS be given the latest tanks and equipment. He believed that if it had the necessary tools it could bring the war in the East to a successful conclusion.*

cycle and sidecar combination. The driver managed to stall the engine and couldn't get it restarted. We ran to another vehicle and were given a lift back. I was particularly annoyed because I had left my camera in the sidecar. So, on the next night, the driver, another comrade and myself went back under cover of darkness on another motorcycle to retrieve it. We stopped before we reached the hill and went the rest of the way on foot. We crept along the ditch at the side of the road and finally saw our motorcycle exactly where we had been forced to leave it. We crept up to it, and it started on the first kick. The Russians opened fire but we made it safely away. The motorcycle, and my camera, were safely recovered.

'The whole battalion now moved forward. With another comrade I was sent forward on a reconnaissance to see if we could spot the enemy. We eventually stopped by a haystack, from where we had a good view of the terrain. We made ourselves as comfortable as possible but remained watchful and alert. In retrospect, we were being rather stupid, for having no field telephone or radio we had no way of contacting our unit. As two German planes flew over, we stood up and waved to them. They spotted us, but thought we were Russians and came into attack. Twice they strafed us. My friend ran forward directly into the hail of bullets but was miraculously unhurt. I threw myself to the ground and got hit by a bullet in the right thigh. I felt the warmth of the blood on my legs and as the planes flew off, I rolled up my trouser leg and could see the bullet. Fortunately, it hadn't penetrated too deep. I dug it out myself and bandaged my leg. We made our way back and reported to the company commander. I thought I would be sent to hospital but it was decided that the wound wasn't serious enough, and so I stayed with the unit.'

ᛋᛋ BIRTHDAYS & CARNAGE

WERNER VÖLKNER

SS-ROTTENFÜHRER

Flak Abteilung

3rd SS Panzer Division *Totenkop*

For the young soldiers of the Waffen-SS, opportunities for any type of celebration were often few and far between, especially when they were fighting for their lives on the Eastern Front. Werner Völkner remembers one of his birthdays, which, because of a later act of kindness, could have been his last.

RIGHT: This photograph, taken at Iwanowka, Russia, in 1943, shows a group of Totenkopf *Division soldiers leaning on a dismounted 3.7cm Flak gun removed from its usual half-track for use in the ground role. Völkner is on the extreme right.*

'On the day we retook Kharkov, it was my birthday. Our company commander appeared to wish me well, bringing with him a bottle of brandy. He took a swig, and then passed the bottle round and wished us a pleasant day before leaving. We certainly enjoyed having a drink and were very cheerful, until the troops started passing us carrying back the wounded from the fighting. The sight of mangled bodies sobered us up quickly and brought us back down to earth. In a sombre mood we put the bottle away, got ourself ready, and it was back to the war again.

'In late March 1943, as we hunted for Russian stragglers after the successful recapture of Kharkov, I had a narrow escape. We had been combing through some woods and villages for the enemy and I came across one Russian soldier who had been very seriously wounded. I think his legs were shattered. He lay there, the snow all around him stained with his blood. I felt very sorry for him, so as I passed by I took my field dressing from its special pocket inside my tunic and threw it to him to enable him to bandage his wounds. As I walked on, something made me turn round and look back at him. He was aiming a weapon at me, ready to shoot me in the back. Luckily, one of my friends was faster on the trigger than he was and shot him dead. You never really knew in those days just how close to death you sometimes came.'

⚡⚡ FIGHTING TO STAY ALIVE

JAN MUNK

SS-STANDARTENOBERJUNKER

SS-Panzergrenadier Regiment *Westland*

5th SS Panzer Division *Wiking*

RIGHT: A Wiking *Division truck struggles through mud and water on its way to deliver much-needed supplies to the front. In July 1943, the division was moved up to the Donetz Front, but was held in reserve during the abortive Kursk Offensive of that month.*

'The order to move came on 11 July 1943. We started in the early evening, travelled all through the night, then slept during the day. Each day we presented ourselves differently to confuse any hostile eyes. First, showing all our weapons, then with no weapons visible at all. Everyone in shirtsleeves, then all in tunics, then all in full camouflage gear. Even the divisional signs on our vehicles were changed at random. The Russian partisans must have gone crazy trying to work out which units were on the move [This tactic was also used during Operation 'Spring Awakening', the German offensive against the Red Army in Hungary in 1945. In an effort to fool the enemy all identifying insignia were removed].

'I could see Russian infantry in front of my trench'

At last we arrived at our destination and deployed into small units. When that happens you don't get a clue what happens to the others to your left or right. Our company met a lot of trucks with Wehrmacht troops who had obviously been thrown out of their positions by the Russians. As we advanced we soon had to stop using the trucks because of enemy gunfire. We got out and started to walk. The route

we followed was very soft and sandy and it made marching, especially carrying a heavy machine gun, really tiring. I was exhausted when our commanding officer caught up with me and carried my machine gun for a while to give me some relief. All the time, he encouraged us to keep going at a fast pace because we were needed urgently.

'We finally occupied the lost positions again and had some peace and quiet at last. The positions we had just re-taken were marvellous: well-made trenches and bunkers. The Russians must have attacked in some strength and very suddenly, because in the bunkers we found loads of unopened German parcels and enormous amounts of equipment and supplies. We had a good time kitting ourselves out in new socks, underwear and so on. In the middle of this paradise, a messenger from company HQ arrived with the message: "Munk and his number two report immediately to HQ." I was furious, having to leave all those goodies and all that food, to go back to the commanding officer. When we arrived, we were told to take up a position in a trench and protect the HQ.

'That was around 1500 hours. At about 1700 hours a prisoner was brought in who told us the Russians would attack with tanks in the early morning of 19 July. He was right! It was soon clear that their attack was succeeding, because I could see Russian infantry in front of my trench moving from right to left. At that time I had a MG34, a beautiful machine gun, very reliable and accurate. My number two was a Rumanian farmer's son. His German was not too good but his willingness to help was enormous, and so was his strength. Where any other number two would carry the regulation two boxes of ammunition, he would carry four and still keep up the pace. There was a great shortage of brass in Germany at that time, so shells for rifles and machine guns were made from steel instead of brass, and then lacquered to prevent them rusting.

'So there I was. I had an excellent machine gun, a first-class number two, plenty to shoot at, but poor quality ammunition. Normally we tried to control our firing and let loose only short bursts. This time, however, the numbers of enemy moving in front of us were so great that much longer bursts were required. That overheated the barrel and,

BELOW: This platoon of the Westland *Regiment was overrun in July 1943 by T-34 tanks, as related by Jan Munk (extreme right, front row) above. The senior NCO (peaked cap) and Munk were the only survivors.*

before I could change to a cool one, the gun jammed. A varnished round had stuck in the hot barrel. In my efforts to put things right, though, I neglected my own cover. I felt as if someone had hit my shoulder with a hammer – I had been wounded. I didn't feel any pain, though, and fortunately could still move my arm.

'My number two had been hit in the left temple and killed instantly'

'Then I heard a noise to my right and saw that my number two had fallen back in the trench, just as he was lifting a full ammunition box. He had been hit in the left temple and killed instantly. The shot must have come from our extreme left. Looking in that direction I could see brown Russian uniforms. As my machine gun was useless I fired my pistol in their direction and then ran back along the trench.

'I soon met several SS soldiers, who I recognised as HQ personnel, cooks, clerks and supply people. They were not

ABOVE: A column of Waffen-SS SdKfz 251 half-track armoured personnel carriers pass through a Russian village as the preparations for the Kursk Offensive get under way. Note the swastika draped over the vehicle in the foreground to aid aerial recognition.

really frontline soldiers and so, unsurprisingly, no one knew what to do next. Lying on the ground was our commanding officer. The others said he was dead but I took a closer look. He had been hit by a bullet just on the outside of his left eye, and the exit hole was in his head near the left ear lobe. It looked very bad and I thought that he was indeed dead, but then he moved. The others pointed to a trench and said they were going to follow it as it should to battalion HQ.

'I picked up my commanding officer and was about to follow them when he managed to tell me not to follow them but to carry on ahead, which would take us to a neighbouring anti-tank unit. The others said he was delirious and took no notice of him. I and another Dutchman decided to believe him, though. I first had his arm around my neck but whenever he heard a shot he would try to walk, with the result that he stepped on my heels and brought us both crashing down. My Dutch friend had been shot in the thigh and could only just walk himself. The best way to get along was to carry my commanding officer in a fireman's hold over my shoulder. That wasn't pleasant because my wounded shoulder was beginning to hurt, but we kept on the move nevertheless. My comrade was behind me and managed to keep the handful of Russians who had followed us at bay with his rifle. They, of course, were just as scared and confused as we were, and a single shot was all that was needed to make them take cover.

'At one stage I had to stop for a breather, which allowed my commanding officer to open his map case to show me where he was heading. I really wanted to believe that he was right because, apart from the three of us and the handful of Russians following, there wasn't a soul in sight. The trench stopped, but we carried on at ground level until at last I saw a group of trees that my commanding officer had said was the anti-tank position. The next moment we came to a big crater and we took cover in it. I told the Dutch lad to get help quickly as I really couldn't go any further. He car-

ried on, and after half an hour or so a Volkswagen vehicle came racing over the terrain to pick us up. I was taken to a dressing station, looked after, and told to my great relief that my wound was superficial, with no real damage. It was there that I met my platoon commander again, who told me a sad tale. He told me that, as far as he knew, the entire company had been virtually wiped out, overrun by Russian tanks in the early morning. I was then moved from the dressing station to a hospital in Dniepropetrovsk.

'Eventually, when I had recovered, I went on leave to Holland on 23 August 1943. When I got back I found the Iron Cross Second Class waiting for me. A rather shy and embarrassed mother handed the award to me with a letter from my company.'

SS CLASH AT KURSK

ERWIN BARTMANN
SS-UNTERSCHARFÜHRER

1st SS Panzer Division
Leibstandarte SS Adolf Hitler

Waffen-SS units at the Battle of Kursk suffered high rates of attrition. Erwin Bartmann was a casualty during the early stages.

Right: Tiger tanks of the Das Reich *Division, part of II SS Panzer Corps, rumble forward during the Kursk Offensive, July 1943.*

'Now, in 1943, the greatest armoured battle in history was about to start. We would attack from the south into the Kursk salient along with Panzergrenadier Division *Grossdeutschland* [the *Leibstandarte* was part of SS-Obergruppenführer Paul Hausser's II SS Panzer Corps, which was in turn part of the 4th Panzer Army. The latter was tasked with driving through the Soviet

defence lines along the Voronezh Front, and then wheel northeast to take Prokhorovka. By the second day of the battle, the *Leibstandarte* had been engaged in fierce battles with the Soviet 1st Guards Armoured Brigade].

'As we attacked we had to pass through a wood, where I was wounded by a shell splinter. We had been lying in shell scrapes, and the shells were exploding in the trees above

ABOVE: Waffen-SS personnel and materiel as far as the eye can see as the Battle of Kursk gets under way. As usual the Third Reich's elite fought tenaciously, but not even supermen could break through the Red Army's six belts of defences of anti-tank guns, mines and infantry positions.

BELOW: Waffen-SS grenadiers head towards Prokhorovka. The clashes in the Kursk salient were particularly brutal, even by the standards of the Eastern Front. No mercy was shown to Waffen-SS soldiers who were captured. Their death's head insignia became a death warrant.

us. There was so much shrapnel and wood splinters flying around that every second man was hit. I was hit by shrapnel in the left shoulder, which went through into my lung, missed my heart by just a few millimetres and lodged between the ribs. I partly lost my eyesight and could only vaguely distinguish between light and dark. Another lightly wounded comrade led me back to the dressing station.

'I felt that if I went under I would never re-awaken'

'There I was bandaged up and waited for transport to hospital. On our way there we had to pass along a road which was in full view of the Russians. They made absolutely no allowances for ambulances, and we came under a murderous fire, but luckily made it through safely. Using a ground-sheet as a stretcher, I was carried out of the ambulance and laid on some straw. There I had to wait my turn as there were many more comrades with worse wounds than mine. I saw many die around me. In the middle of the night I was taken into the operating tent and laid on the operating table. I was given a rather ineffective anaesthetic, but in any case I wanted to stay conscious. I felt that if I went under I would never re-awaken.

[The *Leibstandarte*, together with the *Das Reich* and *Totenkopf* Divisions, made good progress: on the third day of the offensive the *Leibstandarte* and *Das Reich* Divisions engaged the Soviets in a furious tank battle near Teterevino, which resulted in the Waffen-SS being victorious and threatening the entire front of the Soviet 6th Guards Army. By 10 July, the *Totenkopf*, which had been diverted to cover the flanks, had joined *Das Reich* and the *Leibstandarte* for the attack on Prokhorovka. Against Hausser's 600 tanks the Soviets launched the entire contingent of 850 tanks and self-propelled guns of the 5th Guards Tank Army. This mass of armour clashed on 12 July 1943, with over 1500 tanks blasting away at each other at close range. At the end of the day over 700 tanks lay burning on the battlefield. Both sides realised that reinforcements were desperately needed to avoid defeat. However, it was the Soviets who got fresh forces to the area first – Hitler called off the Kursk Offensive on 13 July.]

'The next day I was taken to the station, where I waited for transport with many other comrades. We lay there for a full day, and heard that the Russians had broken through. What now? I had already seen what happened to wounded Waffen-SS men who fell into Russian hands. Fortunately all went well: the train arrived and we were taken farther to the rear, where we were eventually loaded into a proper hospital train. I ended up in a hospital in Krakow and stayed there for a week. Then I moved again, travelling through Czechoslovakia into Austria and to an Army hospital. When we disembarked from the train, everyone who was capable of walking had to make their way to the hospital on foot. This included me. At the dressing station they had taken away my uniform, so all I had on was my shirt and my long-johns. What a sight we must have made as we marched through the town!

By winning at Kursk the Red Army had effectively won the war

'The doctors could not find any shrapnel. Knowing that there was definitely something in my body, I asked if I could be sent to an SS hospital in Vienna. After much fussing this was agreed. There they X-rayed me and found the shrapnel lodged in my ribs. I still have this shrapnel today.'

[The Battle of Kursk was a catastrophe for the Germans on the Eastern Front. German losses were put at 70,000 killed, 2900 tanks, 195 self-propelled guns, 844 artillery pieces, 1392 aircraft and 5000 motor vehicles. The Russians had suffered far more: some estimates placed their casualties alone at 250,000 men. However, by winning at Kursk the Red Army had effectively won the war in the East. Bartmann's *Leibstandarte* Division had done well during the offensive, as had the rest of the Waffen-SS. For example, the *Leibstandarte* had knocked out over 500 Soviet tanks in the nine days up to 14 July. However, from 1943 onwards it and the other German units in the East could only fight a rearguard campaign in a vain effort to hold back the Red Army.]

DEFEAT IN THE WEST

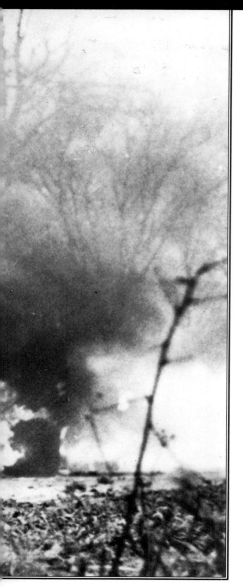

When the Allies invaded France in June 1944, both inexperienced and battle-hardened Waffen-SS divisions were committed to defeating them. However, though they fought with their usual tenacity and courage, the Waffen-SS soldiers found themselves being overwhelmed by Allied material superiority in a grim battle of attrition.

H itler and the German High Command had long realised that the Allies would open a second front in Europe, and had calculated that Allied forces would invade France sometime in the spring or early summer of 1944. What they did not know was the precise date the invasion would take place, or exactly where. A huge Allied deception campaign, involving fake radio traffic and masses of dummy equipment on the ground, successfully convinced the Germans that their main force would land at Calais. For more than a week after the Allies had actually landed in Normandy on 6 June, Hitler was sure that a larger invasion was still to come farther east, and held forces in reserve to counter it.

While the Allies' overwhelming control of the air ensured the success of the initial assault and the securing the beachhead, supplying the front as it expanded east and west was the key to the invasion's eventual success. Therefore, the Allies planned to take Caen on the left, while on the right US forces were to swing right to take the Cotentin peninsula and the port of Cherbourg, and then drive to Brest on the coast of Britanny. All the time, meanwhile, air power would be used to disrupt German troop movements and supply lines, and to prevent reserves moving to the front.

The Germans planned to defeat the invasion by massing forces against it once the initial elements were ashore, then

German troops on the attack during the ill-fated Ardennes Offensive. The campaign was Hitler's attempt to regain the initiative in the West, and he committed his best Waffen-SS divisions to the assault: the Leibstandarte, Das Reich, Hohenstaufen *and* Hitlerjugend, *but to no avail.*

ABOVE: German troops in the Bocage, Normandy, June 1944. Though the Allies had massive superiority in terms of aircraft and materiel when they invaded France, they faced determined opposition from the Wehrmacht and the Waffen-SS. By the end of June, for example, there were six Waffen-SS armoured divisions battling in Normandy.

driving them back into the sea. An alternative proposal, to stop the invaders in their tracks on the beaches, was discarded. Although the time and place of the invasion of Normandy on 6 June 1944 took the High Command by surprise, reserves moved rapidly to block the Allied advance. Among them were several Waffen-SS divisions, most with a core of troops seasoned in the bitter fighting on the Eastern Front. The Waffen-SS panzer divisions that took part in the Normandy battles brought with them a wealth of invaluable and hard-won combat experience gained in the vicious fighting on the Eastern Front, and many were survivors of the great-

est tank battle of all time – Kursk. The Allied tank crews, on the other hand, had nothing like this experience. Many of the armoured units that landed in Normandy were 'green' and inexperienced. That said, not all German units were equipped with the formidable Tiger, Königstiger (King Tiger) or Panther tanks. The mainstay of the panzer armies was still the venerable Panzer Mk IV, with which the Allies could compete on reasonably even terms. In addition, the Allies had huge reserves of men and material, and virtually total control of the air.

The *Hitlerjugend* was the first Waffen-SS division to be blooded in Normandy. From its station at Dreux, between Caen and Paris, it was in position by 7 June to intercept the British and Canadian armies under Montgomery advancing on Caen (fiercely defended and cautiously attacked, the city did not fall to the Allies until 9 July). By 13 June, the *Götz von Berlichingen* division was in Normandy from Tours, to stem the Americans at Carentan. By 17 June, the *Leibstan-*

darte had arrived from Bruges to join the battle for Caen. The *Hohenstaufen* and *Frundsberg* Divisions were ordered from Poland to Normandy on 14 June, when it dawned on Hitler that there would be no further Allied invasions in northern France, and arrived around Caen on 25 June; while the *Das Reich* arrived in Normandy from Toulouse on 10 July to counter the American advance.

The *Hitlerjugend* Division was involved in some of the fiercest of the fighting in Normandy. Its young grenadiers often fought to the death with great bravery. It was often said of them that they were trained to be fighters rather than soldiers. Certainly their training was heavily biased towards combat skills and fieldcraft, with less emphasis on drill

BELOW: US troops clearing hedgerows during the Normandy campaign. The Allied soldiers on the ground had a lack of experience overall compared to their German counterparts. They had to learn quickly to survive, especially when faced by Waffen-SS divisions.

skills. However, even the fanatical young fighters were unable to stem the Allied advance, and by the beginning of August the Germans were facing a crisis in the so-called Falaise Pocket.

The Falaise Pocket had been created by the British and Canadian advance beyond Caen towards Falaise and, farther west, on Vire; and on their right by the American drives on Coutances, Avranches, and then east to Argentan. In the north there were still considerable German forces in the Cotentin peninsula, which were in danger of being cut off by the end of July. Hitler, in an effort to save them, therefore ordered an offensive towards Avranches, in which elements of the SS divisions *Leibstandarte* and *Das Reich* took part. Good initial progress faltered in the face of sheer Allied numbers, and fighting withdrawals and desperate counterattacks became the order of the day throughout the peninsula as the German divisions made their escape through the 50km- (30-mile) wide break in the Allied lines between Argentan and Falaise.

By 21 August 1944, the Allies had closed the Falaise Gap. Some German units had managed to slip through the net, but the battle for Normandy was effectively over. Waffen-SS's losses had been appalling. Divisions that had entered the fray with hundreds of tanks and thousands of men were reduced to little more than battalion strength. The *Leibstandarte* and *Frundsberg* lost all their tanks and artillery; *Das Reich* was left with 450 men and 15 tanks; *Hohenstaufen* had 460 men and 25 tanks; and the *Hitlerjugend* had shrunk to 300 men, 10 tanks and no artillery.

The *Leibstandarte* was sent to Aachen to rest and rebuild. However, it was a journey fraught with difficulties: all movement behind the German lines was harassed by Allied aircraft.

In mid-September 1944, more by accident than design, the Waffen-SS became involved in one of the Allies' greater military disasters on the Western Front. Bernard Montgomery conceived a daring plan to speed the advance of his 21st Army Group into Germany through Holland – Operation 'Market Garden'. US airborne forces would capture the bridges at Eindhoven and Nijmegen, British paratroops would take the bridge at Arnhem, and on the ground the British XXX Corps would advance on a narrow front to link up with them. Little German resistance was expected, especially around Arnhem itself.

The Waffen-SS at Arnhem

Unfortunately, it just so happened that the remnants of the *Hohenstaufen* and *Frundsberg* Divisions had been sent to Arnhem to rest and refit. When the British 1st Airborne Division landed near Arnhem on 17 September, the two battered SS panzer divisions were able to muster themselves into nothing greater than several kampfgruppen. But these – one, at Arnhem, soon reinforced by a detachment of formidable Königstiger tanks – were still armoured units, and more than a match for the lightly armed paratroopers and the strung-out line of XXX Corps. Even so, the airborne troops held out for 10 days, the British 1st Airborne Division losing nearly 8000 out of the 10,000 committed.

It was a major defeat for the Allies, but the advantage to the exhausted German armies was short-lived. Within a further 10 days XXX Corps had overcome the resistance put up by II SS Panzer Corps, and Allied bombers closed the Arnhem bridge to German traffic.

The Ardennes Offensive

Meanwhile, George Patton's Third Army had raced through western France and then swung left to drive past Paris and attack Metz; French and US units had landed on France's Mediterranean coast; Belgium was all but taken; and by the beginning of October 1944 the US 1st Army was attacking the Reich itself along the Siegfried Line north from Aachen.

Hitler now prepared a last attempt to regain the initiative in the West and halt the Allied offensive into the Reich. The key to the offensive was Antwerp, which was the objective of the 6th Panzer Army under 'Sepp' Dietrich. The plan was to strike through the Ardennes forest and across the Maas (Meuse), the spearhead units being the *Hitlerjugend* and *Leibstandarte* Divisions. To the north, 5th Panzer Army would cross the Maas and drive for Brussels. In the south, 7th Panzer Army would secure further crossings on the Maas. If successful, the offensive would break the Allies' front, cut off the their supply line from Antwerp and in theory preserve the Reich.

The assault, launched on 16 December 1944, surprised the Allies and punched a hole through the US 12th Army Group. US airborne forces were encircled at Bastogne, but held out until 26 December. The Germans became bogged down in the narrow network of roads along which they had to advance, and eventually, in a repeat of a pattern that had been seen on the Eastern Front, simply lacked the weight to break through the solid wall of the Allied defence. On 3 January 1945, despite heavy snow, the Allies launched a counteroffensive that proved unstoppable. By 16 January the region was clear. The Germans had lost 120,000 men and squandered their last heavy forces in the Ardennes. By 10 February, the German armies had withdrawn over the Rhine. All they could do was fight persistent rearguard actions in the following months to slow the Allies' relentless advance on the Reich. The end was now in sight for the beleaguered Reich. Soon, the only option for the vaunted Waffen-SS legions would be surrender.

SS WAR OF ATTRITION

EGON SCHULZE
SS TANK RADIO OPERATOR

10th SS Panzer Division *Frundsberg*

On reaching Normandy on 25 June, the Frundsberg *Division was fed into the line between Caen and Villers-Bocage, along with the* Hohenstaufen *Division. However, as Egon Schulze relates, the Waffen-SS faced an impossible task.*

RIGHT: Waffen-SS troops in a Normandy town in mid-June 1944. Even the Führer's finest proved unable to destroy the Allied bridgehead on mainland Europe.

's soon as the invasion of Normandy began, my division was transferred from Russia to Normandy, arriving at the end of June. We went straight into battle against British units that had been pushing southwest from Caen.

'As I had learned a little English in secondary school, I was ordered to establish a prisoner collection centre with a couple of comrades in a village immediately behind the front, near Hill 188, which was then being fought over. The village was empty, so we began looking for a safe house to shelter in, one that offered a degree of protection from the constant enemy artillery fire. We found a house with sturdy cellars, though ourselves and the prisoners were left to fend for ourselves when it came to rations.

'When we had sorted things out the prisoners were brought in. They were young chaps like us, very confused, though glad that for them the war was over. I tried to converse with them, and did manage to reach a level of understanding, agreeing on the pointlessness of war and similar things. All the while shells were landing around us, forcing us to stay in the cellars. The British stayed with us for two or three days, and then they were transferred further to the rear, to be replaced by fresh prisoners. During that 14-day period I met a variety of interesting people.

'I always took a couple of prisoners with me when I went searching for provisions during the quiet spells. As I treated the prisoners fairly I reckoned that I could count on them not trying to escape. There were still cows running around in the meadows surrounding the village, though they had all been wounded by artillery shells. Nevertheless, they could still be eaten so we slaughtered one. One of the prisoners was a cook, and he prepared a wonderful roast for us all. As we sat down to eat it enemy artillery opened up on us and our house took a direct hit, which badly wounded the cook. Fortunately transport arrived that evening to take the prisoners away and he was treated.

'As I have said, when we came under fire we all took refuge in the cellars, and while down there the prisoners would always get out their snapshots and show them to me. We were all in the same boat.'

'After 14 days we were forced to abandon the village and pull back. Soon we were trapped and encircled in the

vicinity of Falaise and things became terribly confused. On 18 August 1944, we received orders to take our tanks and rescue some of our comrades who were encircled by the Americans. On the way there I caught sight of my friend Rudi at a crossroads, but I couldn't say much to him because we were under fire at the time. When we reached our destination, around 60 per cent of the place was already in enemy hands. Unfortunately all our ammunition was located there. Undaunted, we blew up the ammunition to deprive its use to the enemy, despite being under constant fire. By then, however, the whole area had been closed off by the opposition. It was total chaos, with artillery duels going on everywhere, fighter-bombers and fighters in the sky and tank battles raging all around. The area we held got smaller and smaller. We tried to reach our own unit with our tanks, but it no longer existed. It was every man for himself.

'The ground was littered with dead'

'During the evening of 19 August we managed to assemble a few detachments from various units to attempt a breakout, but it was pointless. However, as we advanced into areas which were occupied by the enemy we found we were safe. Though they were full of British and American tanks, they did not shoot at us, they just let us through. The night-time journey itself was eerie. We had no specific destination and radio contact had been lost with the command. The ground was littered with dead German and Allied soldiers, burnt-out vehicles and tanks. As dawn broke my tank and a self-propelled gun reached a crossroads in the forest. In the distance I could hear an MG42 machine gun chattering away – perhaps the location of the frontline! Suddenly firing broke out and the self-propelled gun went up in flames. The enemy was nowhere to be seen. Then there was an almighty jolt and we slewed across the intersection. One of the tracks

had been ripped off by a shell. Amid the destroyed lorries, gun carriages and dead bodies my tank lay helpless, what were we to do?

'I crawled back to the tank'

'There were three of us left. We took the decision to blow up the tank and attempt to escape on foot. As soon as we left the vehicle, though, we came under machine-gun fire from both sides of the road. My two comrades were killed by this gunfire. I was alone. What could I do? As the explo-

sives hadn't gone off I crawled back to the tank, closed the hatch down and waited for whatever or whoever would come my way.

'Around midday I heard the sound of engines, and then a column of vehicles, tanks and lorries full of British soldiers rolled past me heading east. I didn't move. Afterwards two American ambulances stopped at the crossroads. They were driven by German soldiers and medical orderlies. They got out and examined all the fallen who were lying around, but they were all dead. I emerged from my tank to find out what was going on. They said they had been prisoners for four

days and were looking for German wounded. As I wasn't wounded they couldn't take me with them – I was back on my own again. Darkness came. I was still uncertain as to what course of action to take.

'As I was walking I came upon a forester's lodge, which was full of fellow Waffen-SS comrades and some paratroopers. They were organising another breakout, so I elected to join them. However, we were then fired on by British tanks. Resistance was useless: we were in the middle of enemy-held territory and had hardly any weapons. So we surrendered. That was on 21 August 1944.'

⚡⚡ A FEARFUL REPUTATION

EWALD KRASSMANN
SS-UNTERSCHARFÜHRER

SS-Panzer Nachrichten Abteilung 9

9th SS Panzer Division *Hohenstaufen*

The Waffen-SS had a fearsome fighting reputation in the eyes of those Allied soldiers who fought against them in Normandy. However, they were also thought to be brutal towards those they captured, a view which, as Krassmann reports, was more myth than reality.

RIGHT: Ewald Krassmann, here in the uniform of an SS-Sturmmann, of Panzer Nachrichten Abteilung 9 (Armoured Signals Detachment 9), 9th SS Panzer Division Hohenstaufen. *The fighting capabilities of men like Krassmann were attested to by the Allied supremo General Eisenhower himself, when he wrote of their 'ingrained toughness', and among the Allied servicemen the Waffen-SS was generally feared and loathed.*

'The division was ordered to Normandy in the middle of June 1944. It took 10 days to transport the men and equipment to the frontline. The fighting was very severe in that period, with many losses on both sides.

'Once, for a period of two days, we had a captured Canadian pilot with with us in the radio wagon. For these two days we treated him as one of us, sharing the same rations, comforts and dangers. As he could speak some German we got on with him quite well. Eventually we were able to hand him over to a prisoner-of-war collection centre. Just before he left us he turned to us and said he was glad not to have been taken prisoner by the SS! Whereupon, we showed him our field-grey uniforms with the SS runes on the collar. His face went bright red and then very pale. He had been among his most feared adversaries and not realised it – in action we wore camouflage clothing over our uniforms, which hid our SS insignia.'

[The order to form the *Hohenstaufen* Division was given in December 1943, and it spent the whole of 1943 working up, and first saw action in Russia, at Tarnopol, in April 1944. Though its ranks contained mainly 18-year-old teenagers, it performed very well, working in conjunction with the *Frundsberg* Division to enable trapped Wehrmacht and Waffen-SS units to escape from the so-called Kamenets-Podolsk Pocket.]

✠ THE FALAISE POCKET

KARL-HEINZ DECKER

**SS-STURMMANN
(UNTERFÜHRERANWARTER)**

SS-Panzergrenadier Regiment 25
12th SS Panzer Division *Hitlerjugend*

*In one particular action, a kampfgruppe
from the* Hitlerjugend *was cut off by
Canadian troops in the Ecole Supérieur
in Falaise, and was reported to have
fought to the death rather than surrender. However, there was actually a
handful of survivors, one being 18-year-
old Karl-Heinz Decker.*

*RIGHT: Grim-faced but determined, grenadiers of the
Hitlerjugend Division head for the front during the
campaign in France in 1944.*

'On the first day of the invasion we were ordered to move quickly up to the front, and suffered our first casualties from attacks by Allied fighter-bombers. We went into position on the outskirts of Caen, but I can't remember the name of the district. The city had suffered terrible damage as a result of British bombing attacks. We held our positions there for around a month without great losses. I believe it was 7 July when, after heavy artillery fire, we came to grips with the enemy, being pushed back through Caen. From this time onwards we had to change our positions almost every night as the frontline to the left and right was shattered.

'During one attack, I think it was against an enemy bridgehead, we were hit by heavy fire as we came out of a wood. My section received a direct hit from an artillery shell. One comrade had two legs smashed and one arm injured, and another had one leg smashed. There were no medics available so we had to carry them to the dressing station on our Zeltbahn (a waterproof poncho, triangular in shape, several of which could be joined up to make a small tent). Because of this I lost contact with my company and was allocated to a kampfgruppe from the division.

'During the night of 16/17 August we arrived at Falaise. Immediately we came under heavy machine-gun fire, with tracer flying through the darkness at us. We took cover among the houses and occupied one of the buildings. It was the Ecole Supérieur. From this building we had a good view of the crossroads, where Canadian supply columns were passing through. We opened fire on them. They sent in a tank against us, but it was disabled by a *Panzerfaust* and was later towed away. An assault group of Canadian infantry also made little headway against us, eventually occupying the buildings on the opposite side of the street. I can remember there was a long wall, and an orchard on our side of the street.

'In the main building the wounded were treated by our medic aided by a prisoner we had taken. Among the wounded was a badly injured Canadian who needed immediate attention. Under the cover of a Red Cross flag, made by daubing a white sheet with blood to make a red cross, our medic and the Canadian prisoner took advantage of a brief pause in the fighting to carry the injured man over to his own side. In this way our own medic became a prisoner, but he was released a short time later to return to us.

'As our situation was hopeless a breakout was planned. On the evening of 17 August we left our positions and made our way through the orchard to the main building. We said goodbye to the wounded and the medic, who had volunteered to stay behind with them.

'As soon as we went into the street we drew heavy enemy fire, so we plunged into the houses and waited there for dawn to break. Under cover of a German air attack (a real rarity!) we managed to slip past the enemy positions. We followed the sound of gunfire in an attempt to find our own lines, but without success. By now there were only 18 of us left. We marched for hours. We had had nothing to eat and were exhausted, so we went to a farm and asked for some food and a chance to rest. We rested our weary bodies. However, within an hour we were prisoners: the farmer betrayed us to the enemy. I know today that we had been in what was known as the Falaise Pocket.'

⚡⚡ MAKING THE ENEMY PAY

▰▰ **WILHELM FECHT**
SS-SCHÜTZE

SS-Werfer Abteilung 12
12th SS Panzer Division *Hitlerjugend*

The Hitlerjugend *excelled itself in battling to hold the Falaise Gap open for other units to withdraw – and almost destroyed itself in the process. The morale of the young Waffen-SS soldiers, though, remained high throughout the action.*

RIGHT: SS-Schütze Wilhelm Fecht served with Werfer Abteilung 12 (Mortar Detachment 12), Hitlerjugend Division. He is shown here wearing the special black panzer clothing for crews of tanks and certain other armoured vehicles. At the end of June 1944, Fecht and his comrades helped to push Allied forces off Hill 112, which was positioned southwest of Caen.

'When the Normandy invasion started, our detachment wasn't fully equipped. Only one of the batteries had vehicles, so it was only at the end of June 1944 that we in the second battery came into action. We were sent forward at night. Movements were only carried out at night due to the threat from enemy fighter-bombers. Our mortar battery had 36 "tubes" [the *Hitlerjugend* Division had four batteries in its mortar unit], and with these we always gave the enemy a thorough hammering, especially around Hill 112 near Caen. After every second salvo we had to change our positions so that the enemy could not pinpoint our position. Our morale was always good. All we missed was our Luftwaffe – they were nowhere to be seen. From the enemy side we had a lot to put up with, and had to undergo much carpet bombing. Sometimes we had to give indirect fire support against tanks with our mortars. Sometimes the enemy artillery could pinpoint your position to within a couple of metres if you used your radio. We came out of the Falaise Pocket with only 20 men. All the others had been either killed or captured.'

⚡⚡ AN OVERWHELMING TIDE

ERHARD KINSCHER
SS-STURMMANN

SS-Panzergrenadier Regiment 25
12th SS Panzer Division *Hitlerjugend*

Erhard Kinscher, a motorcycle despatch rider with SS-Panzergrenadier Regiment 25, was one of the rearguard left behind when his regiment withdrew from its command post in the Ardenne Abbey.

RIGHT: The man who suggested the idea of a volunteer Waffen-SS youth division, Reichsjugendführer Arthur Axmann. Thus was the Hitlerjugend *Division born*

'During the late afternoon of 8 July, I received an order from Oberleutnant Kaminski of 13 Company to take an MG42 machine gun and, together with SS-Sturmmann Hampel and a runner from 13 Company, to cover the withdrawal of the regiment [each panzer division had two panzergrenadier regiments, each one having three battalions of four companies each. The third battalion also had attached to it a heavy gun company, a flak company, a reconnaissance company and a pioneer company. The *Hitlerjugend*'s panzergrenadier regiments were numbered 25 and 26].

'I hung a belt of 300 rounds around my neck and fitted a further belt of 100 rounds into the breech. The others followed me at short intervals as we went through the shattered buildings and passed the blazing ammunition dump across from the church. To get a good field of fire for the MG42 I went through the northwest door of the Abbey, which was already coming under enemy artillery fire. In front of me I could see a low wall. Beyond it was a meadow, which was surrounded by a hedge. I checked behind me and saw my number three about 50m [55 yards] behind. I wanted to check what was behind the hedge, so I crossed the wall and set off across the meadow. Halfway across I came under heavy fire and could hear Hampel crying, "Erhard, come back, come back." I fired off the whole belt of ammunition in the MG42 towards the hedge and then sprinted back, zig-zagging as I did so, and leapt over the wall and out of sight of the enemy.

'We conferred briefly and decided to cross through the Ardenne Abbey to the northwest side. We could see Cussy lying to the north. What we saw there took our breath away, there were so many enemy tanks and infantry. After a short time the company chief of staff, SS-Untersturmführer Kneip, came to us. The smoke of battle slowly cleared and we could see that the enemy had taken Ardenne. As we sheltered behind a wall, fire came at us from the shattered roof of the granary at the side of our old command post. However, with some return fire from our MG42 and a hand grenade this was soon silenced.

'Then, as SS-Untersturmführer Kneip looked through a hole in the wall in the direction of Cussy, a burst of fire from a submachine-gun caught him in the chest. Through this small gap in the wall he had been hit by seven bullets. My comrade Hampel dragged him back under cover. To try to see where the shots had come from, I carefully went through the door and towards the wall. As I did so an enemy soldier appeared. I stood there with my MG42 levelled directly at his stomach. Fortunately he was alone and passed by without seeing me. After a long wait, Hampel and I made our way around the wall and found the way back to where Kneip lay. He gave each of us his hand, then quietly died.

'Whenever I saw any suspicious movements I let off a burst of fire'

'We lay there for some time, but little or nothing stirred. Whenever I saw any suspicious movements I let off a burst of fire and it soon stopped. In the first light of dawn we could hear artillery and mortar fire, thankfully still some way off. But this didn't last for long – soon shells were landing near us. Under the cover of the bombardment and poor visibility we withdrew. Some 900m [985 yards] to the east we found our assembly point. When we arrived SS-Sturmbann-

führer Milius said to me: "Kinscher, what are you doing here?" Obviously he had already written us off as dead. For my part in covering the withdrawal from the Ardenne Abbey, I was awarded the Iron Cross Second Class on 20 July 1944 [Kinscher was promoted to SS-Sturmmann on 1 August, and was subsequently involved in the chaotic withdrawal through the Falaise Gap].

'By 19 August there were only 20 men left in our company: one officer, one NCO and 18 men. Just before midday, we were ordered to move our two remaining half-tracks to another village. As we were about to set off, a Volkswagen went racing by and hit a pothole. As it bounced a pack of cigarettes fell from it. These were quickly shared out and we took the opportunity to enjoy a smoke before we set out – for many it would be their last. Only 800m [875 yards] out from our start point we came under heavy fire. Both half-tracks were hit and disabled. I quickly moved back into the village with my motorcycle and waited. Our officer admitted: "I think they have us trapped."

'The dead lay all around, charred and shrunken by the heat'

'We finally decided to try another direction in the hope of finding our command post. By the time we reached it there were only two of us from the company left. Later, after my capture, I heard from another of my comrades who had passed the spot that both half-tracks had been terribly burned. The dead lay all around, charred and shrunken by the heat to the size of puppies, the result of being hit by phosphorus shells. So died 14 Company [later, Kinscher managed to hitch a ride on a 3-tonne half-track mounting a 37mm gun and made some progress, until he hit a massive traffic jam just outside a village].

'On reaching the village we found out the cause of the jam on its outskirts. An enemy tank was in an elevated vantage point in the village, and nothing could get past it. A lieutenant was in charge. I asked him if there wasn't something we could do to get at the tank. Looking around, I came across an abandoned 75mm anti-tank gun, but with no ammunition. I did, however, recall seeing some ammunition boxes at the side of the road some way back, so I sent a couple of men back to fetch them. We manoeuvred the gun into position. Here my earlier training on the smaller 20mm gun came to good use, and with the second shot we knocked out the enemy tank.

'The lieutenant sought me out to congratulate me and pinned his own Iron Cross First Class on to my tunic. Shortly afterwards he was kneeling on the wall of a ruined house explaining his plans for our breakout, which entailed splitting the force into two groups. A shot rang out and he fell dead, half his neck blown away by an explosive bullet.

'Some of the soldiers sheltering in the houses had already given up hope by this time. However, with a machine pistol in my hand I persuaded them that it was still worth fighting. I told them to attempt a breakout to the south as the lieutenant had explained. Then an English supply column suddenly appeared in our midst, driving right in among us. Once again we were involved in heavy hand-to-hand combat, and during the melée I was hit by a pistol bullet. I got back behind the cover of a house and pulled off my tunic to have a look at the wound in my chest. The shot had not passed cleanly through my body. I pushed my fist against the bullet hole to try to stem the blood which was pumping out. I quickly realised I had a lung wound!

'After a while a couple of soldiers passed by and gave me a dressing I could press on to the wound. By this time the battle had died down somewhat. After about an hour, another two soldiers came and dragged me into a house where there was a doctor. I couldn't move under my own power by this time because of the amount of blood I had lost. The doctor made an air-tight bandage over the wound and gave me an injection. There were 11 of us in one room.

'Towards evening the doctor managed to organise a damaged truck, with straw on the floor, as transport for us. Those of us who were still alive were laid in the wagon and it set off. After several kilometres we came under enemy machine-gun fire. The doctor waved a Red Cross flag and the firing came to a stop. He then went to try to arrange safe passage for us, but soon came back with the news that it had been refused – if we wanted to carry on we would have to surrender. We tossed our remaining weapons into a brook and awaited the enemy. For us the war was over.

ABOVE: An Allied Typhoon aircraft strafes enemy targets during the Normandy campaign in 1944. Such aircraft made any German daylight movement near suicidal.

'It was already dark when two English ambulances came and carried us off to a dressing station, where an English doctor looked after us. After an examination an English captain came with a padre and asked me what religion I was. The doctor had told him I wasn't expected to survive the night and they wanted to give me the last rites.

However, the next morning I was still alive. They therefore loaded me into an ambulance and took me to a bigger dressing station, then on to a field hospital near Bayeux, where they operated on me on 22 August. At the beginning of September I was shipped to England. My treatment continued. I had 68 penicillin injections to fight the infection, but on 19 October the doctor gave up again and once more called in the padre to my bed to give me the last rites. Once again, however, I survived and my strength began to return. I must say that my treatment was excellent.'

⚡⚡ PANZER DRIVER

MANFRED THORN
TANK DRIVER

SS-Panzer Regiment 1
1st SS Panzer Division *Leibstandarte SS Adolf Hitler*

**Manfred Thorn was a Panzer IV driver
in 7 Panzer Company, II Battalion, SS-
Panzer Regiment 1, the tank unit of the
Leibstandarte *Division*.**

RIGHT: A Panzer IV of the Leibstandarte *Division
moves through a French town on its way to front.
The division first saw action in Normandy at the end
of June 1944, south of Caen.*

'On 18 July 1944, I found myself on the way to Tilly-la-Campagne, in one of the 25 tanks that had left Bully-sur-L'Orne in the early hours of the morning. I was driving tank number 734 and, at 19 years old, was considered one of the "old men" of the unit.

'We moved into a totally evacuated village with no idea of what was to come. All of the houses were intact and the area was surrounded with lush green fields and meadows. Our platoon came to a halt on the east side of the village in an orchard, with our tanks facing northeast towards Bour-guebus. I selected a spot for my tank near to the last house and camouflaged it well. The sounds of battle were still some way off, but every now and again a stray shell would come whistling into the village and make us run for the cover of our tanks. By the next day, the shelling had reduced the orchard to a collection of shattered stumps.

'We gradually learned to tell the difference between artillery shells being fired from land-based guns and those coming from enemy warships lying offshore. As the accuracy of the firing improved we were permitted to move closer into the cover of the houses. By this time our camou-

flage had been blown away by the shell blasts, so we tore down the vines from the side of the house and used this to cover the tank.

'On 22 July the barrage lasted for fully two hours. This was just the beginning, though. The infantry lying in front of our positions had no protection from this shelling, and in our tanks we panzer crews nearly suffocated from the heat and smoke. The temperature inside the vehicles reached 45˚C [115˚F]. The bombardment destroyed the village and also our supply of water for drinking and washing. Luckily for us, in the cellar of our house there was plenty of cider. Washing in cider is a sticky business, though! In any case, for the next two weeks we had little or no opportunity to wash or change into clean clothes, either of which would have been a great treat.

'On 25 July the bombardment started at 0600 hours and came from the air. It was directed at a target just 2km [1.5 miles] from our village. It lasted about two hours and was said to have involved 70 bombers. But that was just the aerial part of the bombardment. These attacks were unnerving to say the least, and we all looked forward to the evenings when it would get a little quieter. The other side seemed to want a break in the evening, too, so their soldiers could be fed and rested. Our meal wagon could only come up under the cover of darkness, so we ate our daily meal at around 2300 hours. That evening the gunner and I were elected to fetch the food for our crew, and as we crossed to the other side of the village to collect it we were shocked at the de-

struction we encountered. Not a single house in the village was left standing.

'During the early hours of the next day, under cover of artillery fire, elements of the North Nova Scotia High-landers reached the village. Somehow around 15 or 16 enemy soldiers had infiltrated past our infantry and were digging in on the other side of the wall that enclosed the garden in which we were positioned. At first we thought they were perhaps some of our own retreating infantry. But, as the light grew stronger, our commander, from his vantage point in the turret, could make out the shape of the distinctive "Tommy" helmets. They, of course, had not realised we were there, as we were still well camouflaged.

BELOW: A Tiger tank in Normandy in July 1944. With a crew of five and an 88mm main gun, the Tiger was more than a match for the Allied tanks it encountered. Waffen-SS Tiger tank ace Michael Wittmann, for example, destroyed 30 Allied tanks on 10 June 1944.

'After the initial shock we quickly realised that speed and surprise could be used to our advantage, so I started the motor and drove away from the remains of the house, bursting through the centuries-old 1.5m- [5ft-] high wall. Then I saw the enemy for the first time, cowering in their trench in shocked surprise, all except for two sappers, who quickly attempted to fire at us at point-blank range with a 3in mortar. However, a high-explosive shell from our gun put paid to that threat. We gave the order "hands up" and most obeyed. However, I could see three or four others cunningly dug into the wall of their trench so they could hardly be seen. I drove towards them until the tracks were only inches from their trench and lowered the gun barrel towards them. They surrendered! 'So, we had our first "Tommy" prisoners. They were young, gum-chewing Canadians, tall and proud as they were marched away.

'On 1 August the Canadians asked for, and were granted, a brief cease-fire to recover their wounded. There were so many dead, wounded and dying by this time. It was not surprising, though, considering the terrain: very flat with no cover. Our own infantry helped to carry the wounded to their transports.

'The barrage began at 0400 hours when thousands of shells hit us all at once'

'The next day, 2 August, brought a furious bombardment intended to finish us off. It began at 0400 hours with thousands of shells hitting us all at once. P-38 Lightning fighter-bombers joined in the attack. No one who took part in that battle will ever forget it. The one remaining wall of the house behind which we were sheltering collapsed on top of our tank, and we had to dig it out.

'One of the tanks from 4 Platoon was badly hit. Some of the armour plating landed on the driver's lap, slicing off both his legs. He begged his comrades to put him out of his misery. All around us were craters so big they could hold an entire tank. We really thought our end had come. It was amazing that no more than 15 of our tanks were hit [each SS panzer regiment usually consisted of two detachments. The first had four panzer companies and a workshop company,

while the second had five companies and a workshop company. The number of tanks could vary from regiment to regiment, especially towards the end of the war, when losses in men and materiel could not be replaced. However, a panzer company was theoretically equipped with 22 tanks].

'We sat in our tanks in the deafening noise, each with his own thoughts, watching intensely the area from where we thought the enemy would come. We knew they would arrive as soon as the barrage ended. Would this be the battle we would not win? That anyone could still be alive in Tilly was something the enemy had not reckoned with. However, we were still alive, and we were still there fighting the next day. The historian of the Calgary Highlanders described us thus: "The Hun is like a rat. You can hit it as many times as you like and it is never enough."

'We were finally released from this hell on 5 August, having held Tilly for nearly three weeks. The 89th Infantry Regiment took over our role in the defence and managed to hold Tilly for another two days.

'The artillery barrages lasting for hours were mental torture'

'Up to this point I had only fought on the Eastern Front. Nothing from my previous experience could have prepared me for what happened at Tilly. The tactic of unbroken artillery barrages lasting for hours was gruesome mental and physical torture. For me, when politicians today toy with the idea of sending young men off to war, they should be made to take part in an exact reconstruction of the action at Tilly-la-Campagne and experience personally what it means to be a soldier, and what is expected of them.'

[The campaign in Normandy was disastrous for the *Leibstandarte* Division. It went into battle with over 200 tanks, but by the middle of August 1944 its strength had been reduced to less than 30 serviceable vehicles: 14 Mk IV panzers, seven Mk V panzers and eight self-propelled guns. For the German Army as a whole battle for Normandy was characterised by high attrition rates. Over 160,000 German troops were lost, either killed, wounded or captured. Replacements amounted to only 30,000.]

SS EXPERIENCE TELLS

RUDI SPLINTER
SS-ROTTENFÜHRER

10th SS Panzer Division *Frundsberg*

The battles in Normandy did not go the Allies' way all the time, and the Germans even took prisoners on occasion. As Rudi Splinter's account shows, the difference between experience and inexperience in battle could make a crucial difference in the reactions of soldiers under fire.

RIGHT: Rudi Splinter, shown here as an SS-Oberschütze in walking-out dress, poses with members of his family. Part of Splinter's division was annihilated in the Falaise Pocket.

'During August 1944 we had just moved into positions in a small wood, dug ourselves a large foxhole and driven our vehicle over it to give us cover. We had hardly time to get settled when the section commanders got the order to report to the company commander for orders. We were going into action to capture a small village, supported by a troop of assault guns. Some of the lads rode on the guns while the remainder trotted along behind them. Then we came under mortar fire. The vehicles stopped and every one dived off and crawled underneath for cover, all jammed in like sardines.

'When the barrage lifted we continued along a road that ran under a railway bridge. On the other side, about 50m (55 yards) back from the bridge, sat two Sherman tanks. We heard the *whoosh* overhead as shells flew by and then saw thick columns of smoke as they hit their targets. We moved along the road and under the bridge and then saw the two Sherman tanks blazing – our assault guns had scored direct hits on them both.

'We continued our march and reached a small hamlet. As I came around the corner of one house I found myself right beside one of the assault guns as it fired. I had never been so close to one before and the blast knocked me off my feet. As I staggered about feeling myself for injuries the hatch opened and one of the crew, highly amused, asked: "What's the matter, lad, did you think you'd been hit?"

'Then we came under fire from a machine gun located on the opposite side of the road, so my officer ordered me and two others to take care of it. We opened fire with our small arms and soon silenced it. A white flag appeared. I didn't speak any English but I knew the words for "hands up", so we all shouted that. I could hardly believe it when they emerged. They came out one after the other until there were over 80 of them. One was an officer who wore a pistol from a lanyard round his neck. He was rather haughty and insisted that as an English officer he shouldn't have to surrender his personal weapon. He was arrogant in his self-confidence and almost had me convinced, but one of our chaps was having none of it. He stepped up to the officer, drew his very sharp combat knife, grabbed the lanyard round the English officer's neck and sliced it off, and then did the same with his pistol belt. The officer's face was a picture of terror. I'm sure he thought my comrade was going to stick the knife in his guts.

'As the prisoners were gathering, I walked around the side of the nearest house and was startled to see a wounded Englishman staggering towards me, holding his hands to his neck, from which was pouring blood. I immediately dragged him over to the side of the house beside the others and started to bandage his wounds. I remember being disgusted that none of his comrades had tried to help him, but had just stood there watching him.

'We were ordered to march the prisoners off towards the rear, making sure they held their hands up in the air. To walk any distance with your hands up is very tiring, so after a little while I gestured to them to put their hands down. We had only gone a short distance when a sergeant from the anti-tank troops leapt from a hedge at the side of the road. His unit was so well camouflaged that we hadn't even noticed it was there. He asked who was in charge then proceeded to give me a real telling off for letting the prisoners put their hands down. The prisoner next to me couldn't speak German, but figured out what was going on and

looked amused at me getting a roasting. I had to indicate to them to put their hands up again, but as soon as we were out of sight I let them put their hands down once more.

'Later, after we had dropped off the prisoners, and while we were enjoying some of the captured English ration packs, with such luxuries as chocolate, white bread, gold-flake cigarettes and even toilet paper, we were alerted by the sound of an approaching vehicle. It was a British Bren-gun carrier. We opened fire with our machine guns and the crew simply bailed out and ran away, leaving it sitting there with its engine running.

'British rations were much better'

'One of our lads was a bit of a mechanical wizard. He soon mastered driving it, and we set off to collect our own rations in it, one of our lads holding his German steel helmet up in plain view so that the anti-tank troops we had seen earlier wouldn't mistake us for the enemy. We got back with our rations, though abandoned them when we moved on as the captured British rations were much better. I always imagine that when the enemy took those positions they must have thought that we had left in such a panic that we left our rations behind. Little would they know we had abandoned them because we had so much captured British food.'

⚡⚡ THE ROUT OF AN ARMY

ERICH HELLER
SS-UNTERSTURMFÜHRER

2nd SS Panzer Division *Das Reich*

Erich Heller's experience shows how tactical withdrawal from France became a total rout and a struggle for survival at every turn.

RIGHT: *A knocked-out Tiger tank in Normandy.*

'On 1 September 1944, I found myself on the Rue de Paris, about 10km (6 miles) outside Hirson [on the French border with Belgium, about 350km (220 miles) from Aachen] along with a disorganised crowd of other soldiers. We had marched all night, the last remnants of the 2nd SS Panzer Division *Das Reich*. Not many remained from the division after Percy, where the entire artillery regiment and the whole of the flak detachment had been lost, and after the escape from Falaise. We were joined by some stragglers from the fallschirmjäger [paratroops], some panzergrenadiers from the 2nd Panzer Division and a Mk IV tank from the Panzer *Lehr* [Tank Training] Division. I also managed to get a Panther tank going again, which had been abandoned through lack of fuel.

'At around 0400 hours, SS-Unterscharführer Peter Cousin suggested that as time was moving on we should get into cover because enemy fighter-bombers would soon appear and shoot us up. At a crossroads I ordered the commander of the Panther, an NCO, to take up position about 100m (90 yards) from the crossroads and secure the junction. I indicated to him where the rest of us would be, pointing on the map to a farmstead about three kilometres (two miles) farther east, on the left side of the road to Hirson. I left behind two of the panzergrenadiers as messengers. We travelled on the Mk IV along the track leading to the farmstead, keeping out of sight of the road (we were hidden from aerial observation by a large wooded area). Before I allowed the men to rest we went over our supplies. There was barely enough fuel left to start the vehicles, but the Panzer IV still had two anti-tank and some high-explosive rounds, and we had sufficient rations. This just left the fuel to organise. Cousin made his way into Hirson in a captured jeep along with a driver. After a few hours he returned to report that there was not a single litre of fuel to be had in Hirson, and there were no German soldiers to be seen anywhere.

'I ordered the gun group leader and the tank commander to me as we began to hear gunfire from fighter-bombers not far away. The attack lasted a couple of two minutes, and then we saw a plume of smoke coming from the direction of our Panther. An hour later, a panzergrenadier brought in the driver. He was burned, his face blackened with powder burns and his hands were bloody. I had him bandaged and

gave him some cognac, then he slept like the dead. But before he went to sleep he reported that all the other crew members had been killed. He was the only one who had escaped. A fighter-bomber had surprised them, attacking out of the sun. It was a miracle that he had escaped with only relatively minor wounds.

'The group leaders were assembled and I asked them for their opinions on what we should do. They were unanimous: disable the Mk IV and the guns and strike out on foot. Suddenly, a panzergrenadier appeared, one of those who was keeping a lookout from the track leading to the farmstead. He reported that American half-tracks and jeeps had appeared round a bend in the road, heading our way. I ordered the men not to make any noise and then went with Cousin to check if the report was accurate. At about 1800 hours the Americans passed us in a large column along the road just 200m [220 yards] away.

'Now we were eager to be gone. We made the larger weapons useless and distributed all the small arms equally among the group: rifles, pistols, machine pistols and our few hand grenades. We filled our haversacks with rations and our canteens with water. All was ready for the move as darkness came. The wounded driver of the Panther we had already sent ahead in the afternoon, along with a driver, who had been instructed to find a Red Cross station. I found out later, when we got back to the division, that he had made it through and that the driver had assisted in evacuating the hospital position.

'A long column of American vehicles had pulled into the side of the road'

'As it grew dark, we got away from the farmstead without any problems, always keeping in the cover of the trees and hedges and parallel to the main highway. After we had travelled three kilometres (two miles) we crossed another road that ran directly north. Considerable noise drew our attention to what was happening a few hundred metres ahead. A long column of American vehicles had pulled into the side of the road for a rest stop. They seemed to feel quite secure – their radios were playing and their lights were exposed –

and soon the smell of hot food reached our nostrils. I ordered complete silence. We just sat there. At around 2200 hours they moved off, allowing us to carry on our journey among the cover of the trees and hedges (the maps I had of the area proved to be very accurate).

'Cautiously we approached'

'At around 0400 hours the next day, we noticed a house with lights burning. Cautiously we approached. The guard appeared to be asleep. With our safety catches off we moved towards the sound of muffled voices. German voices! I ordered the men to lower their weapons and entered a room illuminated by some candles. At the same moment a great commotion arose outside – the guards had noticed the rest of my lads. One of those present in the room stood up; he was an SS-Hauptsturmführer. As I made my report, an SS-Obersturmbannführer entered. With hindsight I know now it must have been Otto Weidinger (commander of the *Der Führer* Regiment). I explained the situation and asked for orders. He advised me to use my own judgement. I therefore told him I intended to take my lads safely back to Germany over the River Maas [Meuse] without losses!

'Our group departed and we marched on without any contact with the enemy in the deserted woods and hedgerows. At around 1100 hours we ran into a German defensive position and a guard took us to a chateau, where the staff of the 116th Panzer Division were located. I quickly explained the position to the senior staff officer, probably a colonel, who reported to the divisional commander in the next room by telephone. I explained to the colonel that their position was unsafe. At the same moment a guard appeared and reported that American tanks had been spotted in the area. I saluted and quickly assembled my men, whom my faithful SS-Unterscharführer Cousin had already arranged in their groups. Within two minutes we were on our way again through the woods. The divisional staff vehicles raced by as they fled east. By now it was midday and we stopped for some rest and some food, being badly in need of both.

'Towards evening we moved on again, near to Eppe-Sauvage, where we heard the sound of engines. On investigating we found a truck full of rations abandoned in the road. By now it was dark, so we topped up our supplies and set off on our march towards the Maas.

'During the night we "motorised" ourselves. To help us move faster, we had requisitioned some bikes, a cart, on which we could load all our packs, and a horse from a local farm. The next day we had to lie up in a wood, as the map showed no more wooded areas and I was not prepared to march in the open in daylight. American troops and fighter-bombers were everywhere, so we had to give villages a wide berth during the night.

'Around daybreak we reached the Maas. I, along with two others, all of us strong swimmers, reconnoitred the river. The banks were of gravel, while the river itself was about 100m [110 yards] across. The current was mild, and we found a good landfall on the opposite side, a place where it seemed cattle came down to the river to drink. Then we swam back.

'Cousin had organised everyone for the crossing and had also found a punt. The good swimmers made their own way across and the others were taken over in the punt. It was already getting light, so when we reached the other side we went straight into the trees. There we ate and slept.

'We were on foot again now'

'The next day we marched through the woods in daylight. From the direction of the road we could hear the usual sounds of troops on the march. We were on foot again now, having left our bikes, horse and wagon on the other side of the Maas. On 8 September 1944 we approached Theux and found an abandoned supply depot. There were still some materials there so we replenished our supplies. We gave Verviers, which lay 30km [20 miles] from Aachen, a wide berth. On the next day we came out of the wooded area just before Erezee and headed south, moving past the south of Francorchamps.

'One experience sticks in my memory. In Erezee, which was free of enemy troops (although I was told that some enemy reconnaissance units had passed through it), I drank coffee with a Belgian family on their terrace. It was getting towards evening and, contrary to our normal practice, we moved through the town itself, naturally with great caution and always ready to fire. At the end of the town stood a large house, and an old lady stood in the doorway. I asked her if she could speak German and she said yes. American troops had passed through earlier, she told me, but she hadn't seen any German troops for some days. They gave me coffee, and my men, all seasoned veterans of the fighting on the Eastern Front, camped out in the garden. It was just like peacetime. The man of the house asked me if I still believed that the Third Reich would be victorious, and of course I had to say yes. I didn't believe it any more, though, as the numerical superiority of the enemy was too great.

'The next day we encountered stragglers from a Volks-grenadier [Home Guard] division. All were older chaps, not exactly battle-hardened. They cried for joy when we agreed to take them with us. Then we pushed on, coming to a forester's house near the German border. Finally, on 11 September 1944, we reached the German border near Losheim.

The Americans were no longer following. Only some enemy reconnaissance troops were sighted, but they kept well out of range of our guns. There was no artillery fire, no fighter-bombers and no tanks – the enemy obviously wasn't interested enough in this area to send in their heavy weapons. We breathed a sigh of relief.

'I searched out the burgermeister and the padre and arranged quarters for my men. Cousin was sent to the rear to report. Whom he would find to report to, and who my superiors now were, I didn't know, as we had been completely out of touch for 14 days.

'It gave me great personal satisfaction to bring back almost 50 men alive. Looking back, I think that was my greatest achievement of the whole war. Above all, though, it was chiefly down to the NCOs and men, whose conduct during the journey made my task easier and allowed us all to win our freedom again.'

⚡⚡ THE ARDENNES OFFENSIVE

▬ HEINRICH SPRINGER
SS-STURMBANNFÜHRER

1st SS Panzer Division *Leibstandarte SS Adolf Hitler*

Heinrich Springer, an SS-Sturmbannführer on the staff of Field Marshal Model, recalls being present at a meeting at which Hitler briefed his senior field commanders on the Western Front on the coming Ardennes Offensive.

RIGHT: Heinrich Springer, here shown as an SS-Hauptsturmführer on the day he was awarded the Knights Cross of the Iron Cross for the capture of a vital bridge over the River Don at Rostov in Russia in November 1941. At the time of the award Springer was a member of the Leibstandarte's *Reconnaissance Battalion.*

'At that time I was first orderly officer to Field Marshal Walter Model. The field marshal asked me to accompany him to a high-level briefing on 11 December 1944 at the Führer's headquarters, the Adlerhorst at Bad Neuheim.

'At the Adlerhorst all of the senior commanders of the Western Front within the area of Army Group B were assembled. Besides the Commander-in-Chief of Army Group B, Field Marshal Model, there was the Commander-in-Chief West, Field Marshal von Rundstedt, the Commander-in-Chief of the 6th Panzer Army, SS-Colonel General 'Sepp' Dietrich, the Commander-in-Chief of the 5th Panzer Army, General von Manteuffel, and many other high-ranking officers – altogether about 50 or 60 people. Everyone knew the reason for this assembly. Adolf Hitler would personally explain to the respective commanders his plans and objectives for this last great offensive in the West, raising their spirits and encouraging them to concentrate all their strength and power.

'As far as I remember, Hitler stood and spoke for just under an hour. It was not a briefing in the normal sense,

BELOW: SS-Sturmbannführer Heinrich Springer (centre, carrying maps) with Generalfeldmarschall Model (extreme left). As Model's orderly officer, Springer attended the meeting at which Hitler briefed his senior commanders in the West on the Ardennes Offensive.

with recommendations and conclusions. It was an address on Frederick the Great at the Battle of Leuthen on 4 February 1757 [when Frederick the Great, outnumbered three to one, defeated the Austrian Army].

'Hitler made a relaxed, calm impression, speaking normally and without pathos. As on so many occasions, he spoke at length on historical matters before bringing himself to the subject of the Ardennes Offensive. He spoke openly and clearly, without gesturing with his hands. On the goal of this operation, the splitting of the US and British forces by a lightning strike via Luttich to Antwerp, the destruction of the British forces in a great *Kesselschlacht* [encircling battle] west of Aachen, he spoke in a lively and convincing manner. I can still clearly recall his closing words regarding what would be the last German offensive in the West. He said: *"Mein Herren,* if we do not succeed with the breakthrough via Luttich to Antwerp we will face a bloody end to this war. Time is working against us, not for us. It is, effectively, the last chance to alter the fortunes of war in our favour. Thank you, gentlemen."'

SS THE END IN THE WEST

HANS-GERHARD STARCK
SS-OBERSCHARFÜHRER

1st SS Panzer Division
Leibstandarte SS Adolf Hitler

The exhaustion of Hitler's armies in the final months of the war reached the lowest levels. It was not a just matter of shattered units and lost equipment. Individuals were also worn out – there was nothing left to give.

RIGHT: Hitler's last gamble in the West. A German Panther tank lumbers forward during the Ardennes Offensive

'After the Ardennes Offensive we had to transfer to the east and headed for Hungary by train. All transport movements were constantly harried by Allied fighter-bombers and we had to evacuate the train four times. Thankfully there were no losses. Then one time I woke up on the train to find it halted and empty. I went to the door and saw all the soldiers down the hill from the train and under some trees. I looked around and the floor of the carriage all around where I had been lying was peppered with 20mm cannon holes. When my comrades came back they could hardly believe that I had remained on the train and was still alive. I had been so weary and tired I had slept through the attack, of which I knew nothing, and miraculously escaped without a scratch.'

THE EASTERN FRONT II: THE LONG RETREAT

From mid-1943 onwards, the Germans were on the defensive in the East along the whole of the front, and Himmler's Waffen-SS divisions were committed to desperate defensive actions in an attempt to stem the Red tide. As the accounts in this chapter show, the military elite of the Third Reich still retained their cohesion in the face of impossible odds.

The German failure at Kursk signalled the beginning of the end of Hitler's fortunes in the East. For the Waffen-SS, however, the period 1943-45 witnessed a rapid expansion in the number of SS divisions, as the Führer desperately tried to stem the Red Army's advance. This was not the only reason for the expansion. Another was that Hitler did not trust the Wehrmacht, whose loyalty to his person he suspected to be less than absolute, a view that was later confirmed when several high-ranking Army officers attempted to take his life in July 1944. The Waffen-SS was to supply an unquestioning and effective alternative. Ever willing to toady to his master's wishes, especially when doing so resulted in his own aggrandisement, Himmler obliged by gathering up volunteers wherever he could. Numbers became more important than quality. And numbers were desperately needed.

By the summer of 1943 the Red Army had a numerical advantage of four to one over the German armies in the East. The Soviets' victory at Kursk allowed them to open offensives on a wider front against the retreating invaders. That said, the German line did not retreat uniformly along the whole front, nor was the fighting easy for the Soviets. In individual actions the Germans showed outstanding tenacity, occasional brilliance and astonishing bravery in the face of their enemy, but there was no doubt that the front was inexorably being rolled

Awaiting the next Russian assault. As friendly artillery shells explode only 50m from their trench, German infantry prepare to defend their positions. By the end of 1943 both the Wehrmacht and Waffen-SS were fighting a grim battle for survival in the East.

up by an enemy superior with regard to manpower and materiel, on the ground and in the air.

By the middle of August 1943, the Red Army had broken out of the northern sector of the Kursk salient and liberated Orel, while Kharkov was being systematically encircled. On 22 August German units began to pull out of the city, lest an attempt to prolong its defence repeat the *débâcle* of Stalingrad. These victories were followed throughout September by a series of successful Red Army assaults along virtually the whole of the southern portion of the front. By the end of September 1943 the German forces in the Ukraine were no longer on the Don, but 250km (150 miles) to the west, on the River Dnieper. In addition, matters had not been improved for the Germans by the concurrent Allied victory in Sicily and the fall of Mussolini: troops were actually withdrawn from the crumbling Eastern Front, including the *Leibstandarte*, to confront the Allied armies that were preparing to invade the Italian mainland.

On 10 October the Red Army crossed the Dnieper, 'bouncing' the natural barrier, racing over it and establishing a toehold so that stronger forces could push across before the Germans massed a firm line on the western bank.

Those Waffen-SS divisions fighting in Russia managed to achieve some local successes, but against the numerically and materially superior Russians had to give ground. The *Leibstandarte*, back from Italy by November, was allocated to XLVIII Panzer Corps of the 4th Panzer Army, and had some successes in the Kiev sector, but was still forced to withdraw. The *Das Reich* Division, attached to XXIV Panzer Corps, was pushed back from Brusilov and conducted a fighting retreat towards Zhitomir. The *Totenkopf*, acting as a mobile fire brigade, was moved up and down the front as and when crises developed. For example, in November and early December it served with Hube's 1st Panzer Army, which was attempting to hold Krivoi Rog and defensive positions on the Dnieper.

During November the German armies in the Crimea were cut off, and on 6 November they were driven out of Kiev, the biggest Soviet city they had held. Armoured reinforcements were brought into the area, some from the West, to cut off the Soviet advance at Zhitomir, and succeeded, but again the German forces had no depth and could not resist the weight of the Red Army's onslaught. In November, too, Hitler issued his Directive No 51, whose import was that forces would now be built up in the West to prepare for the Allied invasion of France, which was expected in the following spring.

In 12 days the Germans lost 25 divisions and 100,000 men

On Christmas Eve 1943, the Red Army in southern Russia renewed its offensive, pushing back the Germans 160km (100 miles). In the fighting that followed 60,000 German troops, including the *Wiking* Division and the SS Sturmbrigade *Wallonien*, were trapped in the Cherkassy Pocket. The breakout began in mid-February, though only 32,000 men got out alive and the *Wiking* Division lost all its equipment.

The Red Army continued its advance, reaching the River Dniester in March 1944, despite the efforts of the *Totenkopf* Division to halt it. The Soviets tore a gap between the 1st and 4th Panzer Armies at Proskurov, trapping the 1st Panzer Army in the Kamenets-Podolsk Pocket. Among the units cut off were the *Leibstandarte* and a battlegroup from the *Das Reich* Division. With the aid of the *Hohenstaufen* and *Frundsberg* Divisions, however, the units in the pocket had been rescued by early April.

In northern Russia the Germans suffered a similar fate, having been pushed back from Leningrad and driven westwards towards Estonia and Latvia. It was in this sector that most of the west and east European Waffen-SS volunteers were concentrated, in III SS Panzer Corps, which contained the *Nordland* Division and the Dutch SS Freiwilligen

OPPOSITE TOP: A typical frontline scene on the Eastern Front in 1944: Waffen-SS troops dug-in and on the defensive.

OPPOSITE BOTTOM: A group of soldiers from the Nordland *Division grab a rare opportunity to relax on the Estonian Front, 1944. Note the 'sunwheel' swastika emblem of the* Nordland *Division worn on the collar patches. Note also the variety in uniforms and headgear, a common feature among Waffen-SS units at this stage of the war.*

Brigade *Nederland*. In the same sector of the front were the 15th and 19th Waffen-Grenadier Divisions from Latvia, the 20th Waffen-Grenadier Division from Estonia, the Flemish *Langemarck* Brigade and the Sturmbrigade *Wallonien*. In early February 1944 the Germans had been pushed back to around Narva, and for the next six months the Waffen-SS held Narva in a heroic battle against overwhelming odds.

In the south, meanwhile, by the end of March the way was clear for the Red Army to sweep into Hungary and Rumania. On 10 April Odessa fell, and the Germans were busy evacuating their troops from the Crimea. A month later they had abandoned the region. Along the rear of the German lines, meanwhile, Soviet partisans disrupted supplies and communications. Throughout May the Red Army succeeded in fooling German intelligence that a massive push was coming in the south, and so the central German armies were depleted to build up defences there. On 20 June, the Soviets launched a huge assault on the centre in Byelorussia. The front broke: in 12 days 25 divisions and 300,000 men were lost to the German order of battle. By 3 July the Red Army was in Minsk, and in Lithuania and northern Poland by the middle of the month.

The fall of Budapest

The second half of 1944 witnessed a similar reversal of fortune for the Germans on the Eastern Front. As ever, the Waffen-SS was at the forefront of the efforts to stop the Red tide, and suffered accordingly. For example, the 21st Waffen-Gebirgs Division der SS *Skanderbeg* and 23rd Waffen-Gebirgs Division der SS *Kama* were annihilated in Yugoslavia. Elsewhere the situation was equally grim. In Hungary Budapest was threatened, and so several Waffen-SS divisions were committed to its defence, including the *Florian Geyer* Division, 22nd SS Freiwilligen-Kavallerie Division *Maria Theresia* and 18th SS Freiwilligen-Panzergrenadier Division *Horst Wessel*. The Soviets, however, proved difficult to stop, and by the end of December 1944 they had encircled the city.

Hitler was determined to relieve the Hungarian capital, and so IV Panzer Corps, comprising the *Totenkopf* and *Wiking* Divisions, attempted to reach the defenders. The Rus-

sians proved too strong, though, and IV Panzer Corps itself was forced onto the defensive. Budapest fell on 12 February 1945, *Florian Geyer* and *Maria Theresia* having been annihilated trying to break out.

The Red Army continued its advance west, and soon threatened the German oilfields in Hungary. In response to this, Hitler launched the last major German offensive of the war. Operation 'Spring Awakening' involved the 6th SS Panzer Army, 8th Army, 6th Army and the Hungarian 3rd Army in a pincer movement designed to crush the Soviet 3rd Ukrainian Front. The 6th SS Panzer Army was commanded by SS-Obergruppenführer 'Sepp' Dietrich, and comprised the *Leibstandarte*, *Das Reich*, *Hohenstaufen* and *Hitlerjugend* Divisions, though they were all understrength and deficient in equipment.

The attack was launched on 6 March 1945. Progress was slow, mainly because of the poor weather conditions. The offensive slowed and then stopped, despite the efforts of the Waffen-SS soldiers, and on 16 March the Red Army launched a massive counteroffensive. In the face of fanatical resistance the Soviets advanced. Waffen-SS divisions were chewed up by the Red Army: the *Horst Wessel* Division was wiped out, *Hohenstaufen* was badly mauled, *Das Reich* was forced westwards, while *Reichsführer-SS* became fragmented in southern Austria.

In the centre and north of the Eastern Front the story was the same: desperate German attempts to hold up the Soviet colossus. On 1 August 1944, the Red Army's advance on Warsaw inspired the underground Polish Home Army (AK) to revolt against the occupying Germans. Three Waffen-SS divisions took part in a counterattack against the Soviets, then joined in crushing the uprising, while the Red Army paused on the Vistula. The fighting went on until the AK surrendered on 2 October, by which time the city was in ruins; and then the Red Army advanced again.

By the end of October 1944, Romania and Bulgaria had defected to the Soviets and Finland had sued for peace. The Red Army, meanwhile, had cut off 33 German divisions in Courland. However, the equivalent of 12 divisions managed to escape, including the survivors from the Dutch SS brigade *Nederland*, who formed the nucleus of the 23rd Freiwilligen-Panzergrenadier Division *Nederland*.

ABOVE: Red Army troops hitch a lift on T-34 tanks during the Russians' so-called 'Right Bank Ukraine' Operations of December 1943 to April 1944.

RIGHT: A weary Waffen-SS soldier awaits the Red storm.

By February 1945 the Red Army had cleared Poland and was preparing for the final drive on Berlin. For this task it amassed 2,200,000 men, 33,500 artillery pieces, 7000 tanks and assault guns and 5000 aircraft. The Germans could only assemble 980,000 men, 1800 tanks and assault guns and 800 aircraft in response. The outcome was inevitable: the German armies disintegrated, and were cut off or encircled all along the Eastern Front. By now, too, Allied forces advancing from the west were inside the Reich. Even at this late stage there were attempts to reform Waffen-SS units, and even establish new divisions, as Hitler came to believe that only 'his' invincible and devoted Waffen-SS could be trusted to turn the tide. On 16 February, for example, *Frundsberg*, *Nordland*, *Nederland* and *Wallonien* attacked in a south-westerly direction and smashed into Marshal Zhukov's northern flank. However, the weakened divisions did not have the strength to halt the massive Soviet assault, and were driven back within two days.

As the war drew near to its inexorable conclusion in the spring of 1945, the German armies were exhausted. The Allied air forces had complete mastery of the sky, and what few remaining supplies of fuel, rations and ammunition were available were usually intercepted and destroyed before they could reach the frontline units, which were in desperate need of them. Those few units still in action put up spirited defences wherever possible, but were usually overrun by sheer weight of numbers. Even in these dire circumstances, there were still a few occasions when individual German units that still retained a reasonable percentage of their original strength would hit back at the enemy, inflicting serious losses. The inevitable could not be avoided, though, and by 25 April Berlin had been surrounded.

The Waffen-SS, true to its creed, fought in Berlin throughout the last days of the Third Reich, though ironically the majority of SS soldiers were non-German volunteers: from the *Nordland* Division, 33rd Waffen-Grenadier Division der SS *Charlemagne* and a battalion of Latvians from the 15th Waffen-Grenadier der SS.

With his world literally crumbling around him Hitler took his own life, and Lieutenant-General Weidling surrendered the city on 2 May. For Germany and the Waffen-SS, World War II was at an end.

For those survivors of the Waffen-SS who fought on the Eastern Front until the fall of Germany, the concept of loyalty burned most strongly in their hearts. While there were some soldiers who still believed that Germany could still rally her crumbling forces, most survivors of the Waffen-SS say today that what held them together, and kept them fighting in these last weeks of the war, was a loyalty to their commanders and to one another, as their writings make clear.

🆘 HOLDING THE DNIEPER

JAN MUNK

SS-STANDARTENOBERJUNKER

SS-Panzergrenadier Regiment *Westland*
5th SS Panzer Division *Wiking*

By October 1943, the Soviets had established bridgeheads over the River Dnieper. The Wiking *Division desperately tried to hold the river line. Jan Munk was wounded in early October in these battles, and returned to the front on 25 October.*

RIGHT: Russians troops haul an artillery piece out of the River Dnieper in October 1943. The Germans blew all the bridges over the river in an attempt to halt the Red Army's advance. However, by November the Soviets were across the river in force.

'By this time a lot of the boys were complete strangers, mostly Romanian. Our positions were still in the Dnieper area, but were rather exposed. There were lots of bushes and undergrowth with a sprinkling of trees. The Russians tried several attacks in what was, for them, very favourable terrain, but we managed to stop them every time. During their night attacks, for example, it was almost impossible for them to move without making a noise, so we had no problems in that respect.

'On 2 November 1943, we knew something was up because we heard the enemy singing and making a lot of noise. In other words, they had had their ration of vodka to boost their courage prior to an attack. Sure enough, at about 1800 hours we received information that an attack was imminent. At that time I commanded a squad, and I sent them all out of the bunker we were in to take their places in the trenches. They all went except for one, a Romanian, who told me that someone had taken his steel helmet, and the one left behind was too small for him. He wanted to stay behind and guard the bunker. I told him what I thought of that, and gave him my own helmet. It fitted. I went out wearing my camouflaged field cap. Then I joined my number two on the machine gun.

'The attack came, a bit fiercer than usual, but we managed to beat it off again. As always, that was the time when our own artillery started shelling, in front of the retreating enemy, catching them in between our shells and machine-gun fire. This time the barrage was very close by. I heard one gun in particular whose rounds landed short and to our left, then the next one was to our left but nearer still.

'The following one was a bull's-eye. It landed right in front of us and destroyed the machine gun. We had been a split second too late in taking cover. It felt as if an enormous weight had pushed me violently down. My number two started to splutter that the bastards had blown his nose off. It wasn't quite that bad, though. A tiny splinter had pierced his nose from one side right through to the other, and he was bleeding like a stuck pig. We decided to go back to the bunker so that I could bandage him properly.

'To my surprise I found that I couldn't move. I thought I had merely cut off the blood supply to my legs by squatting on my haunches. When the next shell came I was pushed, or so I thought, through the trench so fast that I couldn't keep upright, and I scraped my face on the ground. I shouted to my comrade not to be so bloody stupid and to calm down. He helped me to the bunker. Once inside, however, he told me that he hadn't touched me, let alone pushed me. It dawned on me then that something wasn't quite right. My legs were still useless, so I undid my belt and the lower buttons of my tunic and tried to feel along my back. Finding nothing, I loosened my trousers and inspected that area. Still nothing. I dressed again and went back to bandaging my friend. We both had a smoke and then I began to feel all hot and sweaty. I took my cap off and blood poured down over my face. With my fingers I could feel where the blood was coming from – a small cut right on the top of my head. Now I knew why my legs wouldn't work.

'After a while I was carried through the trenches to an area where it was wide enough to use a stretcher. I was then brought to a collection point to wait for proper transport. Quite a few men were there, some on stretchers, some badly injured and others not quite so bad.

'Then the Russians attacked again and all the wounded who could walk were told to man their positions again. Those of us remaining were to be left behind to fend for ourselves as best we could. We were given some grenades and machine pistols and wished "good luck". We fully understood. More than a dozen men would have been needed to carry us away, and they couldn't be spared.

'The Russians shot at us'

The Russians appeared and shot at us – we shot back. They threw hand grenades and we replied. Fortunately, the Wehrmacht counterattacked with the support of some light tanks. We did not lose a single wounded man, although some of us, including me, collected a few more wounds, though nothing serious. I was then taken by stretcher again to a Wehrmacht bunker. It was deep, with a well protected entrance and a very thick roof. Inside were tables and easy chairs. A radio was playing, and it looked almost like something from a propaganda picture. A doctor examined me and then said: "When did you last have a piss?" As far as I could remember that was at noon the previous day – a good seventeen hours before. Before I knew what was happening, I had had a catheter inserted. I didn't feel a thing, though the doctor was pleased that he had done it in time.

'During and after the German counterattack, several Russian prisoners were taken. These were used, as usual, for carrying ammunition and, on this occasion, to carry the stretchers. To go back to the dressing station we had to cross a rather bare, flat field. The Russians were directing some artillery fire on this area and every time a shell landed the Russian carrying the foot of the stretcher I was on would just drop it and take cover. The one at the head end was more careful and lowered me gently. By this time I had a splitting headache and all the dropping wasn't helping. I told the one at my feet that if he dropped me again I would shoot him. I had to warn him twice more. After each warning he would initially lower his end, but soon went back to just dropping me. Eventually I got my pistol out and fired a shot over his head. Everything went fine after that!'

WAFFEN-SS TANK ACE

ERNST BARKMANN
SS-OBERSCHARFÜHRER

5th SS Panzer Division *Wiking*

Famous for his tank-busting exploits in Normandy in 1944. when he won the Knights Cross, Barkmann also fought in tanks on the Eastern Front.

RIGHT: German Infantry Assault Badges in bronze (left) and silver (right).

'The fighting in Russia was extremely savage at times, especially in the Caucasus, but we earned a reputation for ourselves. Even the Russians had a grudging respect for the *Wiking* Division.

'Every soldier who, like me, was first trained as an infantryman, and who later served as such in action, knows all about the difficulties of this branch of the armed forces. It was stipulated that a soldier had to face the enemy three times in battle – and on the Eastern Front it was invariably close-quarter combat – in order to earn the Infantry Assault Badge. You never forgot your first combat experience at the front – it was seared into your mind. Therefore, we never took off our Infantry Assault Badges. The time we spent as infantrymen stayed with us always [Barkmann went on to win the rare Panzer Assault Badge for 25 engagements with the enemy. In Normandy in 1944 he became one of Germany's top panzer aces when he destroyed nine Sherman tanks with his lone Panther in one engagement].'

RIGHT: Panzer ace SS-Oberscharführer Ernst Barkmann in the turret of his Panther tank on the Eastern Front in 1943. In this shot Barkmann is wearing the rare one-piece camouflage overalls and camouflage field cap worn by tank crews. The Panther tank was reckoned to be the best medium tank of World War II, and some 6000 of all variants were built in total.

ss PARTISAN ACTIVITY

WILHELM HILLEN
SS-OBERSTURMFÜHRER

1st SS Panzer Division
Leibstandarte SS Adolf Hitler

In northern Russia the Germans had been besieging Leningrad since September 1941. However, by the end of 1943 they were outnumbered and on the defensive. In addition, behind the lines there was much partisan activity.

RIGHT: *Wilhelm Hillen photographed in Russia in 1943. Note his peaked service cap.*

'It is Christmas 1943. Outside a thunderstorm rages. The wind howls. Somewhere a slamming door beats a regular rhythm. I want to haul myself from my deep sleep but am too weary. Again the slamming – will no one close that dammed door?

'Then a guard roughly shakes me awake and cries: "Untersturmführer, the Ivans!" Instantly I grasp reality. I am not lying in my bed at home, but am a platoon leader in a dugout of the Estonian Volunteer Brigade [the Estonian brigade was formed in May 1943, being titled the Estonian SS-Freiwilligen Brigade 3] east of Lake Peipus. The imagined howling in my dreams is in fact Russian shells, and the slamming of the door the detonations just in front of our positions. The bombardment is cover for a Soviet assault troop who have broken through our lines. But, after vicious hand-to-hand fighting, we manage to throw them back.

'In the battle I had the misfortune to be wounded – some hand grenade shrapnel had hit my right knee. After a few days the wound was so infected that the kampfgruppe [battlegroup] commander, SS-Hauptsturmführer Servet, sent me to the hospital on an ammunition truck. The chief surgeon was an Estonian staff doctor, Dr Poul Esop, a real giant of a man with a thundering voice but a soft heart. He worked round the clock, operating and fussing over the wounded like a father, having a kindly word with everyone. His pipe never left his mouth and he drank vodka by the cupful. I will always remember his eyes: blue-green, like the waters of a mountain lake. I was at the hospital for 10 days, during which time we became good friends.

'Two days before Christmas our kampfgruppe was pulled out of the line. After de-lousing, a wash, sauna and shave we felt like men again. I decided to go and see my friend Poul, who greeted me with a pat around the shoulders that nearly knocked me to my knees. He then asked me if I would escort him on a sleigh ride to a remote farm deep in wooded terrain so he could deliver a baby. As partisans were in the area he warned me it would be dangerous, nevertheless I agreed. My company commander gave his assent, and ordered SS-Unterscharführer Teder and a signaller, SS-Rottenführer Mickelsar, to go with us.

'We climbed onto the sleigh drawn by Russian Panje horses [short, stocky beasts possessing great stamina and endurance] and began our journey. It was painfully cold, and despite our fur coats and felt boots the cold slowly crept into our limbs, especially our fingers. During our journey through the magnificent snow-covered terrain we had our submachine guns at the ready.

'At the farm we were cordially welcomed by the old farmer's wife, who was overjoyed that she was to become a grandmother at Christmas time. Shortly before midnight we heard the first cries of a healthy new baby girl. Poul showed us the little bundle – he was beside himself with joy, describing her as his Christmas baby, full of the eternal wonder of creation on that special holy evening.

'At dawn it was time for the return trip. Poul was snoozing on the trestle, Mickelsar was holding the reins, and Teder and I kept watch. The forest was mysteriously quiet, the only sound being the stamping of the horses' hooves

BELOW: A squad of Waffen-SS soldiers pose for a photograph during a lull in the fighting on the Narva Front, winter 1944. Note they are all wearing the heavy quilted winter clothing over their normal service dress.

and their snorting. As we travelled along, pleasant thoughts of our warm billets filled our minds. Then it happened: shots rang out and a grenade detonated. Teder and I leapt from the sleigh into the deep snow. The horses whinnied and bolted straight ahead in a panic. Everything became still once again. Then we heard the sound of breaking branches in the background, but could see nothing. As we lay there in the cover of the snow I felt a stream of warm blood run down my back – I had been hit by a piece of shrapnel from the grenade next to my spinal column. After two hours had elapsed, though it felt like an eternity, an Army ammunition column coming from the front passed us by and carried us back to the unit.

'On the afternoon of Christmas Day an Estonian police party found the overturned sleigh and the bodies of Esop and Mickelsar, who both had gunshot wounds to the chest. My friend Poul, who always wore his red cross armband, had had his throat cut. All the men's furs, watches, boots and the medical chest had been stolen. I had survived by the skin of my teeth. That's how close living and dying was on the Eastern Front.'

SS TANK BUSTING

REMY SCHRIJNEN
SS-UNTERSCHARFÜHRER

SS Freiwilligen Sturmbrigade *Langemarck*

***Waffen-SS successes on the Eastern
Front in early 1944 became matters of
individual heroism and the extraordi-
nary mutual loyalty that held the best
formations together. None exemplified
this fighting spirit in the face of a lost
cause more clearly than the example of
Remy Schrijnen.***

*RIGHT: Remy Schrijnen is awarded his Knights Cross
in front of his unit for his tank-killing exploits.*

'Whhen Freiwilligen Legion *Flandern* was reor-
ganised and renamed Sturmbrigade *Langemarck*, I became a gunner on a 75mm anti-
tank gun in 3 Platoon, on gun number nine. From 31
December 1943, in the area around Kiev and Zhitomir, the
platoon was in action against Soviet T-34 tanks and succeeded in destroying three T-34s and driving back four others. From 5-7 January 1944, the platoon was in action
around Skhudnov. The fighting was furious and losses on
both sides were heavy. On 6 January, the crew of gun number eight were all killed, then gun number seven was also
hit and the platoon commander, SS-Oberscharführer Grab-
meyer, was killed. Soon, gun number nine was the only one
left to support the infantry against the enemy tanks. Shortly
after its crew also became casualties – only I remained.
Orders were given to pull out, but I ignored them and
stayed behind. I had to load, aim and fire the gun by myself.

'Then the Soviet infantry began to attack and there was
virtually no one left to stop them. However, a radio opera-

tor, who was from the Navy and had been mortally wounded, called down the artillery on his own positions. Behind
the Russian infantry were around 30 tanks, including five of
the new super-heavy Josef Stalin II models. In a furious
exchange of fire, I knocked out three Stalins, four T-34s and
also managed to put some of the others out of action. Then,
from a distance of only around 30m (100 ft), a Stalin tank
scored a direct hit on my gun. The blast threw me some distance and seriously wounded me. I lay there for some time
until I was discovered by our own troops during a counterattack later that day [Remy Schrijnen was found by his comrades on the battlefield, all around him the burning hulks of
the Soviet tanks he had knocked out. He had personally
destroyed over a dozen enemy tanks, and the brevity of his
account here is probably due to modesty – more detailed
descriptions have been published by others. Schrijnen was
awarded the Knights Cross of the Iron Cross for his gallantry during this action, making him the first Fleming to
win the German armed forces' highest award].'

ABOVE: A knocked-out Russian T-34, like the ones Schrijnen battled.

THE WEHRMACHT

HEINZ KÖHNE
SS-OBERSCHARFÜHRER

1st SS Panzer Division *Leibstandarte SS Adolf Hitler*

As a junior NCO with 18 Kompanie of the* Leibstandarte *Division, Heinz Köhne remembers an incident during the battles around Uman in late January 1944 that illustrates the sense of competition between the Waffen-SS and Wehrmacht.

RIGHT: A Waffen-SS column passes through a Russian town in January 1944. Note the SS runes on the number plate of the vehicle in the centre.

'It was during the battles in the Uman "cauldron". We had been fighting a three-day defensive engagement. The Wehrmacht, which had already been retreating for about a week, asked us what we were going to do. We replied that we would hold our positions for three days, after which we ourselves would launch an attack. Somewhat surprised, they thought we would be hard-pressed to even hold the Russians, who had the additional support of fighter-bombers. We replied that we would shoot down the aircraft with our rifles and machine guns. In fact, we did manage to down an enemy aircraft with small-arms fire, after which the air activity in our sector fortunately went quiet. We even managed to counterattack on the third day, pushing the enemy back some distance.

'On another occasion we had a Wehrmacht motorcycle platoon positioned between our Waffen-SS formations. The Russians came charging over the brow of the hill and down the slope in their hundreds. At the sight of so many of the enemy the motorcycle unit made ready to flee. Seeing this, I went straight to the lieutenant in charge and told him we had a machine gun aimed at his men should they try to run away. I left him in no doubt that we would use it.

'The Russians were driven off by our fire, their attack destroyed. Afterwards the Wehrmacht soldiers came to us and said: "You've got some nerve, we would have run." My answer to them was that we all had confidence in our Waffen-SS comrades. We were also single men, whereas they were married and had families at home to worry about.'

⚡⚡ THE CHERKASSY POCKET

RAYMOND LEMAIRE
SS-STANDARTENOBERJUNKER

28th SS Freiwilligen-Panzergrenadier Division *Wallonien*

Raymond Lemaire joined the Walloon Legion of the Wehrmacht in August 1941, being 19 years old. He served alongside Léon Degrelle, before the latter's meteoric rise, and his father, who had joined the same unit to look after him! The Waffen-SS took control of the unit in June 1943, which now became the SS Sturmbrigade Wallonien.

RIGHT: *Raymond Lemaire of the 28th SS Freiwilligen-Panzergrenadier Division* Wallonien, *who fought in the Cherkassy Pocket. Some 32,000 German troops managed to escape from the pocket, though they had to leave most of their equipment behind. However, their efforts effectively saved Army Group South.*

'As a sergeant, I volunteered for the pioneer platoon, as there were only volunteers in that unit. The training was in Dresden and was very hard. I returned to the unit in October 1943, and in November we moved up to the front at Cherkassy. We pioneers had to occupy some of the infantry positions to maintain the line. After numerous actions and battles, I was the only NCO left in my platoon! The fighting continued, and by 26 January

BELOW: A Panzer IV of the Wiking *Division in the Cherkassy Pocket, a photograph that amply conveys the conditions under which German and Russian troops were fighting in southern Russia in the winter of 1943/44.*

1944 we were completely surrounded in the Cherkassy Pocket, together with the *Wiking* Division and around 60,000 German troops in all.

'The Soviets attacked our sector on 30 January, but in two hours of hand-to-hand and close-quarter fighting we managed to beat them off. However, I was seriously wounded by grenade splinters in both legs in the process. Being unable to walk, after a few hours I was evacuated by plane out of the pocket. I subsequently spent eight weeks in hospital, following which I received three weeks' leave. My unit managed to escape from the encirclement, but in all 700 men out of a total of 2000 Walloons died in the period from the end of November 1943 to 17 February 1944.'

SS THE KNIGHTS CROSS

KARL NICOLUSSI-LECK
SS-HAUPTSTURMFÜHRER

SS-Panzer Regiment 5

5th SS Panzer Division *Wiking*

In early 1944 the Red Army was pushing back the Germans along the whole of the Eastern Front. The Waffen-SS fought on regardless, though, and managed to achieve some remarkable results in the face of near impossible odds.

RIGHT: The rare Knights Cross of the Iron Cross, with a frame made from hallmarked silver. One was presented to Nicolussi-Leck for his action at Kovel.

'At the end of March 1944, strong Russian tank forces struck some 30km (20 miles) west of Kovel, a town about 250km (160 miles) southeast of Warsaw, in the middle of the Pripet Marshes. This important rail and road junction was held by supply units, railway troops and around 2000 wounded in various hospitals. The Red Army began to penetrate the encircled town, which was unsurprising when one considers its garrison. In this situation, however, Kovel was declared a 'strongpoint', and I was given the task of striking through the Russian forces in the town and halting them while a counteroffensive could be launched to break through the encirclement.

'Because of the strong enemy forces and the snow-covered, swampy terrain, the breakthrough was very costly and time-consuming. After 10 hours of slow going in the face of resistance, as midnight approached, we had covered only half the distance, having lost a third of our armoured vehicles in the process [a mixture of StuG III self-propelled guns and Panther tanks]. In this situation the breakthrough into the town began to appear hopeless. When my armoured

spearhead was just 2km (1.5 miles) from Kovel, I received an order from my battalion commander to halt. By this time, however, my lead tank was already in action against the enemy defenders to the northwest of the city. Knowing how desperate the situation had become, I disregarded the order and carried on with the attack.

'Thanks to the cover afforded by a blizzard and severe snow drifts that covered our left flank, after 18 hours of battle, and with only half of our armour remaining, we reached the town in the early hours of the morning. We then defended the town against counterattacks by superior enemy forces until an attack by a German panzer corps broke through the encirclement and the troops and wounded could be brought out. Throughout the Luftwaffe had supplied us with rations, medicines, ammunition and petrol.

[A regimental Order of the Day commended Nicolussi-Leck's achievements on 15 April 1944:

'The Führer has awarded SS-Obersturmführer [he was later promoted] Nicolussi-Leck, commander of 8 Company, the Knights Cross of the Iron Cross. Nicolussi-Leck, on his own initiative, and under difficult conditions, succeeded in breaking through to the encircled city of Kovel on 30 March 1944. His reinforcement of the garrison was decisive. He carries a special share in the credit for the city holding out.

'In addition, the Regiment is proud to know that such a deserving, long-serving member is being distinguished. May soldier's good fortune stay with SS-Obersturmführer Karl Nicolussi-Leck.'

SS DUELS WITH RUSSIANS

ERIC BRÖRUP
SS-OBERSTURMFÜHRER

SS-Panzer Aufklärungs Abteilung 5
5th SS Panzer Division *Wiking*

1945 brought fresh reverses for Germany and the Waffen-SS on the Eastern Front, as the Red Army burst into Poland and Hungary. Despite this, the morale of the troops remained remarkably high.

RIGHT: *Waffen-SS soldiers emplacing a 3.7cm flak gun. The retreat of Waffen-SS units on the Eastern Front in 1945 never became a rout.*

'My most memorable encounter took place on St Patrick's Day, 17 March 1945, near Szekefehervar in Hungary. I was adjutant, with the rank of SS-Obersturmführer, to SS-Sturmbannführer Fritz Vogt, holder of the Knights Cross with Oakleaves. The Russians had started their offensive the day before, which was also Fritz Vogt's 27th birthday. Our unit was SS-Panzer Aufklärungs Abteilung 5.

'I had established a command post in a small house and set up communications with a switchboard and radio while shells fell all around us. SS-Obergruppenführer und General der Waffen-SS Herbert Otto Gille telephoned to congratulate Vogt on his birthday and to tell him he had just been awarded the Oakleaves to his Knights Cross. His face

lit up, and I said: "This calls for a drink!" We hoisted a few, then the supply officers showed up bearing some bottles of beer, and all the other officers found time to show up for a quick drink. All the while the war was going on around us.

'One company commander was having some trouble with the enemy, so I suggested to Vogt that I go out and try to straighten things out. Vogt laughed and said: "What's the matter with you, do you feel like a hero today?" I answered that he had just got himself a new medal and should let others have a chance to win one. He replied: "Okay, but watch what you are doing!" By that time, of course, we had all had a good drink and were in excellent spirits!

'I got an SdKfz 250/9 (a half-track armoured personnel carrier with 20mm cannons mounted) and went into battle.

We were firing high-explosive shells and it seemed easy, like shooting fish in a barrel. Then the Russians brought up an anti-tank rifle and shot up my vehicle, forcing us to bail out. We ended up in hand-to-hand combat with them. I had a *Panzerfaust* anti-tank rocket but it wouldn't fire. I therefore used it like a club and cracked one Russian's head with it. I was in trouble, though. However, Fritz Vogt then appeared with a few more armoured personnel carriers and got me out. He told me to take a couple of hours off, and later he and I went off alone on a reconnaissance behind enemy lines. I got the Iron Cross First Class for all this. That Fritz Vogt was some character!'

⚡⚡ FACING IMPOSSIBLE ODDS

JOHANNES HAUSER
SS-STURMBANNFÜHRER

SS-Panzergrenadier Regiment 4 *Der Führer*
2nd SS Panzer Division *Das Reich*

By the end of March the Red Army held most of Hungary and was closing on Vienna. The Soviets would take the city by 6 April. Johannes Hauser lived through these chaotic days – fighting, or attempting to fight, until the end.

RIGHT: *SS-Sturmbannführer Johannes Hauser. An experienced police officer, he also served with the Army police before being posted to the Waffen-SS. As well as being the holder of the Knights Cross (shown here), he was also the recipient of the Close Combat Clasp.*

'In March 1945, I received orders from Berlin posting me a regimental commander in the *Handschar* division. No one could tell me where the division was at that moment, though, so with the help of its field postal number I made my way to Prague. From there I travelled to Vienna. At the information post in Vienna I got my first major surprise.

'By order of a *Führer Sonderbefehl* (special order from the Führer), SS-Obergruppenführer und General der Waffen-SS Felix Steiner was empowered to take from the train any soldier or officer of whatever rank. So, my marching orders annulled, I was taken to the transport school at Schönbrunn. There I was told that because of the perilous situation that had developed in Hungary I was to take command of a newly formed kampfgruppe.

'Every train that passed through Vienna was combed for suitable men, and they were all brought to Schönbrunn on the authority of this *Führer Sonderbefehl*. In the main it affected those returning from leave, on recuperation leave, those only lightly wounded and those, like me, who had

ABOVE: Red Army troops in Poland. As the Russians approached the frontiers of the Reich itself, millions of German civilians fled west to seek refuge. Meanwhile, as the Soviets poured into Germany, the Waffen-SS fought on.

completely different destinations in mind. Fortunately there were some veterans among them with a lot of combat experience, and even some highly decorated soldiers who could help me to form this new kampfgruppe. Within a few days we were organised, but among other things we had to content ourselves with only light infantry weapons: rifles with bayonets, machine guns, machine pistols, grenades and *Panzerfausts* (anti-tank rockets).

'On 1 April 1945, I was given my orders with the rider that, on contact with the enemy, all vehicles would have to be returned as they would be needed to ferry reinforcements to the battle area. During the journey from Vienna towards the Burgenland [Austria's most eastern province] we saw colossal columns of predominantly Hungarian troops, minus weapons, coming towards us on their way towards Vienna. There were so many that they resembled a single huge mass. After a few kilometres we passed fewer and fewer, until there were no more to be seen, and we were alone on the road heading east.

'During the war years we officers developed somewhat of a sixth sense for danger, even if outwardly everything

ABOVE: A group of Waffen-SS soldiers on the Eastern Front in early 1945. Despite the grim military situation they can still manage a smile. In truth, however, there was not much to be cheerful about, as all around them the German war effort was disintegrating.

appeared normal. Now I suddenly had an awareness of danger, and ordered the entire kampfgruppe to disembark and despatched the vehicles back in the direction of Vienna.

'I ordered a reconnaissance to be made of the village of Münchedorf to the south of us, which confirmed it was still clear of enemy troops. We had hardly reached the edge of the village, though, when suddenly the enemy arrived on the scene: three T-34 tanks. They headed towards us, though we couldn't see any infantry support. They clearly hadn't spotted my kampfgruppe - my sixth sense had warned me just in time.

'Directly in front of us was a bridge, around which we dug ourselves well in. The troops awaited my "fire at will" order. This was given only when the first T-34 moved right onto the bridge. A *Panzerfaust* fired and scored a direct hit on the tank, causing it to burst into flames. The wreckage lay right on the bridge and made a good road block for any further attempts to cross. The machine guns opened up at the same time, and the two remaining T-34s, hanging back somewhat after seeing the fate of the first, turned and retreated until they were out of our range and view.

'In the pause that followed we took the opportunity to strengthen our positions and camouflage them well. It was important for us to get well established before it got dark, for we knew that the enemy would be back. Sure enough, that night the Russians unleashed a heavy hail of artillery and rocket fire on the village, which deafened us and effectively ruined our night vision.

'I had to move my command post three times during this period as each one in turn was hit. On the third occasion both my adjutant and my orderly officer were killed. When the barrage ended, the T-34s renewed their assault on our village. The loss of another tank to the *Panzerfaust* took some of the impetus from the Russian attack, though, which faltered as dawn approached.

'While some darkness still remained, a German liaison officer arrived from the north to establish contact with my kampfgruppe. Accompanying him was a Tiger tank that I had designs on, but to no avail. This officer had already heard good things about our kampfgruppe and saw we had defended ourselves with only light infantry weapons and had no heavy armaments or vehicles. However, he also informed me that my men and I were in an exposed gap between the *Der Führer* and *Deutschland* Regiments of the *Das Reich* Division.

'His express instructions were that we were to hold the village of Münchedorf for at least three to four days to enable a cohesive front to be established to our rear. We could arrange the evacuation of wounded as soon as a signals link to the *Das Reich* Division was established. Meanwhile, another furious artillery barrage gave us an idea of what was in store for us. The liaison officer then took his leave towards the rear, but not before assuring me that he would put in an urgent request for reinforcements to be sent to us immediately.

'When the Russian infantry came running over the open ground towards our positions to the south of the village we easily held them off with our machine guns. On that side our positions were especially strong. We then managed to destroy a further T-34 that had made its way forward. The attack then petered out, enabling us to tend to our wounded. By this time the predominantly single-storey houses in the village had become so badly damaged that we had difficulty finding a suitable site for a command post.

'It was obvious to us that the enemy reconnaissance of the village had been very poor. As things were, they could have outflanked us on both sides of the village, where our defence was weakest, and thereby cut us off easily. Instead, they persisted with frontal attacks. Their pressure was relentless, though, and by the end of the second day we had suffered the first enemy break-in: on the southern side of the village. By the third and fourth days we had been forced to give up about half of the village due to our high losses, and we were just able to hang on. At the end of the fourth day we received a message from the division to disengage under cover of darkness and report to the *Der Führer* Regiment. So I could withdraw, which was fortunate because enemy superiority was so great that by the next day our positions would have been overrun anyway.

'What was left of my kampfgruppe evacuated the village at dusk'

'What was left of my kampfgruppe evacuated the village at dusk, and we made our way back unimpeded until I reached the first outposts of the *Der Führer* Regiment. I made my report to the regimental commander, SS-Obersturmbann-führer Otto Weidinger, who instructed me to take command of I Battalion of the regiment as the previous commander had been wounded. He also expressed the thanks and recognition of the divisional commander, and explained that I, on behalf of the kampfgruppe, was to be recommended for the Knights Cross of the Iron Cross.

'After this turbulent period with Kampfgruppe *Hauser*, I was pleased to find a home with the famous *Das Reich* Division. As commander of I Battalion, *Der Führer* Regiment, I took part in the fighting retreat via Modling and the house-to-house fighting in Vienna and over the Florisdorfer Bridge. Then followed transport across Czechoslovakia, where we were supposed to prepare for participation in a relief attack towards Berlin. However, our regiment was pulled out of this proposed attack force and sent with all speed towards Prague to assist in quelling the insurrection which had erupted there [Czech patriots had rebelled against the Germans during the first days of May 1945]. The opportunity was taken, during this forced march through Prague on 9-10 May, to evacuate thousands of German civilians, female anti-aircraft auxiliaries, female signals auxiliaries and stragglers from various Wehrmacht units, who were transported on our vehicles up to Rochizan. It was here that we were encircled by the Americans and surrendered.'

A DISINTEGRATING ARMY

JAN MUNK
SS-STANDARTENOBERJUNKER

SS-Panzergrenadier Regiment *Westland*
5th SS Panzer Division *Wiking*

In the middle of April 1945, the Soviets crossed the Neisse and were advancing relentlessly towards the German capital. Everywhere the forces of the Third Reich were being cut to pieces, and, as Jan Munk recalls, old men and boys could not stop the inevitable.

RIGHT: Jan Munk as an SS-Sturmmann photographed in front of the Officer Candidate Barracks in Ellwangen, June 1944. Note the ribbon of the Iron Cross in his buttonhole.

'In early April 1945, the whole of the Junkerschule Tölz moved to the Todtnau area of the Schwarzwald to form the *Nibelungen* Division [38th SS Grenadier Division *Nibelungen*]. I was given a company of Volkssturm personnel – boys and old men – who were then trained mostly in the use of the *Panzerfaust*. But the new division never really got off the ground. We had no materials and morale in the ranks was poor. I was, however, still convinced that Germany would win the war. After a hopeless few days, we sent everyone home, and the *Nibelungen* Division collapsed.

'We went back to Bad Tölz. There we were issued with orders to find our way back to our own divisions. Mine was the *Wiking*, which at that time was involved in heavy fighting near Graz. The attempts of myself and three other Dutchmen, all of us SS-Standartenoberjunkers, to join our divisions became very hazardous. Bad Tölz had of course issued us with passes, but to travel in those times was diffi-

cult. The Allies had complete control of the air and shot up everything that moved, even people on pushbikes. Our papers were soon out of date and groups of SS maniacs (not Waffen-SS but men from the *Allgemeine*, or General, SS) were roaming the streets and hanging or shooting anyone they thought was a deserter. I even saw Waffen-SS soldiers hanging from trees and lamp posts.

'Our luck held, though, and on 4 April we met an SS-Standartenführer who could use us. This officer had blank orders, all signed by Himmler, which gave him the power to do almost anything. For the next two weeks we confiscated all sorts of materials from the units that we met, and stored and hid them in farms for future use by "Werewolf" units (guerrilla groups who would continue to fight after the war's end).

'This period of relative security ended for us on 29 April. The SS-Standartenführer took us to Landshut where we met the gauleiter, the local Nazi party commander. I was given a company of Labour Corps boys, all 16 or 17 years old and as keen as mustard, to be trained to use the *Panzerfaust*.

'On 1 May, at Eggenfelden near Vilsbiberg, I went with my boys to the edge of a forest. We had to hold that position. We saw about a dozen American tanks approaching, moving in single file along a narrow road. I managed to disable the first one, but I could see that our position was hopeless. I sent all the boys away to make their own way home. They were all crying in frustration that they had not been able to "have a go"'.

SS PARTHIAN SHOTS

EDUARD JANKE
SS-UNTERSCHARFÜHRER

11th SS Freiwilligen-Panzergrenadier Division *Nordland*

In 1945 there were still occasions when a resolute defence put up by a small force of determined Waffen-SS troops could give the enemy a bloody nose, though minor victories could not reverse the impending collapse.

RIGHT: *Eduard Janke as a platoon commander in 4 Kompanie, Aufklärungs Abteilung,* Nordland *Division, January 1945, holder of the Infantry Assault Badge, Wound Badge and Close Combat Badge.*

'My unit was in a small village in Pomerania, on a reconnaissance patrol, when we discovered we were in danger of being cut off by the enemy. My commander ordered me to explain the situation to the commander of a solitary Königstiger tank (a 68-tonne behemoth armed with a high-velocity 88mm gun).

'The tank was commanded by an SS-Oberscharführer, a holder of the Knights Cross of the Iron Cross, who told me to make sure our own anti-tank guns didn't open fire before he did. The Königstiger moved off towards the enemy and positioned itself behind a small hillock. It wasn't too long before the first Russian tank emerged from the wood near the village. One, two, three, four, five, six, seven tanks came out. We became increasingly uneasy.

'Only after the thirteenth enemy tank had appeared did the Königstiger open fire. The leading enemy tank burst into flames, and then our anti-tank guns joined in. One could see the panic break out among the enemy tanks. They turned this way and that trying to avoid the danger, but to no avail. One tank after another was hit. The panic grew as the Königstiger continued to fire. It did them no good. Soon all the Russian tanks were burning [the King Tiger tank was more than a match for anything fielded by the enemy on the Western and Eastern Fronts].

'All the troops who had watched the action were jubilant. The danger of encirclement was still great, however, and we had to pull out of the village later that day. Nevertheless, it was a day to remember.'

ᛋᛋ HITLER'S BODYGUARD DIES

ERWIN BARTMANN

SS-UNTERSCHARFÜHRER

1st SS Panzer Division *Leibstandarte SS Adolf Hitler*

The 'classic' Waffen-SS divisions fought to the very end, but suffered terrible losses. The **Leibstandarte**, *which had been 10,000-strong in June 1941, was reduced to 1500 by April 1945. In the end, the elite of the elite became just another roving band.*

RIGHT: Another German town goes up in flames as the Red Army continues its drive on Berlin. In their tactics the Russians could be ruthless, as Bartmann's account makes clear...

'On 17 April, we arrived at Lichtenberg on the country road between Pillgram and Markendorf, and on the same day were assigned to our positions on the edge of a wood. I was in charge of a heavy machine-gun section. We had two machine guns on mountings and dug ourselves in on the edge of the woods, setting up our weapons as instructed. The night was quiet. We could hear the gunfire in the distance, though, from the direction of Frankfurt-on-Oder, but couldn't tell if it was our guns or the Russians'.

'On 18 April, we prepared for action and in the afternoon we attacked the Russians in our sector. The infantry went ahead and we followed them at a set distance as we had learned in training. Suddenly we heard the sound of "Stalin Organs", and were caught in a heavy barrage and ourselves attacked [these were 82mm rockets whose launchers, known as Katyushas, were mounted on trucks. The rockets could be fired in salvos of 36 at a time and made a distinctive, and unnerving, sound as they flew]. We survived this

attack, and towards evening the orders came to return to our old location and resume our defensive positions. Unfortunately, we lost two dead there to Russian mortars. I got away with a small splinter in my face.

'The next day passed relatively peacefully, allowing us to bury our dead in the Lichtenberg cemetery. That afternoon we saw Russian tanks and troops on the Frankfurt-on-Oder to Mullrose road, going towards Mullrose. The tanks had German women and girls, even children, tied to their gun barrels as they drove past us, so we couldn't do anything. We didn't want to kill our own women and children. All we could do was watch them taking up positions that would cost us dearly the next day.

'At 0230 hours on the morning of 20 April, the Russians made an all-out attack on us in which they suffered heavy casualties. Then, at 0530 hours, they attacked again after a heavy artillery bombardment. We were unable to hold on to our positions this time – our heavy machine gun barrels had become so overheated with constant firing that they were no longer useable – and we moved back to the reserve position that had been prepared for us. At 1800 hours the Russians attacked again, supported by aircraft and tanks. They then dug in opposite us. In the evening orders came to send out a reconnaissance patrol to find out what their strength was. I went forward with two men to find out what was happening in front of us.

'We were in a bad situation: no one was in in charge, our officers had left us, and our company commander was only an 18- or 19-year-old with no combat experience, straight from officer cadet school. Worse was to come. On 21 April I met a senior officer cadet, my platoon commander, who told me that our regimental commander, SS-Obersturmbannführer Rosenbusch, had shot himself.

BELOW: A Waffen-SS half-track retreats through the shattered remains of a village. The early months of 1945 saw a string of Waffen-SS failures in the East, such as the abortive attempt to relieve Budapest. By this time the Waffen-SS divisions were shadows of their former selves.

'We reformed our lines again along the line from Petersdorf to Briesen. We were told in Briesen that a train would be loading at the station to take us where we could be better employed. We waited there a while but the promised train did not come. There were thousands of refugees waiting at the station with their luggage, and a number of soldiers of all arms of the service. We waited a while but eventually gave up when the train failed to arrive. We set off on foot towards the autobahn, where we took up defensive positions with other units. On 21 April we were attacked by the Russians again, with tanks, ground-attack aircraft and *Seydlitz* troops [Seydlitz was a German officer who had fought at Stalingrad; after his capture he recruited Germans to fight for the Red Army]. After some time and some hard fighting we again had to give up our positions and fall back. Meanwhile my little group had grown as we had been joined by Hungarian soldiers fighting on our side. As I remember after all this time, we went on from one German-held village to another, looking for something to eat, as my men only had their iron rations.

ABOVE: *German troops in retreat on the Eastern Front file past a lone Panther tank, April 1945. By this stage of the war even the* Leibstandarte *was reduced to nothing more than a rabble. The Führer's finest were now fighting only for their lives. This meant trying to get to the Western Allies to surrender – Russian captivity could mean death.*

'People need something to eat. Without food, and with hunger in one's stomach, one cannot fight. In one village we found the headquarters of a general. We reported to him, and were given something warm to eat, which improved our morale greatly. We were also given some bread and other items to take with us. This raised our morale even more, and we set off again.

'Near Storkow we met an SS-Obersturmbannführer named Junghans, who took us under his wing. Once more we were part of a unit. He asked me if my men and I would act as his escort, so we agreed and followed him. As his personal bodyguard I stayed close to him always. He had a unit consisting of various companies and battalions and he was trying to re-establish the front in our area, but it was only for a short while. We drove round our old training grounds,

which I knew well from earlier days, and then drove through Markgrafpieske to Spreenhagen. As we came to the edge of the village we saw white sheets of surrender fastened to the windows, and then we came under Russian mortar and rifle fire. We carried on towards Spreeau. There we discovered that the Russians were already in occupation of Spreeau and had shot some German soldiers. Among these killed had been members of the Waffen-SS, who had been betrayed to them by an old man who lived in a house set apart from all the others there.

'Next day, 24 April, our commander went with some tanks to attack a farmstead occupied by the Russians the previous day. He wanted to retake this position, as it formed a strategic point in a commanding position. This undertaking fell through, though, and in the fighting we lost our commander, who was wounded.

'Once more we were without an officer as we set off again towards the west. We then met a long column of soldiers and refugees trying to save their skins, and we followed them. We came to the experimental ranges at Kummersdorf, where we had to fight the Russians once again. After Kummersdorf, a few Waffen-SS comrades and I found ourselves in an endless column of soldiers of all arms of the Wehrmacht: generals, senior officers and their staffs.

'Again we came up against *Seydlitz* troops as we went through some woods. As was later discovered, the *Seydlitz* troops were under the command of Soviet commissars. We were attacked in the woods by Russian infantry. As we went along a firebreak they moved parallel to us and attacked us from the side. The *Seydlitz* troops wore German uniforms but were armed with Russian submachine guns. They kept on attacking us. Those who could not carry on remained behind and mixed in with our column [everyone, it appears, was keen to reach US and British lines!]. One appeared with an armband bearing the words *Komitee Freies Deutschland*, and one of the Wehrmacht officers came up to us shouting: "Where are the SS? This man must be shot!" I personally would have nothing to do with this big cheese. We told them that if they wanted someone shot they should do it themselves. I intensely disliked these gentlemen of the general staff. At that time they were only thinking of saving their own skins.

'We moved from place to place, from south to north and back to the south. The long procession of human beings went from one road junction to another, meeting up with other units. I cannot recall exactly when we went through the radio mast installations at Königs Wusterhausen. I think it must have been after the breakout from the Halbe Pocket.

'Before we came to the Halbe Pocket I came across a container of alcohol that we mixed with apple juice. We then gradually worked our way through it until it was empty. As I see it today, without this mixture, on an empty stomach, we could never have got out of the pocket. We must have been on the edge of it when we emerged from the woods and saw a country road running from left to right with a hillock on either side of the road. On each side of the road was also a Russian gun. The only way was to plough through the middle, so we waited until the gun on the left fired and the one on the right was reloading. We used the slight delay with some success. All my men came through, some with slight wounds, but the main thing was that we all came out of that confusion alive and well.

'Our plan was to get straight through to Berlin. I as a Berliner I thought that it would be better in the city than

here in the confusion of the war. Now that I think about it, it was a godsend that we didn't make it to Berlin. Many of my former comrades lost their lives fighting in the city.

'On 28 April I met up with my last company commander again. He was with other officers from our old unit. We went through Beelitz, Belzig and Ziesar to Genthin, where we rested overnight. Next day we looked around the area to

ABOVE: A Waffen-SS soldier, circa 1945. Though he is kitted out in clothing that is comfortable, his appearance is a far cry from pre-war days and the early period of World War II, when Waffen-SS soldiers dressed and carried themselves according to their elite status.

see how best to cross the River Elbe. Near Jericho there was a half-sunken barge in the Elbe laden with sugar, sweets, chocolate and other fine things. We went aboard and each one of us loaded a pillowcase with sweets. Then we went back ashore and hid ourselves in some bushes so that the Americans, who were on the other bank, could not see us. That evening, at about 1800 hours, an American officer came across on a ferry and, on his own initiative, tried to persuade us to surrender to him. We sent him on his way, though, and looked for a boat that would take us across to the other side.

'On the evening of 29 April a unit arrived with a general's staff and everything that went with it. They wanted to confiscate our boat to save their own lives, but we would not give it up. The general then came to us personally to confiscate the boat, but we agreed among ourselves that we would go first across the Elbe and that two men would bring the boat back so that the general could be saved.

'We landed in an American artillery position on the other bank. There were no sentries to be seen – everyone was asleep. We bypassed the position and set off for Königslutter-in-der-Elm. From the artillery position we went straight into the woods (which are predominant in this area). We slept all day as it was too dangerous to move when it was light. The area was changing its occupants virtually daily – one day Americans, the next British or Russians. So we always had to be careful to avoid falling into the hands of one of our enemies. We reached Königslutter and found shelter in an SS field hospital, where I remained until 13 May. Then, through an error on my part, I was arrested by former German inmates of a concentration camp.

'Those were my last days as a soldier. I then served three years and eight months as a prisoner of the British, being released on 24 December 1948. As a Berliner I could not go back to my old home town, so I voluntarily remained in Britain, where I was nationalised on 5 November 1955.'

SS FIGHTING TO THE END

KARL KÖRNER
SS-HAUPTSCHARFÜHRER

Schwere SS-Panzer Abteilung 503
III SS Panzer Corps

Karl Körner's unit (around 80 tanks) went into action in January 1945 with a full complement of King Tigers. By April it had been reduced to 21 serviceable tanks, though it was still capable of achieving notable victories.

RIGHT: SS-Hauptscharführer Karl Körner, commander of one of the awesome King Tiger tanks, who was awarded the Knights Cross of the Iron Cross in the Reichs Chancellory in Berlin in the closing days of World War II.

'In April I was acting in support of a German infantry counterattack near Bollersdorf when I encountered two of the new Soviet Josef Stalin II tanks a mere 200m (220 yards) away. The crew of the first Stalin must have been half asleep, as they did not see me draw near. I quickly destroyed the first tank and the wreckage blocked the field of view of the second. This tank attempted to reverse back to bring its gun to bear, but ended up reversing into a deep anti-tank ditch.

'On the road from Bollersdorf to Strausberg stood a further 11 Stalin tanks, and away on the edge of the village itself were around 120–150 enemy tanks in the process of being refuelled and re-armed. I opened fire and destroyed the first and last of the 11 Stalins on the road, effectively blocking the remainder, which could not then turn on the narrow road. The crews of the massed assembly of tanks, which were being refuelled and re-armed, began to start their motors in a desperate attempt to get into firing positions. All the while I was firing shell after shell at them.

'As ammunition and fuel trucks exploded into a raging inferno, the Russian crews abandoned their vehicles and fled into the cover of the village. I fired off all 39 shells I had

BELOW: Berlin lies in ruins and Hitler is dead. Those Waffen-SS soldiers still alive face an uncertain future.

on board before I withdrew. My own personal score of enemy tanks destroyed in this action came to 39. By the time we had been driven back into Berlin I had knocked out over 100 enemy tanks and 26 anti-tank guns in total. [For his efforts Körner became one of the last recipients of the Knights Cross.]

'On 28 April 1945, at around 2200 hours, SS-Obersturmführer Oskar Schäfer and I were escorted in a personnel carrier by the adjutant of our heavy tank battalion, SS-Obersturmführer Lemke, from our combat sector in Berlin-Wilmersdorf to the Reich Chancellery. In the bunker of the Reichs Chancellery, Schafer and I were met by Brigadeführer Mohnke [Commandant of the Reich Chancellery and former commander of the *Leibstandarte*].

'On the evening of 29 April, our battalion commander, SS-Sturmbannführer Fritz Herzig, arrived. When we were all assembled the Knights Cross of the Iron Cross was awarded to Schafer, Herzig and myself. The Knights Crosses were brought from the Führerbunker and handed to us by SS-Brigadeführer Mohnke in the presence of General Krebs. Mohnke also signed the entries in our pay books.

'After the awards were made we returned to our units in Charlottenburg, in the Neue Kantstrasse. We got there from the bunker of the Reichs Chancellery once again by way of the Tiergarten in an armoured personnel carrier.'

SURRENDER

'None of you will ever return.' These chilling words were uttered to surrendered Totenkopf Division personnel in 1945 by Russian officers. For the soldiers of the Waffen-SS, the end of the war signalled the beginning of a period of danger and uncertainty. Would they be shown mercy and compassion by their captors, or would savage retribution be administered?

By the early spring of 1945, the much-vaunted Thousand Year Reich of Adolf Hitler was crumbling fast as the inexorable Allied advance continued on both Western and Eastern Fronts. Even the herculean efforts of the remaining few battered remnants of the once mighty elite divisions of the Wehrmacht and Waffen-SS could do little to delay Germany's ultimate defeat. Vast tracts of territory once occupied by the Germans were now under enemy control, and as the Allies advanced, the full horror of the fate of Europe's Jews became clear as one concentration camp after another was liberated. Even the most battle-hardened combat troops were shocked to the core by the horrors they witnessed, and many were filled, understandably, with a terrible desire for revenge, which some would exact against any soldier wearing SS uniform who was unfortunate enough to fall into their hands.

To the Allied soldiers who had witnessed these hellish camps, the guards they captured appeared to wear the same field-grey uniform, the same standard SS rank insignia on the shoulder strap or sleeve, and standard SS cap insignia as Waffen-SS soldiers. Moreover they also carried what appeared to be standard SS paybooks. Therefore, it seemed clear that they were confronting Waffen-SS troops. One could hardly expect the common frontline combat soldiers to have given much consideration to the unique pale brown piping worn on these

US troops escort a batch of German prisoners to a holding camp. In general, those Waffen-SS units that surrendered to the Western Allies were treated fairly. The Russians, however, eager to exact vengeance for the sufferings caused by the Germans, often shot prisoners out of hand.

Abschrift.

Szillat   Im Felde, 2.8.44.
SS-O'Stuf. u.Kp.Fhr.

Sehr geehrte Familie Wacker!

Als Kompanieführer habe ich die traurige Pflicht, Ihnen
Mitteilung zu machen, dass Ihr Sohn. der SS-Sturmmann
Friedrich W a c k e r , seit den schweren Kämpfen bei
Rosignano am 8.7.44. vermisst wird.

Die Abteilung wurde, als Nachhut eingesetzt, eingeschlossen, als
die Kompanie zum Gegenstoss angesetzt werden sollte. Die
Kompanie wurde durch schweren Artillerie-und Granatwerferbeschuss
sowie durch heftige Gegenstösse des Gegners auseinandergerissen.
Seitdem fehlt von Ihrem Jungen jede Spur.

Ihr Sohn hat sich in zahlreichen Kämpfen durch hervorragende
Tapferkeit und ermüdliche Einsatzbereitschaft ausgezeichnet und
war so seinen Kameraden stets ein leuchtendes Vorbild.

Durch sein offenes, ehrliches Wesen, seine stete Hilfsbereitschaft
und Kameradschaft war bei uns allen beliebt. So trifft uns sein
Verlust besonders schwer.

Wir wissen alle um den grossen Schmerz, der Sie, liebe Familie
Wacker mit dieser Nachricht trifft.
Doch wir alle sind in dieser schweren Stunde mit unserem ganzen
Herzen bei Ihnen und in der aufrichtigen Hoffnung, dass Ihr
lieber Junge am Leben ist und eines Tages gesund zu Ihnen in die
Heimat zurückkehren möge.

Möge Ihnen diese Gewissheit die Kraft verleihen, in dieser
schweren Stunde stark und hoffnungsvoll und so tapfer zu sein,
wie Ihr lieber Junge stets gekämpft hat.

Es grüsst Sie im Namen der gesamten
Kompanie in aufrichtigem Mitgefühl

Ihr   gez.: M. Scillat

SS – Obersturmführer
und Kompanieführer.

ABOVE: A registered letter that was sent to the family of Friedrich-Karl Wacker, informing them that he has been officially listed as missing in action (see p 143).

SS guards uniforms, or the death's head or double-armed swastika which adorned their collar patches. As a result, revenge for the atrocities committed by concentration camp guard units was to be visited, on many occasions, on simple Waffen-SS combat troops who fell into Allied hands. There are recorded incidents where camp guards had deserted their posts and ran off as the Allies approached. Waffen-SS combat troops who happened to be captured in the area then bore the brunt of the Allies' wrath, being executed on the spot or turned over to the former inmates, who subsequently beat them to death. Then again, if the Allied soldiers and concentration camp inmates had known that these men were Waffen-SS soldiers, would they have spared them? Probably not, for such were the excesses committed in the name of National Socialism that none of the victors or those who survived persecution were concerned with the minutiae of differentiating between different sections of the SS.

As the war drew to a close, Allied troops became understandably more cautious in their tactics. No one wanted to get killed when it appeared that the war was all but over. Waffen-SS units, however, true to their elite status, almost invariably chose to fight to the last bullet before even considering surrender. Those Allied troops who had seen friends or comrades killed by such last-ditch Waffen-SS defenders often extracted grizzly revenge on them once they did give up. Once again evidence exists of a number of murders of Waffen-SS troops after they had surrendered in these late stages of the war. This sort of behaviour was not restricted to Soviet troops in the East, but was also quite common in the West. On the Western Front, it seems that where Waffen-SS units surrendered en masse, i.e. an entire division, they were able to do so with reasonable certainty

of surviving, but where small groups of men surrendered to equally small Allied units, the risk involved was much greater. On recorded occasions where Waffen-SS men were known to have been executed immediately after surrendering, they were usually in such small groups: at Oberpframmen eight were executed, at Lippach 36; at Eberstetten 17; at Utting six; and at Haar also six. At Webling, however, in one of the more famous cases, 53 Waffen-SS soldiers were gunned down after surrendering to an American patrol.

The war on the Eastern Front – a struggle noted for its savagery

On the Eastern Front, even having one's life spared after surrender was by no means a guarantee of survival. Entire divisions of surrendered Waffen-SS troops disappeared into Stalin's forced labour camps and salt mines, from which very few ever returned. However, the question has to be asked: could Waffen-SS soldiers expect any mercy from a people about whom Himmler had remarked to his Waffen-SS subordinates: 'one can shoot them down without pity and compassion'? The answer is no. To say that many of the excesses committed by Waffen-SS soldiers were also carried

BELOW: A POW tag, as attached to the uniform of captured Waffen-SS soldiers at the front before they were sent to the rear. This tag belonged to Friedrich-Karl Wacker.

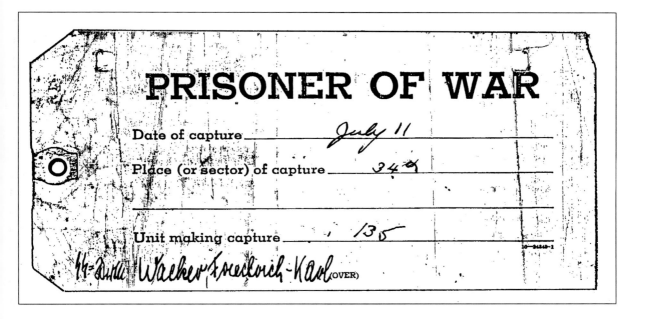

out to revenge the deaths of their own comrades, especially those who were captured by partisans and subsequently killed and often found badly mutilated, is probably a futile exercise. The war on the Eastern Front was notable for its savagery and the absence of the rules of war.

Surrendered Waffen-SS men were often considered by their captors as dangerous Nazi fanatics. This was only true in a number of cases, however. By no means all Waffen-SS men were members of the Nazi Party, though most no doubt sympathised with its ideals to some degree or other. Examination of the captured personal files of even some of the most famous Waffen-SS soldiers reveal them not to have been Party members. Neither were all Waffen-SS men willing volunteers. Many were conscripted in the latter half of the war, and considerable numbers were drafted into the Waffen-SS en masse from the Luftwaffe and Kriegsmarine. Redundant Luftwaffe ground crews or naval shore-based personnel often found themselves wearing the field-grey uniform of the Waffen-SS. Many others who did volunteer either went straight from school or from their compulsory six months' labour corps service into the Waffen-SS, where they completed their basic military training and were posted straight to the front. They had little time to learn anything about the realities of life, let alone political fanaticism.

Most Waffen-SS soldiers spent the closing stages of the war desperately trying to hold back vastly superior enemy forces as the Third Reich crumbled around them. Many had by this time become hardened cynics. Their loyalty was often no longer to the political leadership, and certainly not to their own titular commander, Himmler, whom most of them despised, but to their own unit, their own regimental or divisional commander, and their own comrades.

As can be seen from some of the following accounts, even when, their duty done, they had no option but to surrender, doing so could be just as fraught with danger as being in battle.

A LUCKY ESCAPE

RUDI SPLINTER
SS-ROTTENFÜHRER
10th SS Panzer Division *Frundsberg*

The Poles had seen their country ripped apart by the Nazis. Those Poles fighting in the armies of the Western Allies, therefore, were not inclined to show pity towards their enemies, least of all the soldiers of the Waffen-SS.

RIGHT: Like Splinter, these Germans were captured in the Falaise Pocket. Splinter himself survived captivity – just!

'During August 1944, my unit was helping to hold open the jaws of the Allied pincer movement in Normandy to allow other German units to escape east [out of the Falaise Pocket]. On one particularly wet evening I had crawled under a towed 88mm gun to get out of the rain and get some sleep. I was awakened by someone kicking the soles of my boots warning me we were about to move off. We were to head for safety over the River Seine. Movement was slow, though, with halts every few hundred metres. During one halt I heard the sound of incoming mortar fire. I leapt from the vehicle and hit the ground as a mortar shell landed close by. My leg was hit by several pieces of shrapnel. However, despite the injury – with the shock and the adrenalin rushing through my system – I managed to dash across the road into the doorway of a house before collapsing. When I came to I was inside the house with a number of other German wounded, and my wounds had been bandaged.

'My unit moved on and I was left behind with the wounded. Eventually they tried to evacuate us in a truck, but the truck was too big to negotiate the narrow, hedge-lined roads very smoothly. It kept bouncing off the verges, which caused the wounded to scream in agony. So they decided to take us back to the house and left us there with some medics.

'They came into the room and asked: "Are there any SS troops here?"'

'Eventually some British troops appeared. The officer in charge quickly realised that we were only a group of seriously wounded soldiers and posed no threat to him. He said he had no time to hang around but would make sure someone would come and pick us up. Some time later, other troops did indeed appear: Poles. This made us a little uneasy. They came into the room, heavily armed with Sten guns, and one asked: "Are there any SS troops here?" As I come from Pommerania, and could speak a little Polish, I answered him in his own language. He was taken aback and asked how I could speak Polish. I told him I came from Pommerania but used the Polish word "Pomorze", and that one of my parents was Polish and the other German. He rushed over and shook my hands like I was a long-lost brother. He was from Pommerania, too, from part of the so-called "Polish Corridor". He was very friendly and gave me some cigarettes.

'The Poles took one look at their black uniforms and shot them both'

'I should explain that a few days earlier I and another comrade had passed a destroyed German column. We always checked such vehicles for any food or water, which were always in short supply. We were warned not to use the local water supplies in case they had been booby trapped. Anyway, we discovered a supply of new tunics, unissued with no insignia. As our own tunics were very shabby and tattered, we helped ourselves to the new ones. Because my uniform had no insignia, the Poles hadn't realised that I was Waffen-SS. They even suggested that as one of my parents was Polish I should change sides and join the Free Poles. Of course I had to act as if I thought this was a good idea.

'Meanwhile, the Poles checked the other room. In there were two wounded panzer soldiers from the Army. Both were seriously wounded. One had had a leg blown off and the other had been wounded in the groin. They were in a real mess. The Poles took one look at their black uniforms with the traditional panzer death's head collar tabs, assumed they were SS and emptied their Sten gun magazines into them, slaughtering them as they lay there helpless. When anyone talks of war crimes I always think of that incident.'

[Polish troops took part in the effort to trap German forces in the so-called Falaise Pocket. Units of General Patton's Third Army were ordered to turn north from Le Mans towards Argentan and link up with Anglo-Canadian forces striking south from Caen and Falaise, thus creating a huge pocket of trapped German troops. A contingent of the Anglo-Canadian force was the 1st Polish Armoured Division, which worked in conjunction with the 4th Canadian Division to reach Falaise on 16 August 1944. The Poles and Canadians eventually linked up with the Americans at Chambois three days later. Though it had been a spectacular action, the trap was not airtight: it is estimated over 40,000 German troops escaped from the Falaise Pocket.]

⚡⚡ THE LONG ROAD HOME

KARL-HEINZ DECKER

SS-STURMMANN (UNTERFÜHRERANWARTER)

SS-Panzergrenadier Regiment 25
12th SS Panzer Division *Hitlerjugend*

Karl-Heinz Decker, an 18-year-old grenadier with the Hitlerjugend Division, had a narrow escape after his capture by Canadian troops in the Falaise Pocket.

RIGHT: A camp for Waffen-SS prisoners of war. Photography in these camps was strictly forbidden by the Allies, hence the poor quality of the picture.

'We were taken to a wood and were given spades to dig our own graves. Obviously we were about to meet our deaths. Then, fortunately for us, an English officer appeared and escorted us back on to the road, where we were loaded onto a truck. We were being taken to a holding camp, where we were all accused of being war criminals.

'From this camp I was taken to England – I think it was a race course near London. While I was there I saw the V2s landing on the city. We were told it was an interrogation camp, but I personally was lucky enough not to be interrogated. I must say, however, that I did see some men coming back from interrogation with great red weals on their backs, so that afterwards they could only lie on their stomachs. I, however, was not personally mistreated there.

'After the interrogation camp in London I was taken to America, where I was held in camps in Arkansas and Louisiana. After the end of the war the Americans came into the camp and made us watch a film about what had happened in the concentration camps. We gave them short shrift, though. Right from the start the Waffen-SS has been portrayed as nothing but war criminals, but we knew nothing of the things we were shown.

'After returning from America as a prisoner of war, in early 1946 I was sent to the British POW Camp (No 2228) in Belgium. We received so little to eat and our stomachs were so empty that we only managed to go to the toilet every 10 to 14 days. We sat there on the latrine poles like hens on a perch, tears of pain streaming down our faces as we tried to perform our bodily functions. We lived in holes dug in the ground, with only our tents over the top for cover. We were given very little food and almost left to starve. After a few weeks of this we were shipped out again, this time to England. Initially I worked for Sir Brian Horrocks, who had been the commander of the British XXX Corps at Arnhem. All his domestic staff, except his driver, were German POWs from the Waffen-SS. He was a complete gentleman and we were treated with respect.

'Put to work on the land, I also lived with the farm owners and was given a great deal of freedom. At Christmas 1948/49 we were taken back to Germany to be officially released. We were told that anyone who wanted to return to England as a free man must report back after 14 days' leave. As I knew my family had been broken up when they fled from East Prussia as refugees, and I saw the plight of these refugees myself, and the state Germany was in, I decided to return to England.'

'I have no regrets about serving in the Waffen-SS and am proud to have been in the *Hitlerjugend* Division. Over the years I have worked with, and spoken to, many British veterans, who all admit that atrocities were committed by both sides, even if the media would have us think otherwise.'

⚡⚡ COMBAT AND CAPTURE

ERICH HELLER
SS-UNTERSTURMFÜHRER

2nd SS Panzer Division *Das Reich*

During the fighting in the Ardennes in December 1944, SS-Untersturmführer Erich Heller was actually rescued from the wreckage of a burning house by the American troops who took him prisoner. Heller had had misgivings about his orders from the start.

RIGHT: *The Malmédy massacre, committed by Waffen-SS soldiers. Such incidents made life harsh for captured Waffen-SS troops, as Heller relates...*

'My recommendation that reconnaissance troops go in first was rejected because there was insufficient time to organise them. In these circumstances, as an experienced infantryman, I had severe misgivings about the operation.

'Some of my lads sat on the hulls of the tanks, while others followed behind on foot. I joined these marching troops using the tanks as cover and we progressed across the open plain. However, we had scarcely crossed a quarter of the way over when the enemy opened up with all their weapons. One tank received a direct hit and began to burn.

The one behind which we were advancing also received some hits. Instinctively my men jumped off and sought cover in a ditch. It became apparent that it would be impossible to carry on across some 200 metres of open space with the firepower we had. Besides, we were now coming under attack from enemy fighter-bombers. The fighter-bombers could not see us in the cover of the ditches, which themselves were in the shadows cast by some pine trees. From all around I received news that my own group had not suffered any losses, so I ordered my men to crawl along the ditch to the south, towards the road running into the town. We would make our attack along the road, using the houses and trees that flanked both sides for cover. The weather had also suddenly become very misty and overhead the fighter-bombers had moved away.

'Around 1300 hours my unit assembled west of a bridge we had overrun that morning. It was quiet now, though all our tanks had been knocked out. I sent a runner to the rear with a request for an artillery barrage and another half a company of men with tank support. I arranged my soldiers along the street among the cover (there were many houses, stables, trees and bushes). We first encountered the enemy in the town centre, where a Sherman tank stood. Half an hour later the runner came back from the commander of I Bataillon, SS-Obersturmbannführer Grohmann, with news that there was no artillery or tank support available and only a platoon of grenadiers in reserve. I would have to attempt to take the town with what strength I had.

'The heavy machine guns were behind us to give us covering fire'

'I set my forces out as follows: two-thirds of them on the left of the street and one-third on the right, well separated to keep any losses down. The anti-tank weapons were similarly distributed. The heavy machine guns were behind us to give covering fire and hold back the enemy.

'The reserve platoon under SS-Oberscharführer Drschewianowski went in on my left flank and came under heavy enemy fire, which quickly brought the attack to a halt as there was so little cover where they were. At that moment I gave the order for our attack to begin. We made good progress and the enemy lost possession of the first few houses. However, the group on the right of the street made the mistake of rushing forward and were spotted by the enemy. They soon came under fire from the tank in the centre of the town, as well as machine-gun fire, and quickly suffered heavy losses within just a few minutes. The attack on the right-hand side of the street thus got bogged down.

'Meanwhile, my machine guns had driven back enemy infantry approaching from the left and a *Panzerfaust* team

had managed to shoot up the Sherman. The enemy was now clearly confused, but it didn't take them long to recover. After a brief pause in the firing we suddenly came under tank fire and other gunfire from our left. Through my binoculars I saw two enemy tanks on the western edge of the town. In the middle of the open plain on that flank, the reserve platoon was already meeting its fate. I concluded therefore that the attack would have to be called off. The men were ordered to break off contact with the enemy and withdraw, giving each other covering fire. Three men with *Panzerfausts* and a machine gun would stay behind with me. The action was over in 15 minutes.

'Just as we four were about to make our way back, the house in which we had taken cover was hit by two high-explosive shells and was immediately set on fire. We dashed out and made our way towards the town centre, as I thought that the enemy would assume we would go in the opposite direction and would fan out their artillery fire in the direction of the bridge. I was right. From a new hiding place we could see a Sherman tank dug in, with an anti-tank gun beside it, about 120 metres (394ft) away. We would now have to make our break, but first we would deal with the enemy. Two men fired *Panzerfausts* at the Sherman and scored hits, and I kept the gun crew and tank crew, who had baled out, down with with the machine gun. I later discovered that some were killed or wounded and the tank had to be towed away.

'As we were leaving this house more high-explosive shells burst beside us. Someone had obviously spotted us. I was the last to leave, but as I did so part of the roof crashed down on me and I lost consciousness. I was only out for a few seconds, but when I came to I found I was trapped by a beam from the roof. I tried to extricate myself but couldn't. All the while burning fragments were landing on me and I had to keep throwing them off. I called for my lads but got no answer. Either they had already gone or had been killed. Sooner or later the rest of the house would collapse and that would be the end of me.

'The three American soldiers who suddenly appeared probably got as big a shock as I did. Later I learned that they were from a reconnaissance troop sent out to make sure

ABOVE: Another photograph of a POW camp for Waffen-SS prisoners, taken just after the end of the war. Note the desolate conditions and the lack of cover for the inmates, factors that contributed to the large numbers of deaths in the camps through malnutrition and exposure.

they had cleared all the town. They helped me out, suffering minor burns themselves, and carried me to the rear. I was taken to a house, where they applied some makeshift bandages and gave me some food. Then I fell asleep. Towards evening I awoke, in some pain, and asked for a doctor, but they told me I would be moved farther to the rear.

'The commander of these troops was called Miller and had been born in 1921. His father was a German, from Stuttgart. However, this did not prevent all my decorations and wristwatch being pilfered from me. Fortunately, my collar patches were hidden under my camouflage jacket. However, they fell into the hands of a military police sergeant two days later. He approached me, to the applause of some Belgian civilians, with a huge knife in his hands, saying: "War over, SS kaput". The civilians were delighted, clearly thinking he was going to cut my throat. Fortunately it was just the collar patches he was after.

'The soldiers were not unfriendly to me but were rather uncommunicative. The only one who spoke was an older fellow, the one they called the "Jap-Killer". He was constant-

ly handling these huge knives, with which he would do knife-throwing tricks with great skill and accuracy. He often told me how he had used these knives to send many "damned Japs" to heaven!

'When it got dark a major arrived, escorted by an interpreter in uniform but with no rank insignia. After a few questions about name, rank, unit, the objectives of the attack and so on, I produced my Soldbuch and said that I had nothing further to say. The major appeared to be satisfied. The interpreter, however, said that there had been talk that members of the Waffen-SS were no longer to be treated as regular soldiers.

'After a few minutes I was put into a Jeep and transported to a hospital. Here I was allowed to wash, eat and was bandaged after being examined by a doctor. He told me that my wounds were not that serious and that I could be sent either to a hospital or to a normal camp with medical facilities. I took the latter choice and was driven farther to the rear. Towards evening, in some village or small town, I was received by an officer, again without rank or insignia. He treated me in a very friendly fashion, and gave me a seat, food and drink. To my question as to how I should address him, he laughed and said that I could call him captain if I wished. We talked for a full two to three hours, during which I hardly realised that the first interrogation had started. He was very open with me, even to the extent of telling me he was a Jew from Vienna who had emigrated in 1938, but that I shouldn't feel uncomfortable about it. He was the kindest interrogator I ever had.

'At the end of the interrogation a major and another interrogator appeared. The latter was very intelligent, with lightning-quick reactions and sudden trick questions. The interpreter translated everything for the major. The interrogator told me he could understand me so well because he had studied in Berlin before emigrating with his parents in 1934. It was nearly midnight when they finished. I saluted as they were leaving, in accordance with our standing regulations at that time, with the so-called "Deutsche Gruss", not the normal military salute. My salute was not returned, though the friendly interrogator advised me that I should henceforth refrain from using this salute. I was then given over to a sergeant, who took me to one of the neighbouring rooms where I slept the night.

'He told me that Waffen-SS soldiers were now considered war criminals'

'The next morning, 27 December, I lay and waited, but it was afternoon before they came for me and took me farther to the rear. We eventually stopped in front of a house, from which there was a great deal of noise coming. Inside there were around 10 military policemen singing, drinking and making a great din. I was greeted with a "Hallo", and then the sergeant who had handed me over disappeared. These MPs were real giants of men. They looked at each other, nodded and then quickly arranged themselves on two sides of the room. Before I realised what was about to happen they grabbed me and pushed me from behind with all their strength so that I virtually flew across the room, and cried out: "Superman is flying". The last metre I slid on my belly. Before those on the other side could pick me up and continue the game, a smaller uniformed man entered and shouted at them, at which point they let me go. He signalled that I should follow him. He gave me the clear impression that I was no longer under the protection of the Geneva Convention or the Hague Convention concerning the rules of war, and that Waffen-SS soldiers were now considered war crimi-

nals. On my request that he should explain what he meant by this, he told me about the incident at Malmédy [the murder of US prisoners in December 1944 by the Waffen-SS], which up to that time I had heard nothing about. There was a heated discussion going on among my captors, the upshot of which was that I could well be hanged in the next few days, depending on which unit I had been a member of.

'On the morning of 28 December 1944 I arrived in a prison camp, which was quite small and probably just a provisional camp. Here there were also some 16 German officers, from the 2nd Panzer Division, 116th Panzer Division and the *Brandenburg* Division. They took great pleasure in laughing at the humiliation and discomfiture of a "hero of the Fuhrer". After an hour or so I was taken to a darkened room. I sat on a small stool and in the background I could hear noises, which I felt sure meant that my end was just minutes away. As I sat on my stool the room was suddenly illuminated by a glaring light. Then the Americans, laughing, proclaimed gleefully that this was the light of heaven. They were greatly amused at the sight I made. Then they took me back to the other prisoners, who seemed genuinely happy to see that I was still alive. No doubt they believed that if I had been executed they might be next. This may account for their change of attitude.

'On the same day we were transported farther back in an unheated cattle wagon and with no toilet facilities. For four days we travelled like this, until we arrived at a prison camp near Le Mans. When we left the cattle wagon, we pulled ourselves together and exerted great self-control, determined not to give our captors the satisfaction of seeing us exhibit any weakness. After some waiting around in the icy temperatures, a captain, two sergeants and an interpreter appeared, who told us we would be taken to the nearby camp and treated as prisoners of war. One of the senior doctors who had accompanied us protested about the conditions under which we had been moved, but his complaint was ignored. As the captain and his interpreter withdrew, however, one of the sergeants beat the doctor twice about the head. Then we marched through the camp gate and were led to a tent at pistol point. Thus began our captivity at the hands of the Western Allies, which for me lasted until the second half of 1947.'

⚡⚡ HARSH TREATMENT

FRIEDRICH-KARL WACKER
SS-STURMMANN
16th SS Panzergrenadier Division *Reichsführer-SS*

LEO WILM
SS-OBERSCHARFÜHRER
3rd SS Panzer Division *Totenkopf*

REMY SCHRIJNEN
SS-UNTERSCHARFÜHRER
SS Freiwilligen Sturmbrigade *Langemarck*

RAYMOND LEMAIRE
SS-STANDARTENOBERJUNKER
28th SS Freiwilligen-Panzergrenadier Division
Wallonien

RIGHT: Friedrich-Karl Wacker's testimonial.

246 PRISONER OF WAR WORKING CAMP
BASILDON HOUSE,
PANGBOURNE,BERKSHIRE.

Testimonial in respect of POW AA 112576 WACKER,Fritz

POW WACKER has been employed in the capacity as waiter at 246 Prisoner of War Working Camp for the past eighteen months. During this time he has carried out his duties in a reliable and efficient manner.POW Wacker was at all times clean,honest, hardworking,punctual and soldierlike.

P.O.W. WORKING CAMP No. 246 GREAT BRITAIN

Feb'48   Assistant Commandant 246 Prisoner of War Working Camp   Capt

'By July 1944 I was a prisoner of war in the USA. We prisoners still did not quite believe that we would be defeated, though, and at the end of the year, when the Ardennes Offensive was launched, we all thought Germany would still win the war. We were treated well by the Americans, and the food was fine. We teased and treated the guards like children. We even managed to make a swastika flag, which we hoisted on the highest building in the camp on the night of 30 January 1945. It wasn't noticed by the guards until about 1330 hours the next afternoon. There were no repercussions.

'All this happened while the war was still on, however, when the Germans still held many American prisoners. If the Yanks had treated us badly and word had got back, we might have done the same to American prisoners. After 1945, however, there were no more American prisoners in German hands and the Yanks could treat us how they liked.

In some camps prisoners literally had to live in holes in the ground with no cover, completely exposed to the elements.'

FRIEDRICH-KARL WACKER

'My treatment as a prisoner of war was different in each of the camps I passed through, except for one thing: we were always hungry. Once, during an interrogation by the C.I.C., I was given a beating because I had been assigned to anti-partisan duties. According to the Americans, the people I had been fighting were not partisans but freedom fighters, though the Americans themselves had said that no war can proceed without partisans.'

LEO WILM

'I consider the treatment I got as a prisoner of war to have been absolutely bestial, both from the British and the Americans, but I have to say that this treatment was not at the hands of frontline fighting soldiers. Interned as an SS man and as a "foreigner", I had no POW status and thus was denied the protection this brings. Later, in Belgium, I was badly beaten by the gendarmes with clubs and rifle butts, and kicked in the testicles – anything was permitted. Even Red Cross nurses who had served Germany were given up to 20 years in prison.'

REMY SCHRIJNEN

'On 1 April 1945, I rejoined the *Wallonien* Division at the River Oder, having the rank of SS-Standartenoberjunker, and arrived just in time to take part in the last great retreat. Several of my French comrades went on to take part in the fighting for Berlin and were killed there. We finally surrendered at Schwerin with the rest of Kampfgruppe *Wallonien* on 5 May 1945.

'In September I was sent back to Belgium. In May 1946 I was condemned to death, along with my father [who had served in the same unit]. However, the death sentence was commuted at the beginning of 1947, and I was eventually released in August 1950. My father served a further two years after my release.'

RAYMOND LEMAIRE

SS FAIR TREATMENT

'SEPP' LAINER
SS-OBERSCHARFÜHRER
Panzergrenadier Regiment 4 *Der Führer*
2nd SS Panzer Division *Das Reich*

WERNER BUSSE
SS-UNTERSCHARFÜHRER
SS-Panzer Regiment 10
10th SS Panzer Division *Frundsberg*

GERD ROMMEL
SS-ROTTENFÜHRER
SS-Panzer Aufklarüngs Abteilung 10
10th SS Panzer Division *Frundsberg*

RIGHT: *'Sepp' Lainer (left) photographed as an SS-Hauptscharführer with his friend, SS-Unterscharführer Johan Thaler. Note the Knights Crosses.*

'In August 1944 I entered into American captivity in France, from which I escaped after a few days. After eight days and nights, and just before I reached my own lines, I was captured again, which I considered extremely bad luck. I was then taken to England and then on to the USA. In early 1946, I was transported back to Europe and ended up in France. After some months we were moved to Germany and were actually discharged as POWs. However, we did not gain our freedom, still being held as prisoners and classified now as "internees".

'The Americans in France, just after we were captured, were sometimes fair but also unfair in their treatment of us. In England, however, the British were very, very correct. In the USA, I myself was always treated correctly, but some of my comrades were very badly mistreated.'

'SEPP' LAINER

'I was taken prisoner on 10 July 1944 during the fighting for Hill 112 in Normandy. During the fighting in Russia I had been a radio operator in a tank, but later, in France, I commanded my own tank. A few days before my capture I was promoted in the field to SS-Unterscharführer. My tank was destroyed by a hit from a PIAT [Projector, Infantry, Anti-Tank] round on the turret. I was blown right out of the tank.

'I was picked up by some British medics and taken to a hospital behind the lines. My wounds were only light and so I was flown to London. From there I was taken to Scotland, to a camp called Cultybraggan in Perthshire. It is still in use

today, as a training camp for the Territorial Army. At the end of the war I decided to stay on in Scotland as the Soviets had occupied my home town, and as a former member of the Waffen-SS I did not feel it would be a good idea to return home! My treatment at the hands of the British was always very fair and respectful.'

WERNER BUSSE

'I was in Russian captivity for four and a half years. In the camp we had around 9000 men, with just one Russian doctor to attend to us. He was a Jew. If we hadn't had him as a doctor many more soldiers would have died. There should be a memorial erected to that man. Once, during a medical examination, I asked him how he could speak such good German. He answered that he had studied in Germany and had been treated very well there. He knew of course that I was a member of the Waffen-SS.'

GERD ROMMEL

⚡⚡ FIGHTING TO THE END

HANS-GERHARD STARCK
SS-OBERSCHARFÜHRER

1st SS Panzer Division *Leibstandarte SS Adolf Hitler*

Though the Reich was collapsing in 1945, some Waffen-SS soldiers, men like Starck, fought with determination to the end. However, with surrender came the grim reality of captivity and an uncertain future.

RIGHT: Hans-Gehard Starck, here an SS-Unterscharführer, who was imprisoned at Linz in Austria at the war's end.

'After the failure of the offensive around Lake Balaton in early 1945, the long retreat westwards began. Three divisions of the Rumanian Army had surrendered to the Soviets, which left a huge gap in the front. The panzer units south of Lake Balaton were first withdrawn eastwards to Vorpalota, then moved westwards. By this period of the war, though, the youngsters in the division hadn't the discipline of earlier recruits, they were like little kids. It just wasn't our old, famed division any more. There had been a marked decrease in quality.

'We reached the Austro-Hungarian border near Odenburg and had to pass through the mountains. Anything which broke down was pushed to one side and abandoned. To the south of Vienna we marched towards St Polten. On 8 May we were ordered to cross the River Enns and surrender to the Americans. This was the end of my three-year service as a soldier. At this point my commander asked me why I had pushed so hard for my recent promotion to SS-Oberscharführer. I told him I didn't want to still be a corporal when the next war started!'

'For three months after I was captured I was held in a former concentration camp near Linz, then I was transported to Burgau in Swabia. I went into captivity weighing 80 kilos, but within three months weighed only 52. I was so thin they nicknamed me "Ghandi". In Burgau, a former commander of mine from the *Leibstandarte* got me a job in the office. He was the senior prisoner. Along with three other comrades we did clerical work. Then, in January 1946, we were told to prepare release papers for our younger comrades who had been born in 1928. I took my chance and prepared papers for us as well. The checks were not rigorous and so we were released.'

⚡⚡ DEFENDING ONE'S NAME

▰ KURT IMHOFF
SS-OBERSTURMFÜHRER
9th SS Panzer Division *Hohenstaufen*

Imhoff was an eyewitness to the deaths of thousands of German prisoners held in POW camps due to the indifference of the Western Allies to the conditions in the camps.

RIGHT: Kurt Imhoff as an SS-Untersturmführer in the summer of 1942. Note the ribbon of the Iron Cross in his buttonhole.

'In December 1945, I was transferred from Boston in the USA to Le Havre, France. This marked the beginning of a terrible time for me in two different prison camps in France. They were both under American control but had Polish guards. These camps were in the vicinity of Soissons and Lothringen, and thousands of men died from hunger and illness.

'In early 1946 we were moved to an American prison camp in Germany, near Heilbronn. There I was examined by both American military doctors and former German military doctors and was declared "undernourished" (I weighed 50 kilos; when I had left the USA I weighed 80 kilos). From Heilbronn we were taken to a so-called release camp in Darmstadt. There we were "released" as prisoners of war in one room and then re-arrested in another on the orders of Allied High Command.

'Now the political process started. Everyone was placed in one of five categories; classification into one of the first two categories meant further captivity. As a former officer in the Waffen-SS I was classified in the second-highest category. We were advised that we could retain the services of a lawyer if we wished, though that was no use to me since I had no money. I had also lost my home, which was in the part of Upper Silesia that had been annexed by the Poles, and so had no collateral. Therefore I declined the offer.

'I defended myself, my argument being that from the very beginning of the war and up to my capture and imprisonment I had only been a soldier. Thus they could not charge me with any crimes (I later learned there had already been an investigation into my personal background by the C.I.C. while I was in American captivity). So, in 1947, I was released and found work in the building trade.'

RED VENGEANCE

WILHELM HILLEN
SS-OBERSTURMFÜHRER

1st SS Panzer Division *Leibstandarte SS Adolf Hitler*

For some, capture by the Russians meant not only suffering and ill treatment on their own part, but also being forced to watch the brutalisation and often murder of German civilians by drunken Red Army soldiers bent on vegeance.

RIGHT: *The Red Army in Berlin. The Germans were to reap the whirlwind for their actions in Russia.*

'For several days we had lain with hundreds of other severely wounded German soldiers in a sports hall in an area south of Berlin, where they had collected soldiers captured in the Halbe Pocket.

'After the Russians had robbed us of our last personal effects and had shaved our heads, we were loaded into cattle trucks on 8 May and were transported to a POW hospital in Poland. Next to me lay a 14-year-old youth whose right leg had been amputated. By the door of the wagon stood a tearful, heavily pregnant woman – his mother. The Russian guards pushed her further and further away from the door. As soon as she realised she was unobserved, though, she clambered aboard and hid herself in a corner under a greatcoat. Then the door was shut and the train rolled eastwards.

'Sometime after midnight the train stopped on an open stretch of track. Outside could be heard rifle fire and the howl of drunken Russian soldiers celebrating the end of the war. Then our wagon door opened. Six Red Army soldiers climbed inside and searched us, though their quest for loot was futile as we had already been robbed. Then, I witnessed something that will stay with me to the end of my days.

'They found the pregnant woman, who was repeatedly raped by the soldiers. The screams of the woman and the moans of the wounded, who could scarcely move in their bandages and plaster, were drowned by the howling of the victors. Despite his freshly amputated leg, the youth hurled himself from his cot in an effort to defend his mother. Then came the finale: a Russian drew his pistol and first shot the youth and then the mother in the head. Afterwards, laughing loudly, they threw the corpses from the wagon onto the embankment. I felt paralysed and sobbed unrestrainedly. Now I knew that we had truly been "liberated"'.

AFTERMATH

For those Waffen-SS veterans who survived the war and subsequent captivity, the years since have been difficult. Often ostracised by their communities and denounced as war criminals, former Waffen-SS soldiers have found it almost impossible to disassociate themselves from the atrocities of the Third Reich. This has left a legacy of bitterness.

In 1946, at the International Military Tribunal at Nuremberg, the SS was indicted as a criminal organisation, and the Waffen-SS was included in the indictment. By then the full extent of Himmler's vast SS empire had been revealed. The SS had been involved in a huge range of activities, from the innocent production of soft drinks (the famous Apolinaris mineral water firm was owned by the SS) to the persecution and murder of those seen as enemies of the Reich. In addition to prosecuting the major Nazi war criminals (and as Waffen-SS veterans are quick to point out, none of the senior military figures of the Waffen-SS were indicted personally at the Nuremberg trials, while several high-ranking Army and Luftwaffe officers were tried, found guilty and hanged), the Tribunal had thus, at a stroke, branded the entire SS as criminal. No attempt had been made to differentiate between the different branches of this multi-faceted organisation. Thus, those involved in such obscure and esoteric activities as the production of decorative sword blades or, as mentioned above, soft drinks, found themselves tarred with the same brush as those who served in the murder squads of the Einsatzgruppen or staffed the concentration camps. Also lumped in with all the others were the combat soldiers of the Waffen-SS.

Such was the stigma attached to membership of the Waffen-SS that, long after prisoners of war from the Wehrmacht

The grim reality of the Nazis' racial policies. As the Allies liberated the concentration camps and the world became aware of the atrocities committed against European humanity, everything associated with the Nazi state was deemed evil.

were released, many Waffen-SS soldiers continued to be held in captivity. The conditions in which they were held were sometimes quite shocking. They were often totally lacking in sanitation, with little or no cover from the elements and with the inmates on little more than starvation level rations. These camps would certainly have found the Allies in danger of censure by the International Red Cross, were it not for a rather cynical and deliberate move by the Allies. Waffen-SS prisoners had been released from POW status, and then immediately re-classified as 'Internees'. With their rights as prisoners of war under international law thus removed, they were at the mercy of their captors.

This is not to suggest that every single former Waffen-SS soldier was badly treated, far from it. Indeed, some speak with gratitude of the chivalrous manner in which they were treated, especially where their guards had been combat soldiers themselves and knew that, whatever else they had been, Waffen-SS soldiers were usually extremely tough and often very brave soldiers. Many, however, were treated extremely harshly, with beatings and starvation by no means uncommon. This was to be a traumatic time for all German prisoners, and deaths while in Allied captivity through disease and malnutrition was not uncommon.

The destitution of veterans

When release from captivity finally came, former Waffen-SS men found themselves ostracised by their own communities. The SS had indeed become the 'Alibi of a Nation'. Deprived of pension rights, unable to find work because of the stigma of having served in the Waffen-SS, many veterans were virtually destitute. On top of everything else, many could no longer return to their homes and families as they now lay in areas controlled by the Soviets. In any case, having experienced such cavalier treatment at the hands of the Western Allies, few would now be willing to place themselves at the mercy of the communists. Therefore, many decided to remain in the countries in which they had been held as prisoners, and subsequently settled in the USA, Canada and the UK.

While in captivity, all Waffen-SS soldiers had gone through some degree of screening to establish whether they were wanted in respect of any war crimes. The fact that well over 90 per cent were released without any sort of charge being brought against them did little to remove the stigma of their having belonged to what was now technically considered an illegal organisation.

The treatment of non-German SS

The HIAG was formed by former Waffen-SS soldiers to aid comrades who had fallen on hard times, such as those who were unable to work due to war wounds and were being denied a state pension or benefits. In addition, the organisation also assisted the widows of fallen Waffen-SS soldiers struggling to bring up their children. Germany had turned its back on these men, so they turned to each other, and veterans associations sprang up for almost every former Waffen-SS unit. The intensity of the post-war comradeship between former Waffen-SS soldiers is perhaps best illustrated by events such as the funeral of Josef 'Sepp' Dietrich in 1966, when some 7000 former Waffen-SS soldiers attended the ceremony.

Today, the vast majority of former Waffen-SS soldiers live quietly in retirement, their pension rights now fully restored, and are loyal to the democratic traditions of the Federal German Republic. For many, however, a bitterness does remain towards the harsh treatment they received for carrying out their duty.

The treatment of non-Germans who had volunteered for service in the Waffen-SS varied greatly. On the Eastern Front, the Russians made no effort to establish whether those who has served in Waffen-SS uniform had done so willingly or had been conscripted. Most were simply shot on the spot as they surrendered, and those who did not suffer this fate were put to work in forced labour camps, where the majority perished.

In the West, foreign SS volunteers were segregated and were initially usually treated with considerable brutality as the populations took out their frustrations (ironically, most Waffen-SS foreign volunteers had served solely on the Eastern Front and had had no part in aiding the Germans to suppress their fellow countrymen). Their families often found themselves ostracised, and when the men were released from prison they were often unable to find jobs. Many in fact moved to Germany on release from prison. That said, though considered as traitors in their own countries, few of them were actually executed.

In Holland, former Waffen-SS volunteers were held at the grim prison at Veluuwe or the former concentration camp at Vught. They were forced to dress in the striped concentration camp garb and were treated ruthlessly: over 60,000 Dutch people were stripped of their citizenship.

Flemish Waffen-SS volunteers were first held under British control at the former concentration camp at Neuengamme, before being transferred to Beverloo in Belgium in cattle trucks. Their numbers included Red Cross nurses who had served on a purely humanitarian level in hospitals on the Russian Front. From Beverloo station to the

camp was a distance of some 5km (three miles), and along the way the prisoners received continual beatings. On arrival at the camp they received further beatings and harsh treatment from their captors, and over 200 were executed in front of baying crowds.

Danish volunteers in the Waffen-SS suffered rather less than their other west European counterparts. This was probably due to the fact that the Danish crown had consented to these volunteers serving. They did, however, lose their pension rights.

In the final analysis, though, could elite soldiers who fought with a savage ferocity, who were ruthless in battle, and had a low regard for human life in general, including their own, expect mercy from the peoples of Europe who had suffered at their hands?

⚡⚡ THE BITTER LEGACY

WERNER BUSSE
SS-UNTERSCHARFÜHRER

SS-Panzer Regiment 10
10th SS Panzer Division *Frundsberg*

For many veterans of the Waffen-SS, the continual protrayal of them as genocidal fanatics is a constant source of bitterness. In their eyes they were just soldiers.

RIGHT: SS-Unterscharführer Werner Busse, shown here as an SS-Schütze in field-grey service dress. He would later wear the special black panzer clothing as a tank commander in the Frundsberg *Division.*

'We ex-soldiers of the Waffen-SS feel very bitter about the treatment we got after the war, even from our own people in Germany. Most people class the Waffen-SS in the same category as the guards in the concentration camps and that is not true. We

were fighting soldiers, probably a bit more dedicated to our cause than others because at least until the end of 1944 the Waffen-SS contained mostly volunteers. Many of our former counterparts in the Wehrmacht were glad enough to have had the divisions of the Waffen-SS fighting alongside them.

'Today we are sad at the way we have been portrayed by historians and the media. That said, we are at the same time glad that now more and more people are interested in the real, military role our former units played in the war. Our officers were tough and led from the front, like officers in today's armies. The Waffen-SS also pioneered the extensive use of disruptive-pattern camouflaged clothing used today by all armies, and most modern forces have also adopted the more rigorous and aggressive style of combat training we used.'

A PLEA FOR OBJECTIVITY

LEO WILM
SS-OBERSCHARFÜHRER
3rd SS Panzer Division *Totenkopf*

GERD ROMMEL
SS-ROTTENFÜHRER
SS-Panzer Aufklarüngs Abteilung 10
10th SS Panzer Division *Frundsberg*

HANS-GERHARD STARCK
SS-OBERSCHARFÜHRER
1st SS Panzer Division *Leibstandarte SS Adolf Hitler*

RIGHT: SS-Oberscharführer Leo Wilm pushes his motorcycle through the mud on the Eastern Front.

'The victors held prosecutions against Germans and forgot their own criminals. One should think of the case of Lieutenant William Calley who, in Vietnam, killed the inhabitants of a whole village. However, it is not for me to talk of American war crimes. War has its own laws, though these laws should not to be used to judge one side only!'

LEO WILM

'First, I think the media are to blame for not differentiating between the Waffen-SS and the security forces, all are generalised under the title "SS". Who was Eichmann, who carried out the persecution of the Jews in such great numbers? He was in the Allgemeine-SS, and is therefore seen as one of us. So long as they don't try to make any differentiation between us, the fighting troops, and them, the truth has no chance. Just ask the soldiers who fought against us. The enemy frontline soldiers who have experience of us know – like the British soldiers at Arnhem who fought against us – they know what the Waffen-SS were like.' [Gerd Rommel refers here to the fighting in Arnhem being conducted in what was generally accepted as being a very fair manner by both sides. British wounded airborne troops were evacuated during a cease-fire by Waffen-SS troops using captured British Jeeps, and the injured then tended by Waffen-SS medics. A letter of thanks for this chivalrous behaviour was sent to the German officers responsible after the war.]

GERD ROMMEL

'People today can't or won't see the difference between the Waffen-SS and those who murdered the Jews in the concentration camps – we are all tarred with the same brush. We frontline soldiers were very shocked when he heard reports of what had happened. No one could explain why it had been done. We certainly all regretted that it was possible that some of the concentration camp personnel could be transferred to us in the Waffen-SS.

'However, I don't let myself become too disturbed by the condemnation of the Waffen-SS. My feelings are for my fallen comrades and the fallen soldiers from the other side.'

HANS-GERHARD STARCK

✠ MYTHS AND REALITIES

JAN MUNK
SS-STANDARTENOBERJUNKER

SS-Panzergrenadier Regiment *Westland*
5th SS Panzer Division *Wiking*

The Waffen-SS has often been portrayed as waging a policy of extermination against the peoples of eastern Europe. However, as Jan Munk indicates, this picture is very misleading.

RIGHT: *Survivors of Buchenwald concentration camp. Many German civilians and veterans of the Waffen-SS maintain they never knew of the mass killings in the camps.*

'In general, when people talk of the SS they think of concentration camps and the brutal killing of prisoners and civilians alike. We all know of policemen who have treated arrested persons very badly. We all know of people who murder or torture their victims, and we all know of the armies that have committed atrocities, but that does not make everyone a who wears a uniform a beast.

'The terrible thing, however, is that with the SS everyone in either the Allgemeine-SS or Waffen-SS has been labelled as bad. The Waffen-SS was composed of volunteers who were soldiers with minimal political affiliations, whereas the All-gemeine-SS contained Nazi Party members and not soldiers. Most people who talk of the SS really mean the Allgemeine-SS: they do not know there were two groupings. We in the Waffen-SS were just soldiers, maybe a bit better than the ordinary Wehrmacht soldier, but that was probably because we were volunteers. I never personally saw any misbehaviour on our side.

'In Apolinowka, for example, north of Dniepropetrowsk, the local Russian population was treated completely free of charge by our doctor, a Dutch SS-Hauptsturmführer. At another time we were located near Losowaja, and the *scheishaus-parole* (latrine gossip) consistently mentioned that we would be moved either to France or Italy. Eventually we were told to make wooden sledges to aid the movement of our equipment. We already had it well planned: our 12-man section needed four sledges, big ones. We knew that the grandfather in one of the local farmhouses was planning to build a house for his daughter and, armed only with an axe, he had made a beautiful square beam from a tree trunk. We bargained with him and bought the beam for two Army blankets, 20 roubles, cigarettes and a few sewing needles and flints. We had a saw brought over from the supply unit and in no time at all we had our four sledges (the ones left over we sold to other sections).

'We were ordered to report to him and explain our behaviour'

'Next day, though, a Rumanian, a fellow who could speak some Russian and was used as an interpreter by the Kompanie, was gloating when he told us the grandmother had been to see the company commander. According to him, she had complained bitterly because her old man had slaved away for weeks making that beam and now it had been taken away by some soldiers of his Kompanie.

'If our SS-Untersturmführer had been the sort of SS officer that is commonly portrayed, he would have shot the old woman there and then. Instead, we were ordered to report to him and explain our behaviour. We couldn't say anything about the Army blankets we had traded as they were Army property, but the rest we admitted. He decided that we could keep the sledges as the beam had been cut up anyway, but we had to hand the old couple another 40 cigarettes and 10 roubles. It served us right as we should have known better than to make any deals with the locals. So much for inhuman treatment of the local population by the Waffen-SS!

'I do very much regret that I had become part of a regime that was able to establish concentration camps and to order mass slaughter. But I, my comrades and the Germans I talked to knew nothing of this. It sounds pathetic, I know, but it happens to be true.

'On my last home leave, my father told me he believed that Jews were being killed in concentration camps. I told him that at the Junkerschule at Bad Tölz we had many inmates from Dachau [the supply of concentration camp labour to industries and institutions was common throughout the war]. They were dressed in their blue and white striped trousers and jackets and were put to work in the gardens and keeping the roads clean. When we passed them they had to stand to one side and take their caps off, no more, no less. If we dared touch them they could complain to their Kapo and we would be reprimanded. They were issued with three cigarettes per day, we got two. In addition, they started work later in the morning than we did and all looked reasonably well fed. Should I believe my father or my own eyes? Of course I know now that all of it was just a huge and elaborate deception, but at the time none of us knew that.

'I have no regrets about joining the Waffen-SS. I am grateful to have had the experience of the camaraderie and I am proud to have belonged to a group of men whose loyalty to each other was beyond question. I remember the days when everyone in Europe agreed that communism was evil. Everyone knew about the Siberian camps for political prisoners and of the regular purges held by Stalin to get rid of Communist Party members who did not toe the line. I believed then, and I believe now, that my motives in opposing that system were right.

'I fully admit that Nazi Germany had to go'

'The Soviets and the Western Allies joined forces and they won the war. All that was bad and all that was wrong was blamed on the losers. I fully admit that Nazi Germany had to go, as the atrocities committed with the knowledge and approval of its government are unforgivable. But, I also remember the outcry in the civilised world when Germany bombed Warsaw and Rotterdam at the beginning of the war, denouncing it as uncivilised. However, just a few years later the Allied nations adopted the same practice when they bombed German cities.'

SS OLD ENEMIES

ERNST BARKMANN

SS-OBERSCHARFÜHRER

SS-Panzer Regiment 2
2nd SS Panzer Division *Das Reich*

Ernst Barkmann, holder of the Knights Cross, illustrates that the Waffen-SS fought a hard but honourable war against its foes. Both he and the men he fought recognised that one's duty was to kill the enemy. But war was never a personal matter.

RIGHT: SS-Oberscharführer Ernst Barkmann, winner of the Knights Cross for his tank-busting exploits in Normandy in 1944. Veterans like Barkmann have been appalled at the way they have been associated with the Gestapo and death camps. They regard themselves as having been mere soldiers.

'The SS had many aspects and many tasks. Today, however, everything is put into one pot and thus the Waffen-SS has become tarnished. Before 1933, after World War I, Germany lay in ruins. A lost war, a terrible economic situation, seven million unemployed, hunger, homelessness and poor social security. Then came Hitler and the Nazi Party and all these grievances were abolished for all to see.

At that time I was a 12-year-old schoolboy and a drum-major in a youth band. We often marched at the head of the SA and SS parades during election times. The prevalent propaganda at home, in schools and in public against the communists, socialists and Jews may have been common in the big cities, but it was far removed from our farmhouse. Because I was Waffen-SS I am associated with all the crimes of Nazi Germany.

That the Waffen-SS were fair and brave fighters is even attested to by Soviet veterans who have invited us back to visit the Caucasus. And during the war even the Red Army regarded us in the *Wiking* Division as brave soldiers.

'Once, many years after the end of the war, I discovered an old Russian adversary from the battles in Hungary and Vienna in 1945. We had a good understanding with each other. He informed me that during the war he had been a company commander and also the commander of a Josef Stalin II heavy tank. I was his former enemy, who had been the commander of a Panther tank. It was pure chance that we found each other again after so many years. But there we were, facing each other across a table in a bar. On that day, though, there were no more arguments or enmity. We were just two old soldiers, and so we sat there and drank many glasses of vodka together.'

UNJUST ACCUSATIONS

JOACHIM PEIPER
SS-OBERSTURMBANNFÜHRER

1st SS Panzer Division *Leibstandarte SS Adolf Hitler*

Many Waffen-SS soldiers were genuinely shocked at the constant attempts to portray them in the blackest possible light once the war had ended. Even very simple and seemingly insignificant matters were often twisted in an attempt to further blacken the reputations of some of the better-known personalities. Before his murder by French communist terrorists in Traves in 1976, Joachim Peiper recalled one such incident.

RIGHT: Although no personal guilt was ever established against him, Joachim Peiper accepted responsibility for the actions of his men.

'For a long time I commanded III Bataillon, Panzergrenadier Regiment 2 of the *Leibstandarte SS Adolf Hitler*. This unit had made quite a name for itself for its night attacks in Russia and was known in divisional and corps areas as the "Blowtorch Battalion".

'Our troops used this highly practical tool in winter to pre-heat the engines in our vehicles, to heat water quickly for cooking and many other things. There was also a saying among the soldiers in those days when they were given a task: "we will soon torch that." The vehicles even used a blowtorch as their tactical symbol.

'During post-war interrogations, however, this name was twisted from the "Blowtorch Battalion" to the "Arson Battalion". It was suggested that the blowtorches were used to burn down houses. In action our armoured personnel carri-

ers were in the habit of going into the attack at full speed and with all guns blazing. As the Russian houses mostly had thatched roofs, it was inevitable that they would catch fire during the battle. It would certainly be unnecessary for troops to dismount from their vehicles and use blowtorches to set houses on fire when they would almost certainly have already been set on fire as the result of the shooting that was going on, but it was one more allegation with which to blacken the image of Waffen-SS troops.'

[Peiper, although he himself had not given the order, was condemned to death after the war by the Allies for his unit's killing of US prisoners at Malmédy in December 1944, during the Ardennes Offensive. However, the sentence was commuted to life imprisonment and he was in fact released on 22 December 1956.]

⚡ PROUD TO BE WAFFEN-SS

FRANZ RIEDEL
SS-OBERSTURMFÜHRER
10th SS Panzer Division *Frundsberg*

HANNS-HEINRICH LOHMANN
SS-OBERSTURMFÜHRER
SS-Freiwilligen Panzergrenadier Regiment 49
De Ruiter

ERHARD KINSCHER
SS-STURMMANN
SS-Panzergrenadier Regiment 25
12th SS Panzer Division *Hitlerjugend*

RIGHT: SS-Obersturmführer Franz Riedel, commander of 7 Kompanie, SS-Panzer Regiment 10, Frundsberg Division. Veterans such as Riedel are proud to have fought in the Waffen-SS.

'We old soldiers have only fought in battle and today stand completely in support of our democratic state in Germany. We have nothing to do with right-wing radicalism and completely abhor what they do.'

FRANZ RIEDEL

'Anyone who takes an interest in the subject of the Waffen-SS must realise that we were soldiers just like any others. They have condemned us at Nuremberg as a "criminal organisation" and we have had to fight against this defamation for over 40 years. We, as old soldiers, have become the scapegoats of the nation, and this is what has made us bitter.'

HANNS-HEINRICH LOHMANN

'After a great deal of medical treatment for my severe lung wound, I eventually ended up in Camp 106 in Stamford. There, an English captain brought my Soldbuch, which had been left behind in my tunic pocket in the ambulance when I had first been brought to an English field dressing station in Normandy. He could see that I had been in the Waffen-SS. We got talking as it appeared that he had been directly opposite me in the fighting. Because I was not medically fit to work I became his batman, and we became such good friends that we are still in touch to this day. He kept my Soldbuch safe for me until I visited him in England in 1958, when he returned it to me.

'Although, as soon as I had been captured, I identified myself as a soldier of the Waffen-SS, I did not have any problems. Several interrogations and written questions followed after the war's end, but it wasn't really so bad. Today, though, the military achievements of the Waffen-SS are not recognised. We are all seen by the greater part of the population, especially the media, as war criminals.'

ERHARD KINSCHER

⚡⚡ RIGHTING WRONGS

MATHIEU KLEIN
SS-HAUPTSTURMFÜHRER
2nd SS Panzer Division *Das Reich*

The injustices and false accusations levelled against the Waffen-SS prompted Mathieu Klein to establish an organisation to represent Waffen-SS veterans and their dependents.

RIGHT: SS-Hauptsturmführer Mathieu Klein was a long-serving SS officer who was instrumental in the formation of the Waffen-SS ex-servicemen's association after the war.

'In 1952 I formed the HIAG in Bonn. In the immediate post-war era there was much for the HIAG to do. There were, in captivity in Belgium, France and especially in Russia, many thousands of comrades who needed our help.

'In December 1994, I was 84 years old, and for many years I still have dreams of the terrible experiences in Russia, the wind and the minus 40 degrees of frost. Then, to be treated like criminals in our own Fatherland because we were in the SS. That is something none of us from the Waffen-SS can comprehend. Today we are treated like second-class citizens, not by the people but by the government. But this just serves to make us still as proud as we always were!'

[The HIAG, the Mutual Aid Society of the Waffen-SS, was established to lobby for personal, political and financial rehabilitation from the German government and populace in general. The HIAG has achieved some major successes since its formation. For example, in August 1953 Chancellor Adenauer of West Germany stated in a speech that members of the Waffen-SS fighting divisions had been soldiers like any others. In addition, General Heinz Guderian, a much-respected member of the Wehrmacht, praised the conduct and fighting capabilities of the Waffen-SS frontline divisions in his memoirs published after the war. Despite the efforts at rehabilitation, though, Waffen-SS veterans are still looked upon by many with disdain.]

OPPOSITE TOP: The motto of the SS, Meine Ehre Heisst Treue, was not only engraved on the blades of SS dress daggers, but was also carried on the belt buckle worn by every Waffen-SS soldier. Shown here is the Waffen-SS officer's service belt and buckle with the motto surrounding the central eagle and swastika device.

OPPOSITE BOTTOM: The Panzer Assault Badge, here seen in its higher grades for 25 and 50 individual days of combat against the enemy. The higher grades were introduced in 1943 to recognise participation in 25, 50, 75 and 100 separate actions. Many such awards were won by Waffen-SS soldiers fighting on the Eastern Front, testimony to their martial virtues.

REFLECTIONS

What did Waffen-SS soldiers think of the Russian, British and American troops they fought against, what were their views on the peoples of the territories Germany occupied during the war, and what were their views regarding their own leaders? In this chapter, Waffen-SS veterans reflect on their thoughts during their service in the field-grey SS uniform.

Today the Waffen-SS has an unenviable reputation. As described in previous chapters, the soldiers of the Waffen-SS have often been branded as nothing more than war criminals. But what did Waffen-SS soldiers think of their opponents, of the Russian, British and American troops who eventually defeated them, and of the peoples of countries they occupied?

The contributors to this book agreed that many grave errors were made by Waffen-SS troops, and that some committed atrocities. They do not seek to deny this; rather, what they look for is the recognition that Waffen-SS troops were not alone in perpetrating such excesses. Indeed, is is difficult to deny that the combatants of all nations fighting in World War II were occasionally guilty of dishonourable acts.

However, it is also true that, for many years after the war, atrocities committed by Allied troops were hushed up. Reports of brutalities, murder and rape by Soviet troops were well known, but among the Western Allies any atrocities that had not already come to public attention tended to be omitted from the official histories or glossed over as 'mopping-up operations'.

In recent years, however, more and more accounts have come to light of looting, rape and the murder of captured German soldiers by Allied troops, not just from the Red Army but

Two SS-Oberscharführers of the Totenkopf Division. Although both are of the same substantive rank, note that the soldier to the right wears the double-braid rings on his sleeve, denoting his appointment as 'Der Spiess', or senior NCO, of the unit. Note also the death's head collar patches.

also among the Western Allies. In one case American troops cold-bloodedly shot down German troops who were unarmed and surrendering under the cover of a white flag. Cameramen were on the scene to film the atrocity, and the film has subsequently been seen in television documentaries. Contrary to Allied claims, no written order has ever been found from a German commander to his troops that no prisoners be taken. On the other hand, such orders by Allied commanders to their troops were issued in writing and are a matter of record.

No one, least of all the combat soldiers of the Waffen-SS who have contributed to this book, would seek to condone or excuse what happened in the Nazis' concentration camps, or would attempt to justify the hundreds of thousands of brutal murders carried out by Heydrich's Einsatzgruppen (Special Action Groups) on the Eastern Front. Waffen-SS soldiers were by no means always Nazis. According to most, joining the Waffen-SS was a way in which to serve their country as a member of a famed, elite force in a crusade against communism. Other less conscious motives have been discussed in Chapter One.

The Waffen-SS as liberators

Like the elite units of other nations, the soldiers of the Waffen-SS fought ferociously, intent on killing the enemy before the enemy killed them. Undoubtedly some Waffen-SS soldiers went too far and overstepped the bounds of acceptable behaviour, even in the heat of battle. That said, so did Allied soldiers. After the Normandy invasion, for example, over 400 American soldiers were court-martialled for rape and murder. Almost 200 cases of rape against French women resulted in courts martial, and 49 American servicemen were hanged.

The murder of a number of Canadian prisoners by members of the *Hitlerjugend* Division in Normandy during the first few days of the invasion is well known. The division has been roundly condemned for this atrocity and its reputation has been irrevocably tarnished. However, it is now admitted that the Canadians also killed unarmed German prisoners. Kurt Meyer, 'Panzermeyer', the commander of SS-Panzergrenadier Regiment 25, one of the principal units of the

ABOVE: SS-Oberstgruppenführer Josef 'Sepp' Dietrich. Of humble origins, he rose to command the Leibstandarte *and 6th SS Panzer Army. He was held in great esteem by the men he commanded. Some 7000 Waffen-SS veterans attended his funeral in Germany in 1966.*

Hitlerjugend Division, was tried, found guilty and sentenced to death for the part his troops played in the murder of Canadian prisoners. One distinguished Canadian officer, Brigadier Harry Foster, was honest enough to admit his feelings in regard to the death sentence passed on Meyer. He said: 'I don't believe that Meyer pulled the trigger or gave orders to execute any of them, although I'm sure he knew what was happening. But does that make him any more guilty of murder than I am guilty for knowing about the German soldiers my troops killed?'

This is not an attempt to make two wrong deeds into a right one; rather, it is to put the lapses of both sides into context, and to recognise that anger, indoctrination and the darker side of human nature will affect soldiers everywhere, whatever the rights or wrongs of the cause in which they are fighting.

Many people have strong opinions on the Waffen-SS. However, it is interesting to hear the opinions of the Waffen-SS soldiers themselves, expressed here in print for the first time. In the pages that follow, we will see what former Waffen-SS soldiers thought of their enemies, the civilians they met in occupied countries, their Wehrmacht counterparts and their own leaders. In the summer of 1941, for example, as Hitler's armies poured into the Soviet Union following the start of Operation 'Barbarossa', Waffen-SS troops often found themselves welcomed as liberators, especially in the fertile countryside of the Ukraine where the farming communities loathed the collective system forced upon

them by the communists. German soldiers were no doubt pleasantly surprised to find the population friendly, and the indigenous population were equally relieved to find that the average German soldier was not the brutal fascist monster that Soviet propaganda had led them to expect (Himmler's racial policies quickly destroyed this goodwill).

We will also see what several respected figures in the German military thought of the fighting qualities of the Waffen-SS. Their opinions do not gell with the common belief that the Wehrmacht and Waffen-SS were forever at loggerheads and had little respect for each other.

Above all, the quotes listed below reveal that those who wore the death's head badge had the same feelings, emotions, desires and fears as the soldiers of other nations who fought in World War II.

⚡⚡ THE RED ARMY

LEO WILM

SS-OBERSCHARFÜHRER

3rd SS Panzer Division *Totenkopf*

REMY SCHRIJNEN

SS-UNTERSCHARFÜHRER

SS Freiwilligen Sturmbrigade *Langemarck*

EDUARD JANKE

SS-UNTERSCHARFÜHRER

11th SS Freiwilligen-Panzergrenadier Division *Nordland*

ERIC BRÖRUP

SS-OBERSTURMFÜHRER

SS-Panzer Aufklärungs Abteilung 5
5th SS Panzer Division *Wiking*

RIGHT: Red Army soldiers, 'Ivans' to the Germans.

'As far as my views about the enemy are concerned, I can only say that all of them – the Russians, British, and Americans – did their duty. When it came to cruelty, however, the Russians and the Poles were top of the list.'

LEO WILM

'In my opinion the Russians were good soldiers, but they had terrible leaders, officers who squandered them in massive numbers in suicidal frontal attacks. They suffered the most terrible losses, and this always had a great demoralising effect on them. As for the British, Americans or French, I can't really express an opinion as I never actually fought against them. I only ever fought against the Soviets on the Eastern Front.'

REMY SCHRIJNEN

'I only ever fought on the Russian Front in the Waffen-SS, and in my opinion the Russians were very good fighters.'

EDUARD JANKE

'The Russian soldier was pretty tough, but in some cases very poorly led. Their commanders were obliged to "go by the book": they weren't allowed much flexibility. If you could get them running they would just keep on running as long as you didn't let up the pressure.'

ERIC BRÖRUP

⚡⚡ THE WESTERN ALLIES

WERNER BUSSE
SS-UNTERSCHARFÜHRER
SS-Panzer Regiment 10
10th SS Panzer Division *Frundsberg*

HANS-GERHARD STARCK
SS-Oberscharführer
1st SS Panzer Division *Leibstandarte SS Adolf Hitler*

WILHELM FECHT
SS-SCHÜTZE
Werfer Abteilung 12
12th SS Panzer Division *Hitlerjugend*

RIGHT: A GI of World War II. The Waffen-SS first encountered American troops during the Italian campaign in 1944.

'I reckon the British were the best soldiers, then the Soviets, but the Americans came last.'

WERNER BUSSE

'The first British soldiers I encountered were at Caen in Normandy. They were not like us: they had huge amounts of materiel. They were very wasteful: we often used to pick up things that they had discarded. The Soviets were tough fighters and very good soldiers all in all. As for the Americans, at the time of the Normandy invasion I don't think their leadership was very good – think about the shambles at 'Omaha' Beach. They were dropped too far out from the beach in deep water and really struggled. They didn't have the same intensive training we had. Later, in the Ardennes, I came up against Americans who were every bit as tough as we were. The Canadians were very hard men, but personally I had my doubts about them as far as soldierly qualities, such as discipline, were concerned.'

HANS-GERHARD STARCK

'I cannot commend the behaviour of the Western Allies at all. I know for certain that about 20 members of the replacement battalion of the *Hitlerjugend* Division were executed by the British at Solltau just before the end of the war. Further, the French General Leclerc, in American uniform, had some 13 members of the *Charlemagne* Division shot. He had asked them why they wore Waffen-SS uniform. They answered back with a comment about him wearing an American uniform. That was reason enough, apparently, for shooting them.'

WILHELM FECHT

SS ATROCITY IN NORMANDY

ERHARD KINSCHER
SS-STURMMANN

SS-Panzergrenadier Regiment 25
12th SS Panzer Division *Hitlerjugend*

Erhard Kinscher, a despatch rider at the regimental command post of SS-Panzergrenadier Regiment 25, **Hitlerjugend** *Division, did not personally witness the shooting of Canadian prisoners near the command post which led to the post-war trials of many soldiers from the division. However, he was told of the incident by a comrade and shown the bodies.*

RIGHT: *'Panzermeyer', a hard soldier but no butcher, as Kinscher makes clear in his account.*

'On or around 9 June 1944, in the late forenoon, after reporting with a message to the regimental command post, one of the runners from 13 Company said to me: "Come with me". He showed me the bodies of five Canadians. When I asked him what had happened, he said to me that he had been told that as SS-Obersturmführer König was leading these men back as prisoners, one of them had produced a hidden pistol and shot at him. All the Canadians were subsequently killed. At the time of the shooting the officer in charge at the command post would have been the regimental adjutant, but whether he gave the orders for the shooting or not I don't know. When "Panzermeyer" returned, however, there was an almighty row and the adjutant was posted to I Battalion, at the front, as punishment. He was killed in action soon after.

'I must say that I myself found the bodies of two of the *Hitlerjugend* Division who had been similarly executed by the enemy, with pistol shots to the back of the neck. But this does not excuse what our men did to those five Canadian prisoners of war.'

SS CANNON FODDER

JAN MUNK
SS-STANDARTENOBERJUNKER

SS-Panzergrenadier Regiment *Westland*
5th SS Panzer Division *Wiking*

The soldiers of the Red Army often displayed a reckless bravery on the Eastern Front, similar to that shown by the Waffen-SS. At other times, however, as Jan Munk remembers, Russian soldiers could behave like dumb animals.

RIGHT: Red Army soldiers firing an artillery piece on the Eastern Front. Though Russian soldiers could display incredible bravery, they were also often poorly led. Worse, they appeared to show suicidal tendencies at times.

'In our opinion the Russian soldiers were regarded as little more than cattle for the slaughter. They just kept coming, regardless of casualties. I'll give you an example.

'We were once on the edge of a wood. We saw the Russians coming out of the trees pulling some sort of anti-tank gun. It was not a heavy calibre piece, but no doubt it could shoot. There were about five Russians, and we just watched as they turned the gun around and started to get ready to load, aim and fire it. At that point we opened fire and shot them all. A second group then came out of the wood, not running, but walking casually as if on a Sunday stroll, and approached the gun. The same thing happened: we shot them all. One more group followed in the same way and we shot them, too, before they gave up and left the gun alone. These were actions we just could not understand. It was as if, without complaint, they all willingly committed suicide.

'Our greatest fear was not so much being hit but being taken prisoner. The Russians could be really bestial. We once had a Russian youth, a deserter, whom we kept in the unit because he was intelligent, very helpful and knew a few words of German. In short, he was a much-needed extra pair of hands. Some nights he would go off into no-man's land and come back with a few of his countrymen whom he had persuaded to desert. One morning, though, he failed to return. We thought he had simply gone back to fighting for the Red Army.

'Some days later we captured a village from the Russians. In the centre of the village there was a small tree, and there we found our "Ivan". Someone with some medical knowledge had nailed one end of his intestines to the tree and then spun him round until there was no more gut left.'

SS HARRIDANS

ERWIN BARTMANN

SS-UNTERSCHARFÜHRER

1st SS Panzer Division *Leibstandarte SS Adolf Hitler*

The Red Army employed large numbers of women in its ranks. These women lived, fought and died side-by-side with their male comrades. They fought just as hard as the men, as Erwin Bartmann remembers.

RIGHT: *SS-Unterscharführer Erwin Bartmann, who had a frightening encounter with a group of female Russian soldiers. In this shot he is wearing the rare M38 headgear with its distinctive cloth-covered peak. Such items are now highly sought after by collectors.*

'In the winter of 1942 we were in our prepared positions before Kharkov. The snow was very deep and it was very cold. I had been ordered to take my telephone cable reel and lay a line to the next unit. It was a simple task so I didn't think anything about it. So far, so good, but then I ran into the enemy. In fact I was up against a battalion of Russian women soldiers. What a clamour, it was terrible! They sprang from the edge of their trench, screaming like banshees. I thought my time had come. I ran like hell and was fortunate enough to get back to my unit unhurt. A lucky escape!

'A couple of days later they attacked our positions. We were forced to withdraw and had to leave our wounded behind. When we retook the positions, we found our comrades had all been murdered. One was a friend of mine who, like me, worked on the field telephones. We carried various tools in our haversacks, such as screwdrivers, pliers and the like. His pliers had been rammed down his throat as he lay there helpless, choking him. I was the one that had to collect the identity discs so that the bodies could be buried. Who knows what would have happened to me that day if they had caught me? It still makes me shiver to think of it.'

⚡⚡ RUSSIAN CIVILIANS

LEO WILM

SS-OBERSCHARFÜHRER

3rd SS Panzer Division *Totenkopf*

RICHARD FUCHS

SS-UNTERSCHARFÜHRER

Panzerjäger Abteilung 5
5th SS Panzer Division *Wiking*

JAN MUNK

STANDARTENOBERJUNKER

SS-Panzergrenadier Regiment *Westland*
5th SS Panzer Division *Wiking*

RIGHT: Waffen-SS and a Russian family.

'During my time in Russia I often helped wounded Russian soldiers, and took Russians prisoner in combat. It never occurred to me to do them any harm. One would offer captured Russian soldiers a cigarette and clap them on the shoulder to calm them down.

It was the same with civilians. Once in southern Russia, for example, I saw cherries growing for the first time (we certainly didn't see them in central or northern areas of the Eastern Front). I went to a Russian woman who owned the trees they were growing on and asked her if I could take some cherries. I gave her some bread in exchange. Of course I could have just taken the cherries, but we could be very severely punished for looting. I even remember an old Russian woman kissing my feet in gratitude when I once helped some Russians. There was quite a difference when we were the ones in captivity, though. They stole everything: money, watches, anything they could lay their hands on. But that was different, of course, as our politicians would say. They were our "liberators"'.

LEO WILM

'In the Caucasus, during our advance, one evening we entered a village and camouflaged our self-propelled gun to prevent it being spotted by enemy aircraft. The gun barrel was released from its travel lock and ended up, purely by chance, pointing directly at a large bush. As we began to prepare our positions for the night, there came a rustling from that bush, and then a uniformed Russian appeared with his hands up. Naturally this caused great excitement.

'I undertook a recce of the river'

'Our commanding officer asked me to translate the words of our captive Russian. I asked him where he came from. He pointed to the nearest house and said: "There". My chief ordered me to send him home, and I went with the Russian to his house. He disappeared quickly into the house and came back shortly afterwards dressed in smart civilian clothes. He very proudly introduced his wife and his many children. By way of thanks, he offered me a goose. I stood back and told the delighted "homecomer" that he and his family should eat the fat goose themselves. The whole peasant family stood there, eyes brimming with tears of relief and gratitude.

'On another occasion during the advance, we had to cross a river which was swollen. Some of the retreating Russians were already established on the other side, and we came under heavy fire from their machine guns. I undertook a recce of the river and its banks and fortunately reached the other side without difficulty. A Russian soldier lay on the opposite bank, badly wounded in the thigh. I went towards him and he begged me not to shoot him. In my uniform pocket I had a field dressing. I gave this to him and he tried to kiss my feet in gratitude – he could hardly believe that I was not going to shoot him.

'I was able to help the family to exchange sunflower seeds'

'Later, in the winter of 1941/42, together with three comrades, I was quartered with a Russian family in a small village in the southern sector of the Mius Front [the *Wiking* Division had pulled back to the west bank of the River Mius at the beginning of December 1941]. The primitive clay houses had only two rooms. The family consisted of four people: father, mother and two children aged eight and twelve, who were named Ivan and Jura. They all had very little to eat, so soon we began to give them all we could spare. I quickly became great friends with the children and, because of this, I was able to pick up quite a bit of their language. I was able to help the family to exchange sunflower seeds for oil at a local mill which was under German administration. The father also got tobacco from me, which really delighted him. I also helped to organise contests with the children from the village in shooting with a bow and arrow. Eventually, I became almost like a village schoolmaster. Then, in the spring, we got our marching orders. Our wagon was made ready to leave and I went to take leave of my young friends, but they weren't there. Everyone looked for them and eventually we found them sitting on a large stone behind the house, crying their eyes out. It was a very upsetting to leave them and their family.

'Later, in the Donetz basin near Stalino, I contracted an infectious illness and was therefore quartered separately from my comrades with an old Russian mother. My canteen had to be hung on the garden fence, and every day my comrades would come by and fill it with food.

'The old mother told me about her daughter, who had been evacuated when the Red Army pulled back so as not to fall into the hands of the German *Untermensch* [subhumans], or so they had told her. I was very ill indeed at that time, and the old lady tended me and looked after me as if she was my own mother. She would often get up very early, about 0400 hours, and walk into Stalino to get me some sort of powdered pudding in order to make me a meal.

'Then, once again, came the order to move on. I packed my kitbag into one of the vehicle lockers and went to take my leave of my "nursing sister". I found her outside the rear of the house. It was a very tearful departure for us both'.

RICHARD FUCHS

'The Soviet population that we met in the Ukraine was in my opinion very pleasant and did not show any animosity towards us. For example, when we were finally settled in Slavyansk on 24 April 1943 we were allocated a house to stay in. When another boy and I entered our billet we were met by the grandparents of the house, their daughter and her children. Her husband and brothers, too, were absent, probably fighting with the Red Army. Grandma put a big wooden tub filled with warm water in the main room then told us to get undressed. While she scrubbed our backs the daughter washed and mended our underwear and the children were told to polish our boots.

'Any sexual contact was forbidden'

'We often shared our meals with them and in exchange got eggs, fried potatoes and gherkins. All this fraternising was allowed, but any sexual contact with a Russian woman was strictly forbidden. That was not too difficult to obey as I never saw an attractive looking one, a good-looking a face that is. As for the figure, we could only guess what has hidden under all those layers of skirts.'

JAN MUNK

SS   EAST EUROPEANS

FRIEDRICH-KARL WACKER

SS-Sturmmann
16th SS Panzergrenadier Division
Reichsführer-SS

It was not always the case that the Waffen-SS had cordial relations with the local civilian population of a conquered country. Some of the more ideologically indoctrinated Waffen-SS soldiers treated eastern Europeans as less than human. Wacker's account illustrates the diversity of types found among the Waffen-SS's ranks.

RIGHT: Friedrich-Karl Wacker as an SS-Sturmmann in 1943 while serving with the Reichsführer-SS Division. This photograph was taken after his release from hospital.

'Once, during my time with the convalescent company in Warsaw (I was still recovering from being wounded), I was assigned to anti-partisan operations. There was this one particular character doing guard duty at the same time as me. He was tall, a real big chap, with big scars on his neck. Talking about the Poles one day, he said: "I am going to get one of those bastards." The next morning we found the body of a Pole lying in the street. He had been shot dead, obviously by the guard on duty with me. Some guys in the SS certainly thought they could do anything and get away with it, even murder.

With regard to the east Europeans in general, I remember the Hungarians as being very friendly. They were simple people, peasants, with just dirt floors in their homes, but they invited us in and treated us like lords. I suppose that between us and the Soviets we were considered to be the lesser of two evils.

[Though many Waffen-SS soldiers got on perfectly well with east European civilians, as the accounts in this book illustrate, the Nazi Party and the SS as a whole regarded eastern Europe as an area ripe for colonisation by a racial and biological German elite. To SS ideologues such as Himmler, the indigenous population would be useful in providing forced labour, but ultimately they had no future in the occupied areas. To soldiers such as Wacker, who were often billeted with them, the civilians of eastern Europe and Russia were just like themselves, but to the SS they were merely 'racially and biologically inferior elements'.]

⚡⚡ THE YANKS DROP IN

ERIC BRÖRUP

SS-OBERSTURMFÜHRER

SS-Panzer Aufklärungs Abteilung 5
5th SS Panzer Division *Wiking*

One of the least documented of the combat units of the Waffen-SS was the Parachute Battalion, whose exploits included a glider-borne attack on Tito's partisan head-quarters at Drvar in Yugoslavia. Eric Brörup spent some months with the training company of the Waffen-SS paratroops in the late summer of 1944, and came face-to-face with captured US airmen.

RIGHT: *Members of the crew of an American bomber after a mission. Eric Brörup encountered men such as these when he was being trained as a paratrooper.*

'Because of my flying experience as a civilian and my general interest in aviation, and because of my dislike of life in the infantry (I had been in cavalry and reconnaissance units before joining SS-Panzer-grenadier Regiment 24 *Danmark*), I volunteered for the SS-Fallschirmjäger. In any case, *Danmark* still had too many "politicals" from the defunct Freikorps *Danmark* for my liking. My request for a transfer was granted.

'Initially, some of the personnel sent to the SS-Fallschirm-jäger were penal troops sent to the paras to redeem themselves in action. When I reported to the training company, though, there were none of these penal troops; the majority were volunteers. The unit was stationed at Papa, Hungary, alongside a Luftwaffe transport squadron, some personnel

from one of the parachute schools, the usual administrative staff and a Hungarian Army parachute unit under the command of a major.

'Although we were issued with full paratrooper kit – jump boots, smock, para helmet and so on – lack of fuel for the aircraft meant that I never actually got started on jump training.

'The duties were not particularly demanding and the weather at that time was good. Time off was spent at the pool, or at local hostelries sampling the wine, listening to music and eating goulash. One morning we were watching an American bomber formation flying high overhead, moving towards Wiener-Neustadt and the factories located there. As we were discussing the apparent ease with which the enemy could penetrate German air space, a large number - perhaps 30 or 40 - of our own aircraft appeared and went straight into the attack. We could see the spent cartridge cases from all the gunfire glittering in the sun as they came down to earth. In the action three of the bombers were shot down.

'Then, one of the Messerschmitt 109s that had just scored a victory flew over, waggled its wings and landed (we subsequently learned it was out of fuel). We half expected the pilot to be an ace wearing the Knights Cross, but it turned out to be a 19-year-old private first class. Grinning from ear to ear, he reported that it was his fourth victory in three weeks, which would make his father, a test pilot himself, very proud. We invited the pilot into the officers' mess and treated him like a prince.

'Having full bomb loads on board, all of the American aircraft shot down exploded on impact when they hit the ground. However, some crew members bailed out and were picked up by the Hungarians. Later that day, I was ordered to go to the Hungarian barracks. Someone had heard that I could speak English, and so I was asked to help in the interrogation of the airmen, though technically this should have been the Luftwaffe's job.

'The Americans were nervous when they saw the death's head insignia'

'An SS-Obersturmführer from Intelligence was there, as well as SS-Obersturmführer Leifheit and SS-Untersturmführer Dräger from our unit, and of course the Hungarians. The Americans were very nervous when they saw the SS death's head insignia on our caps. As we were in shirt-sleeve order and our shoulder straps were of Army pattern, only the cap insignia immediately identified us as Waffen-SS. The Americans obviously thought they were really in for it, but I allayed their fears and told them we were not police or Gestapo, just ordinary fighting soldiers. I asked them for their names, dates and places of birth, the usual stuff, which they gave willingly.

'Then I tried asking for information about their unit, intended target, aircraft type and so on. Naturally there was

no reply, then a second lieutenant spoke up: "Sir, if you were in our position would you answer these questions?" "Absolutely not!" was my reply, "and I don't expect you to, either."

'They asked what would happen next, and I explained that their next of kin and the International Red Cross would be informed, and that they would probably be turned over to the Luftwaffe.

'Bailed-out bomber crews were often torn apart by the inhabitants of towns'

'I told them they were very lucky to have been picked up by regular soldiers. Bailed-out bomber crews were often torn apart by the inhabitants of the towns and cities they had been bombing if the civilians got to them first. Even our own airmen were issued with armbands with the words *Deutsche Luftwaffe* on them to make sure they weren't killed by irate civilians if they were unfortunate enough to be shot down over their own territory.

'A few days later I was ordered to the SS-Führungs Hauptamt [SS Command Head Office] in Berlin, where I was given a real dressing down about alleged fraternising with enemy prisoners. I replied that I had merely treated them in the way that I myself would hope to be treated if I was unfortunate enough to be taken prisoner!'

[Thanks to a bureaucratic error, Brörup's name was not removed from the nominal roll of the SS-Fallschirmjäger training company. This unit later became 1/SS-Fallschirmjäger Battalion 600 and served in the Ardennes Offensive (the Battle of the Bulge) under Otto Skorzeny. During the offensive a number of Skorzeny's men roamed behind Allied lines dressed in US uniforms, causing considerable alarm and consternation with their activities. There were even rumours of an intended assassination attempt on General Eisenhower. Skorzeny was much feared by the Allies and considered most dangerous. He and all men identified as serving under his command were placed on a 'wanted' list by the Allies. After the war, Skorzeny told Brörup that his name had also been on this wanted list, but that he, Skorzeny, had set the record straight with the Americans.]

SS BITTER LEAVE

WILHELM HILLEN
SS-OBERSTURMFÜHRER

1st SS Panzer Division *Leibstandarte SS Adolf Hitler*

Hillen was wounded in action on the Eastern Front in early 1943. During his convalescence, he was temporarily assigned to the Waffen-SS welfare service. The emotional stress of such duties were in many ways worse than the stresses of combat.

RIGHT: *Bitterness and despair were also present on the home front. Perhaps mothers with sons fighting at the front, women such as these often bore terrible grief for lost ones.*

'The medical officer arranged a temporary attachment for me to the Welfare Officer of the Waffen-SS in Denmark. It was based in Copenhagen, where I was to stay for six weeks while recovering. If I had know what was in store for me, though, I would have resisted this posting by all means possible.

'I reported enthusiastically enough – a newly created SS-Untersturmführer – and was met by SS-Sturmbannführer Berger. He explained to me what my duties would be, which gave me a weak feeling in my stomach, despite the excellent breakfast I had been given. I had been given the task of breaking the news of the deaths of members of Freikorps *Danmark* to their next of kin and returning their personal effects. A Danish SS-Oberscharführer was assigned to me as a driver and interpreter.

'I had to visit a family in the area around Hadersleben/Aperade, who lived in a large farmhouse. The memory of that visit remains with me to this day. All four sons of the family served in the Freikorps, three of whom having already been killed. It was my job to break the news of the death of the fourth and last son.

'It was a beautiful Sunday morning. The sky was blue and the cornfields around the farm had a golden shine. I lingered for well over an hour, trying to pluck up the courage to approach the house. Even in my foxhole at the front in Russia I never felt as miserable as I did at that particular moment. However, I pulled myself together and knocked on the door of the house.

'The farmer's wife appeared, a large blonde woman, who led me into the living room. There, in a show case, were four photographs, each of a young man in the uniform of our forces. Three were surrounded by black crepe and from the frame hung their Iron Crosses. I didn't know how to put into words the news I had for her.

'To this day I can see that grief-stricken lady standing before me. She did not cry when I broke the news I had for her, but in those short minutes her face aged by years. To me she was the epitome of the heroic mother whose sacrifices cannot be reflected by any award or medal. Immediately upon my return to the office I reported myself as being fit for frontline service, and was soon on my way back to the fighting in Estonia.'

▟▟ HOME TRUTHS

JAN MUNK
SS-STANDARTENOBERJUNKER

SS-Panzergrenadier Regiment *Westland*
5th SS Panzer Division *Wiking*

Not surprisingly, attitudes in the occupied countries towards the Waffen-SS were often most strongly expressed against those of the local population who had elected to serve with the Germans.

RIGHT: *A happy Waffen-SS foreign volunteer. However, many people in the occupied countries were far from happy about their young men being in the SS.*

'During my first leave in Holland, on reaching the railway station of my home town Leiden, I said goodbye to another Dutchman with whom I had spent many hours on the train. His destination was Alkmaar, a town about 65km (40 miles) or so north of Leiden. Months later I heard that when he arrived in Alkmaar he first went to the barber in order to look decent before he saw his parents. When he was sitting in the barber's shop, the Dutch underground emptied a Sten gun into his back. I myself took no chances. If I ever travelled on a bus or train, I always stood with my back against a wall or window, otherwise people would burn holes in my uniform with their cigarettes or cut it with a razor.

'During my first leave I wanted to see the family of a Dutch boy who had been killed in action. As his home was near Leiden I went there on my pushbike. It wasn't too warm, so I wore my old motorcycle coat, a beautiful, made-to-measure, long black leather coat. I think I must have looked a bit like one of those sinister Gestapo fellows you always see in war movies.

'I cycled quite a long way on the road, but then had to carry my bike over my shoulder to cross over a tramway bridge. I was halfway across, balancing from sleeper to sleeper, when I was shot at. I put my bike down and drew my pistol (normally when we went on leave we only took our bayonet, but having heard stories I thought it wise to have something more lethal). A second shot was fired. It was useless firing my pistol because I could not actually see anyone. Anyhow, fortunately no more shots were fired at me and I carried on with my journey.'

SS FRENCH LEAVE

WERNER VÖLKNER
SS-STURMMANN

SS-Flak Abteilung
3rd SS Panzer Division *Totenkopf*

HANS-GERHARD STARCK
SS-OBERSCHARFÜHRER

1st SS Panzer Division *Leibstandarte SS
Adolf Hitler*

*RIGHT: Members of Werner Völkner's unit
photographed on the Eastern Front, after
they had been transferred from France.*

M any of the Waffen-SS divisions were reformed during their lives. In most cases this was accomplished by transferring the divisions to occupied France, away from the fierce fighting and horrendous weather on the Russian Front. Not until later in the war did the French Resistance pose any real threat to the safety of German troops.

'My division was moved from Russia to France for rest and refitting. We arrived at the railway station and began to unload our vehicles and weapons. Unfortunately there were too few vehicles to tow all the guns, so I was left there to guard one of the guns for which there was no tractor. A couple of hours went by, then four hours, then it began to get dark. All the while I was becoming an object of curiosity for the local population. I had no food and no money to buy any. All I could do was take a few apples from the adjacent orchard, and boy did my stomach suffer for that over the next few days. It was only when they held the roll call at the camp next morning that they realised I was missing. I had been totally forgotten!

'On another occasion I was on guard duty, patrolling the area around the garage where the vehicles were kept. I was feeling dreadfully unwell. By the time I was relieved next morning I was almost on the verge of collapse, and so I was rushed into hospital. The sergeant-major came to see me, though I certainly didn't get any sympathy from him. He gave me a real roasting. He said I was not in a fit state to do my duty properly. I tried to explain that I couldn't leave my post, but all he said was that I should have fired a shot in the air to attract help!

'While I was in hospital, a beautiful young French girl took a real interest in me. One day she told me that my division was being posted back to Russia. The rumour among the troops was that we were about to be issued with tropical kit to go to North Africa, so I told her she was very wrong. She wanted me to desert and said she had friends who would hide me. She was a lovely girl for sure, but I decided my duty to my country came first. Then, one day after I had been released from hospital, I was ordered to go to the railway station to help collect some new kit, which we thought would be our new tropical issue. When we saw it we got a bit of a shock. Felt overboots, padded anoraks and extra blankets – winter kit! It was true, we were going back to Russia!'

WERNER VÖLKNER

'While our regiment was in France in 1942, because I spoke good French, I was elected to go and buy some supplies for my comrades at the local stores in the city of Laigne. One woman, who ran a store where I shopped regularly, got to know me and invited me to dinner one night. She told me her own son had died at the start of the French campaign in 1940. She was like a mother to me, and she even offered to hide me if I deserted. I could stay with her until the Allies appeared. I refused, of course, but I was still amazed that she felt so confident that I would not report her to the authorities.'

HANS-GERHARD STARCK

⚡⚡ ON THE WEHRMACHT

▰ JAN MUNK

SS-STANDARTENOBERJUNKER

SS-Panzergrenadier Regiment *Westland*
5th SS Panzer Division *Wiking*

By and large the Waffen-SS respected their Wehrmacht comrades in the field. They were both, after all, doing the same job. However, at times there could be a degree of friction between the two organisations.

RIGHT: Wehrmacht soldiers. Competition between them and Waffen-SS soldiers is often exaggerated.

'The rain started, a typical Russian affair, i.e. a deluge! The countryside turned into a huge field of mud and roads ceased to exist. Regulations stated that if one track was getting too bad, another track should be made running parallel to it. However, all this was to no avail. In such mud even four-wheel drive wasn't enough. If your truck bogs down, you have to get out and push. We were up to our ankles, or higher, in that terrible sticky, gooey mud. Our squad, about 10 men in a truck, was extremely lucky, though. In dry conditions our driver, a Belgian, would always be clipping the edge of a building, scraping a tree or reversing into a wall, but he was never told off. When it rained, though, it was our truck that always got through. He was an incredible driver in the mud. No one ever complained about the busted mudguards or the broken lights if it meant you could stay on board when the occupants of other trucks were having to push their vehicles through the mud.

'Our platoon, having four trucks, was ordered to be the last one in the enormous column. We had strict orders from the battalion commander not to let anyone pass, and to use force if necessary to ensure they didn't. A column of that length moves slowly, the drivers keeping an eye on the vehicle in front and following it. If a vehicle from another unit overtakes and pulls in front, and then turns off, it might instinctively be followed by the driver behind it and the rest of the drivers behind him. In this way a column can be split up. So no overtaking by anyone!

'On such a journey our trucks would form a kind of diamond shape. One in front, then two side by side, then one behind. Each truck had a soldier standing on the step of the cab and facing the rear. If he saw someone trying to overtake he would tell the driver, who would pull out and block him. That worked quite well in most cases.

'Once, a staff car came into sight. It was a Citroën with a driver and a high-ranking Wehrmacht officer sitting beside him. The driver tried several times to overtake, and I could see that the officer was getting very annoyed because his way was repeatedly being blocked. At one stage he would have passed us with his superior acceleration, but I, as number one on the machine gun, was told by my platoon führer to fire a burst in front of him. That did the trick. I don't know if that officer ever reported the incident. At the time he was mad as hell and said he would, but we all just grinned at him.

'We regarded the Wehrmacht as being of the same calibre as ourselves. On some occasions we did meet Wehrmacht soldiers when we were called in to plug a gap or to retake a position lost by them. We would meet them retreating, as we ourselves were driving forward in our own trucks. I don't think we ever considered them as weaklings or cowards. We never really discussed the Wehrmacht. We knew that the reason we were there was often to retrieve a position. That said, the Wehrmacht or the Luftwaffe also often got us out of a mess. It worked both ways.

'Our own officers, our Waffen-SS officers, we regarded without exception as men you could trust and as men to be respected. There was nothing unusual to see an officer relieving one of his men carrying a heavy machine gun or heavy ammunition box to make things easier for him. They were always in the thick of the action, and not way back to the rear where it was safe.'

⚡⚡ HITLER AND HIMMLER

JAN MUNK
SS-STANDARTENOBERJUNKER

SS-Panzergrenadier Regiment *Westland*
5th SS Panzer Division *Wiking*

RICHARD FUCHS
SS-UNTERSCHARFÜHRER

Panzerjäger Abteilung 5
5th SS Panzer Division *Wiking*

HANS-GERHARD STARCK
SS-OBERSCHARFÜHRER

1st SS Panzer Division *Leibstandarte SS Adolf Hitler*

RIGHT: Hitler (right) and, ever at his side, Heinrich Himmler (left), the leader of the SS. Many Waffen-SS soldiers had respect for Hitler, the former soldier, but grew to dislike and ridicule Himmler.

The feeling of respect for Hitler but contempt for Himmler seems to have been widespread within the Waffen-SS. As soldiers themselves they respected the military achievements of Hitler as a junior NCO in World War I. His winning the Iron Cross in both Second and First Classes, as well as other decorations for combat bravery, while holding the lowly rank of corporal was an uncommon feat. Himmler, on the other hand, had no frontline experiencer, and his prim schoolmasterish appearance did little to enhance his standing among these tough combat soldiers.

'As for the political leadership, all I can say is that we believed in what Hitler said, and I myself was convinced that Germany would win the war right up to March 1945. I only really knew the war was lost for sure when we heard that Hitler was dead.

'As far as Hitler was concerned, we regarded him as a true man. He was only a corporal when he earned the Iron Cross First Class in World War I. In those days that was quite an achievement. When he spoke at meetings or rallies he managed to captivate his audience. He was able to get us in a mood where we believed everything he said and we left fired with enthusiasm. Everyone I met respected and trusted Hitler, and I myself shared these feelings and opinions.

'As for Himmler, he certainly was not a man. He gave the impression that he could not be trusted, and he certainly wasn't a shining example of an Aryan super-race, either in appearance or character. We thought Himmler a miserable-looking person to be head of the Waffen-SS.'

JAN MUNK

'The Waffen-SS had no love for Himmler. To us he was more or less a stranger. We called him *Reichsheini* [meaning he was a man obsessed with his own importance]. About Hitler, today I think he must have known he could not win a war against the whole world. Our Luftwaffe was too weak and our supplies were insufficient. The order always to hold firm in the last few months of the war cost the lives of very many German soldiers.'

RICHARD FUCHS

'My feelings about *Reichsheini* were the same. To me a Heini is a man who is not trustworthy, a juggler, an illusionist, a weak little man who is nothing without his uniform.'

HANS-GERHARD STARCK

BELOW: The fate of countless thousands of Waffen-SS soldiers: burial in a foreign field a long way from home. Note the SS runes in white stones on the central grave.

⚡⚡ THE EXPERTS' OPINION

GENERAL EBERHARD VON MACKENSEN
COMMANDER III PANZER CORPS

GENERAL FRIEDRICH KIRCHNER
COMMANDER LVII PANZER CORPS

GENERAL OTTO WÖHLER
COMMANDER 8TH ARMY

FIELD MARSHAL VON MANSTEIN
COMMANDER ARMY GROUP DON

GENERAL HEINZ GUDERIAN
COMMANDER 2ND PANZER GROUP

RIGHT: Heinz Guderian spoke highly of the fighting qualities of the Waffen-SS, and the Leibstandarte *in particular.*

Although it has often been suggested that senior Army commanders looked down upon the Waffen-SS as arrogant upstarts and considered their tactics as being reckless and wasteful of lives, they soon grew to value the reliability of Waffen-SS troops. Some of the testimonials that the Waffen-SS received from distinguished Wehrmacht commanders illustrate the point:

'I can assure you that the *Leibstandarte* enjoys an outstanding reputation, not only with its own superiors but with its Army comrades also [referring to the *Leibstandarte*'s achievements during the winter of 1941/42 in Russia]. Every division wishes it had the *Leibstandarte* as its neighbour. Its inner discipline, cool daredevilry, cheerful enterprise, unshakeable fortitude even when things become difficult or serious, exemplary toughness and its camaraderie, all of these are outstanding and cannot be surpassed.'

GENERAL EBERHARD VON MACKENSEN

'To the SS-Panzergrenadier Division *Wiking*. Today [19 September 1942] the SS-Panzergrenadier Division *Wiking* leaves the units attached to my Panzerkorps [to switch to the East Caucasus]. From the very first day of its attachment up to the last, the division has been admirably successful in bold attacks and determined defence in continual weeks-long battles under unfavourable weather conditions and against an enemy always numerically superior. It has proved itself to have an outstanding fighting spirit, which has caused great damage to the enemy. Thanks to the excellent steadfastness of the division, the enemy has been prevented from achieving his goal of breakthrough and envelopment. So, today, I watch the brave men of the *Wiking* Division leave my forces with a heavy heart. My thanks and full recognition go equally to its officers and men. My best wishes go with the division on its way to new battles and new successes.'

GENERAL FRIEDRICH KIRCHNER

Medals and decorations of World War II are today of interest mainly to the collector of military memorabilia. However, it is often forgotten that many of them had to be earned, and that the higher decorations in particular did not come cheap. No one, for example, wins the British Victoria Cross or American Congressional Medal of Honor for simply wearing a uniform. It is the same in the German Army. Many veterans of the Waffen-SS, men who have contributed to this book, hold numerous awards for gallantry, awards that were won in many instances during the bitter fighting on the Eastern Front. Decorations such as the Wound Badge (above), awarded in black, silver and gold grades dependent on the number or severity of wounds received, were bought with blood. Similarly with the Deutsche Kreuz in gold (left), which came above the Iron Cross First Class in terms of seniority.

'In the past few days the Corps has recorded two great successes. First, the defensive victory by the SS-Panzergrenadier Division *Wiking*, which after the engagement by the Tiger detachment resulted in the destruction of 84 enemy tanks. Second, the daring advance across the Merla by SS-Panzergrenadier Division *Totenkopf*. My thanks and appreciation to the command and to the troops.'

GENERAL OTTO WÖHLER
[Headquarters of the 8th Army, 20 August 1943]

'I had it [the 3rd SS Panzer Division *Totenkopf*] under my command on frequent occasions later on, and I think it was probably the best Waffen-SS division I ever came across.'

FIELD MARSHAL VON MANSTEIN

'My old Chief in Stettin, former Army General Paul Hausser, was tasked with the development of the officer corps of the Waffen-SS. General Hausser was an exceptional officer, an intelligent and gallant soldier and an outstanding, honest and blameless character. The Waffen-SS had much to thank this distinguished officer for. I have encountered the SS divisions *Leibstandarte* and the *Das Reich* in battle and later, as General-Inspector of Panzer Troops, have inspected the Waffen-SS divisions many times. They always distinguished themselves through their self-discipline, comradeship and good soldierly behaviour in battle. They fought shoulder-to-shoulder with the Army panzer divisions and became, the more so the longer the war lasted, "one of us".'

GENERAL HEINZ GUDERIAN

SS THE LAST WORD

GERD ROMMEL
SS-ROTTENFÜHRER

SS-Panzer Aufklärüngs Abteilung 10
10th SS Panzer Division *Frundsberg*

On the whole question of friends and foes, allies and enemies, and the upshot of the war, Gerd Rommel deserves to have the final comment.

RIGHT: *Gerd Rommel as an SS-Schütze in a photograph taken in Angouleme in France in June 1943. He is wearing the special black service dress for tank crews.*

'In my opinion, everyone in World War II fought for his own fatherland, for his family, and for his children in the belief that he was doing right. What has come out of it?

'We have all experienced and seen, throughout the world, suffering and misery. This is true of World War II and the conflicts that have been waged across the globe since 1945. There has still not been a war that has brought the results that the politicians have hoped for at the time they started it. Think of Iraq. Even though the Iraqis lost, Saddam Hussein remained in power. The war in the Gulf brought only death and corruption, and, as ever, it is the "little man" who has suffered. It was the same when I fought and it is the same now.'

GLOSSARY

Abteilung: detachment, usually battalion-sized

Abzeichen: badge or insignia

Armee: army

Armee gruppe: army group

Armee Oberkommando: Army High Command

Artillerie: artillery

Aufklärung: reconnaisance

Ausbildung: training

Ausbildungs und ersatz abteilung: training and replacement battalion. Each division had such a battalion, to which new recruits were initially posted awaiting assignment. Soldiers rejoining their divisions after recovery from wounds were also usually posted first to the 'A u E Bataillon', which was the reserve pool from which battle casualty replacements were taken.

Bataillon: battalion

Batterie: battery

Befehlshaber: commander

Begleit: escort

Brigade: brigade

Brigadeführer: brigade commander

Ersatz: replacement

Ergänzungsstelle: recruitment office

Einheit: unit

Feldgendarmerie: military police

Feldbluse: field blouse, tunic

Feldlazarett: field hospital

Feldmütze: field cap

Flak: anti-aircraft artillery

Freikorps and Freiwilligen Legions: the early Germanic volunteers units of the Waffen-SS were the Volunteer Corps or Volunteer Legions, such as Freikorps *Danmark* and Freiwilligen Legion *Norwegen*. These units served with the Waffen-SS but their members were not accorded the same status as Waffen-SS soldiers. The SS prefix to the rank was not used. Thus, a soldier would be a Legion-Scharführer rather than an SS-Scharführer. As the war progressed, however, such units were disbanded and all volunteer units became part of the order of battle of the Waffen-SS proper.

Freiwillige: volunteer

Führer: leader, used to denote officer status in the SS

Führung: leadership

Gefechtstand: command post

Genesenden kompanie: recuperation company. Soldiers recovering from wounds were often posted to this company for light duties until fully recovered.

Geschütze: gun

Gewehre: rifle

Heeresgruppe: army group

Hitler Jugend: the Hitler Youth movement, usually expressed as two words, while the SS panzer division was usually referred to as one word: *Hitlerjugend*.

Infanterie: infantry

Infanterie Lehr Regiment: infantry training regiment. The 'Lehr' regiments, however, were more than just training regiments. The term 'Lehr' also means demonstration, or display. These units were examples of the highest levels of achievement in their particular discipline. Some, such as *Panzer Lehr*, also acquitted themselves with distinction in battle.

Jäger: rifleman, light infantry

Jabo: JAgd BOmber, fighter-bomber

Junkerschule: officer training school

Kampfgruppe: battle group, a combat group of indeterminate size

Kaserne: barracks

Kavallerie: cavalry

Kommandeur: commander

Kompanie: company

Korps: corps

Kradschutzen: motorcycle troops

Krankenhaus: infirmary

Lazarett: hospital

Lehr: see Infanterie Lehr Regiment

LKW: LastenKraftWagen, a motor lorry, truck

Marschstiefel: marching boots, jackboots

Maschinegewehr: machine gun

Maschinepistole: machine pistol

Nachrichten: signals

Nahkampf: close combat

Nebelwerfer: literally, smoke discharger. Actually a multi-barrelled rocket projectile launcher, nicknamed 'moaning minnie' because of the low moaning sound the projectiles made when fired.

Oberbefehlshaber: commander-in-chief

Oberkommando: High Command

Panzer: armour, tank

Panzerfaust: single-shot anti-tank projectile launcher

Panzergrenadier: infantryman trained to operate tactically within an armoured formation.

Panzerjäger: tank destroyer

Panzerkampfwagen: armoured fighting vehicle (tank)

Polizei: police

Racketenbusche: bazooka

Reiter: horseman, cavalryman

Ritterkreuz: Knights Cross of the Iron Cross

Ritterkreuzträger: Knights Cross bearer

Rollbahn: main traffic highway. In Russia, many rollbahn were formed by constant heavy traffic passing over dirt roads, compacting the soil until it was hard as concrete. In the spring, however, the rains turned them into seas of glutinous mud.

Sanitäter: medical orderly

Scheisshaus Parole: shit-house gossip. Soldiers would escape from their NCOs to the latrines for a quick smoke and to catch up on the latest gossip. The term was used for all sorts of unfounded rumours.

Schützenpanzerwagen: armoured personnel carrier

Salbstfahrlafette: self-propelled gun carriage. Usually an open fighting compartment based on the chassis of an obsolete or obsolescent tank

Soldatenheim: literally, 'soldiers' home'. A German body directly equivalent to the British Navy, Army and Air Force Institutions (NAAFI) or US Post Exchange (PX).

Stab: staff

Stahlhelm: steel helmet

Standarte: SS unit equivalent in size to a regiment

Stiefel: boots

Sturmgeschütz: self-propelled assault gun. A highly successful type of weapon. Based on a tank chassis but with a fixed, closed superstructure and low silhouette. The Germans produced a number of different types of these vehicles and used them to considerable effect throughout the war.

Stellungswechsel: rapid redeployment from one position to another

Tarnung: camouflage

Tarnmütze: camouflage cap

Tarnjacke: camouflage jacket

Unterführer: NCO

Unterführerschule: NCO training school

Wache: guard

Wachregiment: guard regiment

Zug: platoon

Zugführer: platoon leader

WAFFEN-SS ORGANISATION

Army Group: The largest Waffen-SS field formation during World War II was the armeegruppe (army group), such as Armeegruppe *Steiner*. Commanded by a senior general or colonel-general, in Waffen-SS terms an SS-Obergruppenführer or SS-Oberstgruppenführer, theoretically this formation would consist of a number of corps-sized units. However, by the latter stages of the war, when such units were formed, their status was never as impressive in reality as it was on paper.

Corps: At the next level organisation was much more efficient. Each corps, or group of divisions (usually a minimum of two), was commanded by an SS-Gruppenführer or SS-Obergruppenführer. As well as the divisions it controlled, each corps had its own permanent elements, such as headquarters staff, military police, transport and so on. Divisions within the corps were not permanently assigned. For example, I SS Panzer Corps during the period of its existence contained at various points in time the 1st SS Panzer Division *Leibstandarte SS Adolf Hitler*, 2nd SS Panzer Division *Das Reich*, 3rd SS Panzer Division *Totenkopf*, 12th Panzer Division *Hitlerjugend*, 17th SS Panzergrenadier Division *Götz von Berlichingen*, the Luftwaffe's 11th Fallschirm Division, the Army's 117th Jäger Division and the Führerbegleit Division. There were a total of 18 Waffen-SS corps formed, some of which existed on paper only.

Division: At the next level was the division. A typical panzer division circa 1944 would be commanded by an SS-Brigadeführer or SS-Gruppenführer, and would consist of divisional staff elements, one panzer regiment, two panzergrenadier regiments, an artillery regiment, a reconnaissance battalion, an engineer battalion, an anti-aircraft battalion, a signals battalion, plus military police, transport, medical support and so on. A total of 38 Waffen-SS divisions were formed during the war. In standard military nomenclature, the division would be numbered with an Arabic numeral, designated according to type, with its honour title following, such as the 2nd SS Panzer Division *Das Reich*.

Regiment: Next came the regiment, commanded by an SS-Standartenführer or SS-Oberführer. In a typical 1944 panzer division, for example, the panzergrenadier regiment would contain a regimental staff, three battalions of armoured infantry, one heavy gun section, an anti-aircraft defence section, a reonnaisance section and a combat engineer section. The regiment would be described by its type, followed by its number in Arabic numerals and its title, if any. Thus SS-Panzergrenadier Regiment 6 *Theodor Eicke*.

Battalion: At battalion level, the commander would normally be of the rank of SS-Sturmbannführer or SS-Obersturmbannführer, and the average battalion would be comprised of four companies. A battalion was indicated by using its number in Roman numerals before the parent regiment's designation: II/SS-Panzergrenadier Regiment 25.

Company: The company, or kompanie, would be formed from a number of platoons, or zuge, and would be commanded by an SS-Obersturmführer or SS-Hauptsturmführer.

Platoon: The platoon, or zug, would usually be commanded by a junior officer, such as an SS-Untersturmführer, or a senior NCO, such as an SS-Oberscharführer. Within the platoon were numerous squads, or gruppe, commanded by a senior corporal or junior sergeant (SS-Unterscharführer or SS-Scharführer). The section, or rotte, would be commanded by a junior NCO, such as the SS-Rottenführer.

The above are, of course, only rough guides. Battlefield expediency often required very junior ranks to assume the command of much larger units. The intense and realistic battle training given to Waffen-SS troops often resulted in those junior ranks who had had considerable responsibility thrust upon them performing very well. Unlike in the Red Army, where the loss of an officer would often totally demoralise a unit, Waffen-SS units suffered no such problems. In view of the high losses in officers suffered by the Waffen-SS, this was perhaps just as well !

WAFFEN-SS RANKS

SS-Oberstgruppenführer........*Colonel-General*

SS-Obergruppenführer ....*General*

SS-Gruppenführer.................*Lieutenant-General*

SS-Brigadeführer ....*Major-General*

SS-Oberführer ....*A senior colonel, entitled to wear the grey lapel facings on the greatcoat as worn by generals, and to wear a general's silver braided cord cap piping.*

SS-Standartenführer ....*Colonel*

SS-Obersturmbannführer.......*Lieutenant-Colonel*

SS-Sturmbannführer..............*Major*

SS-Hauptsturmführer ....*Captain*

SS-Obersturmführer..............*First Lieutenant*

SS-Untersturmführer.............*Second Lieutenant*

SS-Sturmscharführer ....*Senior Warrant Office (after 15 years' service).*

SS-Standartenoberjunker ....*Officer candidate with substantive rank of SS-Hauptscharführer.*

SS-Hauptscharführer.............*Warrant Officer*

SS-Oberscharführer ....*Staff Sergeant*

SS-Standartenjunker..............*Officer candidate with substantive rank of SS-Scharführer.*

SS-Scharführer ....*Sergeant*

SS-Junker..............................*Officer candidate with substantive rank of SS-Unterscharführer.*

SS-Stabsscharführer ....*The senior NCO of a unit. This was an appointment rather than a rank, and was denoted by two rings of braid on each lower sleeve of the tunic. The appointment could go to any NCO rank from SS-Unterscharführer upwards.*

SS-Unterscharführer..............*Senior Corporal/Lance Sergeant*

SS-Rottenführer ....*Corporal*

SS-Sturmmann.......................*Lance-Corporal*

SS-Unterführeranwarter.........*Soldier nominated as NCO candidate. Must have signed on for at least 12 years' service.*

SS-Oberschütze.....................*Senior Private, attained after six months' service.*

SS-Schütze............................*Private. SS-Schütze was the basic rank, but where the soldier had a specific trade speciality this was reflected instead, i.e. Panzerschütze.*

ORDER OF BATTLE OF THE WAFFEN-SS

The following list gives the final order of battle of the 38 divisions of the Waffen-SS, together with each division's principal component units (the numerical strength of a Waffen-SS division was around 19,000 men, though the later divisions never approached this level of manpower):

1st SS Panzer Division *Leibstandarte SS Adolf Hitler*

SS-Panzergrenadier Regiment 1
SS-Panzergrenadier Regiment 2
SS-Panzer Regiment 1
SS-Panzer Artillerie Regiment

2nd SS Panzer Division *Das Reich*

SS-Panzergrenadier Regiment 3 *Deutschland*
SS-Panzergrenadier Regiment 4 *Der Führer*
SS-Panzer Regiment 2
SS-Panzer Artillerie Regiment 2

3rd SS Panzer Division *Totenkopf*

SS-Panzergrenadier Regiment 5 *Thule*
SS-Panzergrenadier Regiment 6 *Theodor Eicke*
SS-Panzer Regiment 3
SS-Panzer Artillerie Regiment 3

4th SS Panzergrenadier Division *SS-Polizei*

SS-Panzergrenadier Regiment 7
SS-Panzergrenadier Regiment 8
SS-Artillerie Regiment 4
SS-Sturmgeschutz Abteilung 4

5th SS Panzer Division *Wiking*

SS-Panzergrenadier Regiment 9 *Germania*
SS-Panzergrenadier Regiment 10 *Westland*
SS-Panzer Regiment 5
SS-Panzer Artillerie Regiment 5

6th SS Gebirgs Division *Nord*

SS-Gebirgsjäger Regiment 11 *Reinhard Heydrich*
SS-Gebirgsjäger Regiment 12 *Michael Gaissmair*
SS-Gebirgs Artillerie Regiment 6
SS-Sturmgeschutz Batterie 6

7th SS Freiwilligen-Gebirgs Division *Prinz Eugen*

SS-Freiwilligen Gebirgsjäger Regiment 13 *Artur Phleps*
SS-Freiwilligen Gebirgsjäger Regiment 14 *Skanderbeg*
SS-Freiwilligen Gebirgs Artillerie Regiment 7
SS-Sturmgeschutz Abteilung 7

8th SS Kavallerie Division *Florian Geyer*

SS-Kavallerie Regiment 15
SS-Kavallerie Regiment 16
SS-Kavallerie Regiment 18
SS-Artillerie Regiment (mot) 8
SS-Panzerjäger Abteilung 8

9th SS Panzer Division Hohenstaufen

SS-Panzergrenadier Regiment 19
SS-Panzergrenadier Regiment 20
SS-Panzer Regiment 9
SS-Panzer Artillerie Regiment 9

10th SS Panzer Division *Frundsberg*

SS-Panzergrenadier Regiment 21
SS-Panzergrenadier Regiment 22
SS-Panzer Regiment 10
SS-Panzer Artillerie Regiment 10

11th SS Freiwilligen-Panzergrenadier Division *Nordland*

SS-Panzergrenadier Regiment 23 *Norge*
SS-Panzergrenadier Regiment 24 *Danmark*
SS-Panzer Abteilung 11 *Herman von Salza*
SS-Panzer Artillerie Regiment 11

12th SS Panzer Division *Hitlerjugend*

SS-Panzergrenadier Regiment 25

SS-Panzergrenadier Regiment 26

SS-Panzer Regiment 12

SS-Panzer Artillerie Regiment 12

13th Waffen-Gebirgs Division der SS (kroatische Nr 1) *Handschar*

SS-Waffen Gebirgsjäger Regiment 27

SS-Waffen Gebirgsjäger Regiment 28

SS-Waffen Artillerie Regiment 13

SS-Panzerjager Abteilung 13

14th Waffen-Grenadier Division der SS (ukrainische Nr 1)

Waffen-Grenadier Regiment der SS 29

Waffen-Grenadier Regiment der SS 30

Waffen-Grenadier Regiment der SS 31

Waffen-Artillerie Regiment der SS 14

15th Waffen-Grenadier Division der SS (lettische Nr 1)

Waffen-Grenadier Regiment der SS 32

Waffen-Grenadier Regiment der SS 33

Waffen-Grenadier Regiment der SS 34

Waffen-Artillerie Regiment der SS 15

16th SS Panzergrenadier Division *Reichsführer-SS*

SS-Panzergrenadier Regiment 35

SS-Panzergrenadier Regiment 36

SS-Artillerie Regiment 16

SS-Panzer Abteilung 16

17th SS Panzergrenadier Division *Götz von Berlichingen*

SS-Panzergrenadier Regiment 37

SS-Panzergrenadier Regiment 38

SS-Panzer Artillerie Regiment 17

SS-Panzerjäger Abteilung 17

18th SS Freiwilligen-Panzergrenadier Division *Horst Wessel*

SS-Panzergrenadier Regiment 39

SS-Panzergrenadier Regiment 40

SS-Artillerie Regiment 18

SS Panzerjäger Abteilung 18

19th Waffen-Grenadier Division der SS (lettisches Nr 2)

Waffen-Grenadier Regiment der SS 42

Voldemars Veiss

Waffen-Grenadier Regiment der SS 43

Heinrich Schuldt

Waffen-Grenadier Regiment der SS 44

Waffen-Artillerie Regiment 19

20th Waffen-Grenadier Division der SS (estnische Nr 1)

Waffen-Grenadier Division der SS 45

Waffen-Grenadier Division der SS 46

Waffen-Grenadier Division der SS 47

Waffen-Artillerie Regiment 20

21st Waffen-Gebirgs Division der SS (albanische Nr 1) *Skanderbeg*

Waffen-Gebirgs Division der SS 50

Waffen-Gebirgs Division der SS 51

Waffen-Gebirgs Artillerie Regiment 21

22nd Freiwilligen-Kavallerie Division der SS *Maria Theresia*

Freiwilligen-Kavallerie Regiment der SS 52

Freiwilligen-Kavallerie Regiment der SS 53

Freiwilligen-Kavallerie Regiment der SS 54

Freiwilligen-Kavallerie Regiment der SS 55

23rd Waffen-Gebirgs Division der SS *Kama*

Waffen-Gebirgsjäger Regiment der SS 56

Waffen-Gebirgsjäger Regiment der SS 57

Waffen-Gebirgsjäger Regiment der SS 58

Waffen-Gebirgs Artillerie Regiment der SS 23

This division was disbanded in late 1944 and its remnants allocated to the 23rd Freiwilligen-Panzergrenadier Division *Nederland*, though the latter never exceeded regimental strength. *Nederland* comprised the remains of two existing regiments, SS Freiwilligen Panzergrenadier Regiments 48 (*General Seyffardt*) and 49 (*De Ruiter*).

24th SS Gebirgs Division *Karstjäger*
Waffen-Gebirgsjäger Regiment der SS 59
Waffen-Gebirgsjäger Regiment der SS 60
Waffen-Gebirgs Artillerie Regiment 24

25th Waffen-Grenadier Division der SS (ungarische Nr 1) *Hunyadi*
Waffen-Grenadier Regiment der SS 61
Waffen-Grenadier Regiment der SS 62
Waffen-Grenadier Regiment der SS 63
Waffen-Artillerie Regiment der SS 25

26th Waffen-Grenadier Division der SS (ungarische Nr 2) *Hungaria*
Waffen-Grenadier Regiment der SS 64
Waffen-Grenadier Regiment der SS 65
Waffen-Grenadier Regiment der SS 66
SS-Panzer Bataillon 26
This division never reached full divisional status.

27th SS Freiwilligen-Panzergrenadier Division (flämische Nr 1) *Langemarck*
This was a division in name only, and never exceeded regimental strength.

28th SS Freiwilligen-Panzergrenadier Division *Wallonien*
This 'division' never exceeded regimental strength.

29th Waffen-Grenadier Division der SS (russische Nr 1)
This unit was formed from Kaminski's infamous brigade (Kaminski, a renegade Russian, commanded a brigade of criminals and disgraced servicemen; his men committed many atrocities while participating in the crushing of the Warsaw uprising of August 1944). It was never a true division, and was subsequently absorbed into the Free Russian Army.

29th Waffen-Grenadier Division der SS (italienische Nr 1)
This unit is not thought to have exceeded regimental strength. It received its number when the other 29th Division was absorbed into Vlassov's Army.

30th Waffen-Grenadier Division der SS (weissruthenische Nr 1)
Waffen-Grenadier Regiment der SS 75
Waffen-Grenadier Regiment der SS 76
Waffen-Grenadier Regiment der SS 77
Waffen-Artillerie Regiment der SS 30

31st SS Freiwilligen Grenadier Division
SS-Freiwilligen Grenadier Regiment 78
SS-Freiwilligen Grenadier Regiment 79
SS-Freiwilligen Grenadier Regiment 80
SS-Artillerie Regiment 31

32nd SS Freiwilligen Grenadier Division *30 Januar*
Formed late in the war and never reached full strength.

33rd Waffen-Kavallerie Division der SS (ungarische Nr 3)
This division was never fully formed and was overrun by the Soviets when Hungary fell in 1945.

33rd Waffen-Grenadier Division der SS (französische Nr 1) *Charlemagne*
Formed from a Waffen-SS volunteer brigade, which in turn had originated from volunteers from the Army's *Legion Volontaire Français*. It never reached full divisional strength.

34th Waffen-Grenadier Division der SS *Landstorm Nederland*

SS Freiwilligen Grenadier Regiment 48
This unit originated from the home guard Landwacht *Nederland*, being taken into the SS in 1943. Between November 1944 and March 1945 it was expanded and reformed as a division, but saw little action.

35th SS Polizei Grenadier Division

Formed from policemen in the closing months of the war, this unit never reached divisional strength.

36th Waffen-Grenadier Division der SS

The infamous *Dirlewanger* Brigade (Oskar Dirlewanger was a criminal whose anti-partisan brigade committed many atrocities), this unit thankfully never reached divisional strength. It was of extremely dubious military value.

37th SS Freiwilligen-Kavallerie Division *Lützow*

Little is known of the composition of the unit, which was formed in the closing days of the war and committed to action around Vienna.

38th SS Grenadier Division *Nibelungen*

Formed from staff and cadets of the Bad Tölz officer training school, this unit never exceeded regimental strength.

By the time the war ended, most of the Waffen-SS foreign volunteer units had been disbanded or amalgamated with newly formed divisions in the above order of battle.

Those which were not included in the order of battle of the Waffen-SS divisions, but which still existed by 1945, included such oddities as the Indische Freiwilligen-Legion der Waffen-SS, with its Indian volunteers; the Kaukasicher Waffenverband der SS, comprised of Azerbaidzhanis, Armenians, Georgians and volunteers from the Caucasus region; and the principally Moslem Osttürkische Waffen-verband der SS. None of these units proved of great military value to the Waffen-SS.

INDEX